GAME CHANGER

Improving the Outcome in Severe Autism
using Personalized Medicine

Peter Lloyd-Thomas

Copyright © 2023 Peter Lloyd-Thomas. All rights reserved.

No part of this book may be reproduced, or stored in a retrieval system, or transmitted in any form or by any means, electronic, mechanical, photocopying, recording, or otherwise, without express written permission of the publisher.

The contents of this book should not be construed as medical advice. This book is for informational purposes.

ISBN: 9798847843287

Cover design by: Miloš Končar

Website: epiphanyasd.com

Dedications

James L-T
Better known as Monty, as seen on the front cover.

Monty's 1:1 Assistants over a 15 year period, in order of time served
Irena, Vera, Nela, Dule, Nevena, Nada and Žarko

Monty's understanding class teacher during his awful year-long regression
Bojana L. Thanks also to Angie, Biljana, Marija, Bojana S, Miloš, Eric, Aleksandra and all his teachers and friends at school over the years, in particular Linge, Chloe and Klara.

My most prolific emailers/collaborators
Agnieszka and Yi

Inventor of bumetanide as a therapy for autism
Yéhézkel Ben Ari

Monty's ABA consultants
Lilian, Erin and Tony

Most prolific commenter on my blog
Tyler. Thanks to all the many hundreds of other people who have made comments

Thanks to all the people who helped to proofread/edit this book
Matthew (Monty's big brother), Sue (one of my big sisters), David (my big brother), Natasa (prolific emailer/networker), Anita (prolific editor) and Tara.

Thanks to everyone!

Praise for the Companion Blog – Epiphany ASD

Peter, thank you very much for all the information you provided in this blog! I find it x-times much more useful than a USD1500 consultation with a so-called "top-rated autism doctor".

M.11 July 2022 at 16:36

My daughter is an older kid, and what I have seen is that, every autism intervention, including doing nothing, has about one percent of kids who 'recover'. This blog is the only one that is completely rational and systematic. By translating so much research into practice, Peter is bridging the chasm and offering something completely unique. He gives us all a chance to succeed. Peter, just cannot thank you enough for all that you do, it is invaluable.

RG10 October 2015 at 06:19

Hi Peter. Thank you very much for your work. This blog is a beacon in the midst of the lack of information on autism.

Anonymous25 July 2022 at 03:09

Hi Peter, I am a parent of a 21 yr old. We have tried so many things…Your model of looking at autism treatment is exactly what I wish the myriad of doctors we have seen would use.

Anonymous14 July 2015 at 00:39

Thank you for fighting the good fight. I have worked in the US medical field (in management) for 30 years, so I'm not surprised that physicians take a pretty passive approach toward autism. They do better with diagnostic certainty and with treatments where the effects and side-effects are well-known. Obviously not there yet with autism.

Anonymous15 December 2019 at 21:57

Dear Peter, thank you very much for sharing your findings and for giving us hope for a better future.

Anonymous21 December 2019 at 20:27

Peter, my son is 25-mo and diagnosed ASD on ADOS-2 in Oct 2020. I started to throw myself into the myriad of journals and with my A-Level Biology my understanding has been stretched. I was drowned. Then I found your page while I was searching intensively around GABA switch. You are a godsend.

TC 16 December 2020 at 12:25

Hello Peter. I've been checking your blog for a while now and it's absolutely eye-opening. Thank you for all the effort to share your experience. I am from Egypt. Research on autism treatment is not very common here. I must say I'm not from a scientific or medical background but I am a parent who has two eyes and a brain and I want the best for my child. So I'm reading your words and a lot of what you say rings a bell.

M 3 January 2022 at 01:09

Hi Peter. Thanks for publishing this great resource. I'm a young adult just diagnosed with high functioning autism / Aspergers. I'm starting to research treatments for my Aspergers, but I'm overwhelmed.

B 5 June 2022 at 05:58

I am working with our doctor to evaluate Bumetanide for my daughter. I found Bumetanide should have no effect on non-mutated neurons and the impact on the overall Rett's neurological excessive synchrony can be huge. Thank you for your blog. I have zero science background and would never have come to this without your inspiration

P 10 September 2022 at 06:24

I pride myself by knowing the story of Monty and you. Your insights in autism and sharing of your experience deserve an "A". The autism and NT world need to hear your perspectives - i strongly hope that you can do a TED talk.

Anonymous 9 September 2022 at 21:22

How to use this book and what it offers

(this is based on feedback from those who read the draft version of the book)

- This book is written for those people who want to treat any debilitating symptoms of autism and common comorbidities, including intellectual disability.

- The book is much less complicated than the associated blog. It is written in the style of a novel not a scientific paper.

- There are plenty of topics covered and personal anecdotes that have no science involved.

- Read only what you want to; skip over any parts that don't matter to your circumstances. The book does repeat itself sometimes because it is assumed that people will read selectively, based on what is most useful to them.

- Understand that this book is focused on personal experiences, including interactions with a wider community of people looking for answers. This means a lot of ground is covered but some is left out.

- Understand that this book is focused on what can be done for the brain, which is, of course, connected to the rest of the body; however, that focus means that some information is not included.

- Make use of the blog, which is searchable, and contains far more detail and information. Throughout the book you will be given suggestions as to how to use search terms to access specific information on the blog but you can do this this for any topic. https://www.epiphanyasd.com/

- Google terms that are new to you, but don't be concerned if you cannot understand the more scientific ones. Not completely grasping terms like DHCR7 will not impede your understanding of the book.

- The index is meant to benefit you for finding all the references to a single topic.

Contents

The Author	1
Preface Why I wrote this book	3
Part 1 – Living in a Bubble A personal journey into adulthood	7
Part 2 – Tips and Tricks learnt along the way Another easy read	41
Part 3 – Autism 101 A simplified overview of the science and its application to better understand autism	131
Part 4 – Treating Autism using Personalized Medicine An introductory perspective to a complex subject	195
Part 5 – A to Z of Drugs used in Autism Clinical Trials Who thinks there isn't enough autism research?	243
Part 6 – Preventing Autism What to do about the autism tsunami	291
Take Home Message	309
Index	311

The Author

Peter Lloyd-Thomas has a Master's Degree in Engineering from Imperial College in London and was on the Dean's List at INSEAD, Paris where he gained his MBA. He is experienced as a strategy consultant, developing solutions to ill-defined problems.

His younger son, nicknamed Monty, was born in 2003 and has classic autism. For several years Peter was a parent governor at the small mainstream international school, attended by both his sons. He gave this up and used the time to research autism and translate the science into therapies for his son.

Peter comes from a family of doctors, including medical researchers, who were all taught that autism is untreatable. The Baron score, still used today to grade the severity of inflammation in ulcerative colitis, is named after one of them.

Peter discovered after trialing bumetanide in 2012 that his son's autism does respond to drug therapy. He then developed a personalized polytherapy, the autism Polypill, to treat his son's specific sub-type by repurposing existing drugs.

He shares the published research and his own insights via his blog Epiphany ASD, with parents, doctors and some researchers.

Peter is not a doctor, but has a lot to say about the science of autism and its translation into medical therapy.

He is a practical person; he designed and then supervised the construction of his family's home and he does mend a lot of things. For him treating autism is another project to tackle and a challenge to overcome.

PETER LLOYD-THOMAS

Preface

Game Changer is an introduction to the world where severe autism is viewed as a treatable medical condition, based on translating existing science into therapy. In my autism science blog, I have been shining a light on the usually hidden world of autism science since 2013, all the while fine-tuning a personalized medical therapy for my own son. Monty was diagnosed in 2007 with what now would be termed level 3 severe autism, the kind that requires lifetime care.

The purpose of this book is to highlight how many readers of my blog are significantly improving their child's life prospects, based on existing peer-reviewed science. The book does not go into all the complex details and cite the scientific literature; for that look no further than my Epiphany ASD blog, where thousands of research papers are reviewed and are but a click away.

I have been using personalized medicine for a decade and in 2019 started presenting at international autism conferences. My blog has had two million page views and tens of thousands of comments since 2013.

Many people reading my blog are doctors trying to figure how to help their own child with autism. At medical school they were taught that autism is untreatable and to date all clinical trials have failed to get past the final stage. There is no singular autism and in fact we now know that there are hundreds of possible causes of autism. There cannot be a one size fits all solution; no therapy can possibly benefit everyone.

With such a wide variation in what is now diagnosed as autism, what makes a game-changer? For some people it is getting their five-year-old to talk. For another it is stabilizing a child's behavior so he does not get excluded from school. For an older parent it might be stopping their adult child being violent, so that they can finally go on a holiday together.

In our case, game-changing was raising cognition so that Monty could follow the standard curriculum in a mainstream school without an IEP (Individualized Education Plan), although with an assistant. He went from being unable to maintain any attention and learn anything at school, to being the pupil with model behavior and fully includable. He left high school in 2022 with exam grades (English IGCSEs) that were better than some of his peers. Science was a B, Maths a C, English a C and Geography a C.

Later on, after our game-changer and the many improvements it brought about, it became necessary to develop pharmacological solutions to problems that presented over the years. This included violent summertime raging, verbal and motor tics and most recently acute sound sensitivity.

The science behind how your brain works is very complicated and still only partially understood. Even the simplified version in my blog, Epiphany ASD, is overwhelming to most people. *Game Changer* is not going to tell you exactly how to treat your particular case of autism, for that you need to read the blog and prepare coffee for late-night reading. *Game Changer* will certainly give you plenty of ideas, since it does include an A to Z review of most science-based medical therapies.

Most people's favorite posts in the Epiphany ASD blog are the ones without any science. This book is written with that in mind. Parts 1 and 2 are easy reading, parts 3, 4 and 5 are a bit sciencey, but we finish with part 6 which will be plain sailing for all. There is some repetition in the book; my assumption is that most people are not going to read it from cover to cover.

Having read the book, you then need to find a helpful doctor, or two. This will be much easier in the United States than in Europe.

This book tends to apply spelling from American English, even though the author is English. It is assumed that most people reading this book will be from North America. Some UK English spelling looks very unnatural (e.g. oesophagus vs esophagus) in comparison.

Why call the book *Game Changer*? That is what some readers of my blog call their discoveries. Rather more cryptic options would have been *Hiding in Plain Sight*, or perhaps *The Risk of Doing Nothing*. Some autism interventions have existed for up to 50 years in the scientific literature. They are mostly common drugs that are sitting in your local pharmacy right now. *The Risk of Doing Nothing* is being so worried about doing harm that you neglect to do some good.

GAME CHANGER

PETER LLOYD-THOMAS

Part 1

Living in a bubble
A personal journey into adulthood

A tearful beginning – read on, it does get better

It wasn't really a surprise.

"I am sorry to tell you, my colleagues and I all agree that your son fits a diagnosis of autism. You will receive our full report in a few days' time."

I still remember the ensuing floods of tears – not mine, Dads don't cry.

That was way back in 2007 when we took our three-year-old son to meet a neurodevelopmental pediatrician and her multi-disciplinary team for an autism assessment in central London. Perhaps not the best ending to a Christmas visit to see relatives in England.

Many of those relatives had medical degrees, but nobody knew anything about autism. My mother, a retired general practitioner, looked things up and asked if the diagnosis was autism or autism spectrum disorder. "It looks like one is worse than the other – which way round is it?", she asked. "I am afraid it says autism", I replied, "that's the bad one". To which my mother added, "never mind it's just a label, he is still the same little boy he was."

Another pearl of wisdom, I later received was "just make sure he doesn't get violent, when he gets older." We were later to discover that this is easier said than done.

What difference did a diagnosis make?

In the check-in queue at the airport to fly home, I did wonder whether we were supposed to cut in front of everyone else, like people nowadays do at Disneyland.

Nobody really notices a three-year old with autism. People will assume he is just another badly behaving toddler. You can get away with a lot at that age. Fast forward 16 years and try taking your untreated adult-sized child with severe autism on a plane. People are a lot less understanding and the struggles of trying to travel will likely have multiplied.

Fortunately, after all the therapy you can read about in this book, we can now take our adult son anywhere, from the Great Wall of China to the Wailing Wall in Jerusalem. There were of course some pretty difficult moments along the way, but, so far at least, for every big problem there has been a solution.

Back in 2007 the autism assessment team saw a little boy who jumped a lot, cried a lot and did not speak a word; the big surprise for the developmental pediatrician was that he was already toilet trained. Be thankful for small mercies she told us.

I think like most parents in this situation, our priority at that time was speech. During the assessment in London, we had been told about PECS, the Picture Exchange Communication System. Behavioral intervention using approaches like ABA (Applied Behavioral Analysis) was almost non-existent in Europe at that time.

In parts of North America it has long been relatively easy to enrol in intensive early intervention programs, they have existed for decades, it is just a question of who is going to pay for them.

We had to make our own early intervention program.

The first step was a trip to Brighton, on the south coast of England, where the office of the PECS people was and then enrolling in their three day training course. A few weeks later, I was back in London to learn how to make my son communicate. There were very few parents, it was mainly speech therapists and teaching assistants. Using picture cards stuck on a velcro strip in a little red folder sounds like a simple thing to learn; however the training manual was a few hundred pages long. This was the first of many books that you would not really keep on your coffee table.

PECS, when carried out correctly, is a surprisingly powerful means of communication. I just hoped that our son would be one of those for whom PECS triggers at least some verbal communication. We were lucky and it did.

Once you have single words emerging, you have the basis for other methods that will, over the years, encourage the use of more complex speech.

We used a method called Verbal Behavior, which like PECS, is based very much on the principles of ABA, which is Applied Behavioral Analysis. ABA is a huge business in the United States, because many insurance companies will pay for it. In the rest of the world people generally cannot afford ABA, so it is much less common.

We had to fly in experts and hire and train our own therapists, because there were none.

Kindergarten and then elementary school

Monty's big brother joined a local kindergarten when he was three years old; he did not really like it. He soon moved to a tiny international school with only a dozen children of all ages in a small house. 18 years later, the school has several hundred pupils, from two years old through to 19 years old.

We enrolled Monty quite young in the same school, in its then tiny kindergarten.

A tiny school is naturally the perfect environment for children with special needs and at my PECS course in London they all told me how lucky we were to have this option. Don't come back to England, was their advice.

I ended up helping out as a parent governor of the school for several years, before it became a for-profit private business. This served us well because I got to know all the teachers and there was never a worry of automatic exclusion when Monty got diagnosed with autism. Many parents encounter great difficulty with schools, over the years, until their child becomes an adult. The situation varies greatly, but much of the United States and Scandinavia have very good provision.

As his nineteenth birthday approached, Monty completed his public IGCSE exams and we called it a day with academic schooling. This remains an amazement to the teachers who knew him before he started personalized medicine at the age of nine. A lot has changed, the school became much larger and stopped accepting pupils with special needs long ago. Monty was there for 16 years.

During those first years, the school was like a magnet for kids with special needs that the large international schools would not admit. A family from the US Embassy had their daughter at the US international school, but only our much less well-resourced school would accept their son. The boy would arrive every morning in his wheelchair, pushed by his assistant, who came overseas with him from the US. It never seemed fair that the school with a lot of money would expect our, poorly resourced, school to take their difficult cases. Life tends not to be fair.

Later, twins with autism from the US Embassy came to our small school; one twin more affected than the other. Again, their sister went to the big US international school; so much for inclusion and togetherness. Life was not easy for the mother and eventually the twins were sent to a residential special school in upstate New York. The rest of the family continued their diplomatic tour of duty seeing the sights of Europe.

Some of the teachers really liked having the special needs kids around, perhaps they thought it was fulfilling a moral duty to care for all, other teachers were less keen. One told me she would refuse to have a teaching assistant in her class, to which the then Principal said she would not have a choice.

In TV shows like South Park and in kid's playsets, there is a child in a wheelchair and some variation in skin colours. The idea is that kids should grow up surrounded by all types of people and hopefully become more tolerant adults.

I did ask an Irish teacher at our school how he thought the kids accepted their classmate with non-verbal severe autism, who came to school in a wheelchair. I was really surprised by his answer. "They are frightened of him." That was not what I was expecting to hear.

For about 12 months people were frightened of my son Monty, when he had a severe regression at the age of eight. I did ask one of his classmates what he thought of the situation. He was very rational and understanding. "Monty has a brain illness and this is why he is behaving like this; we have to be understanding and it will pass." I am still impressed that an eight-year-old boy can think like this.

Many little boys with autism get adopted at school by a little girl, with strong mothering instincts. It is extremely common. Monty first had a little Dutch girl take a protective interest in him and then when she left the school, a South African girl followed. What tends to happen is the cute little boy grows into a much bigger boy, the girls approach puberty and priorities change.

Monty is 19 and still some of the girls from school want to hang around with him. Big brother finds this hard to understand and asks me why this is still the case.

Parents are naturally biased and so I asked Monty's assistants why the girls in his class are still so nice to him. "Oh, but he is so cute" is the kind of answer I get.

I recall that in my elder son's class they were not so nice to the boy with Asperger's syndrome (level 1 autism), or the one that wanted to touch the hair of all the girls with long hair. Many people with autism are fascinated with hair – pigtails, ponytails, men with beards, men with moustaches. It is a sensory issue, but one that can get you into trouble when you are older.

Unlike the boy with autism in my elder son's class, Monty was trained by his assistants that you cannot touch another person, without asking permission first. It is all part of teaching the concept of personal space. So, if his blond Czech classmate had made a nice ponytail, he might well ask if he can he touch it; invariably she said yes. In my elder son's class, the boy with much less severe autism, but with the same desire to touch long hair, was viewed by the girls as a stalker/predator.

We had one assistant who had just graduated from University and she had long blonde hair. This is already a big plus in Monty's eyes, but she was always changing her hairstyle, which for Monty was even better. She was educated to be a teacher for deaf people, so I got to learn all about things like cochlear implants. She was a real natural with ABA, hugely energetic and she herself was the reinforcer, no gummy bears required. The local schools for the deaf are very dated and not a good fit for her bubbly personality. She went to work on cruise ships in the Caribbean.

I mentioned many times in my blog that it is really important who is your teaching assistant. Monty has had seven different assistants over a 15-year period. In our case the assistants also worked at our home, so we got to know them all quite well. They were all very different but we did figure out what makes a successful assistant.

We had two males and five females. There is no reason why a young man cannot be a teaching assistant, but it is much more often going to be a better match with a young woman. Yes, women are more likely to look for work like this, but there is much more to it than that. Qualities required include caring, patience, tolerance, adaptability, reliability and empathy – our experience was these were more commonly found in women. Does being young matter? You certainly need to be young at heart, with boundless energy.

If you want your assistant to learn specific instructional methods, this should be a key criterion at recruitment, some people are much more willing to learn new skills than others.

As your child gets older, and you want to promote social inclusion at school, you need to have an assistant who the other classmates see more like one of them, rather than being a teacher. Monty's assistant at high school was only a decade older than him, so she looks more like a big sister.

We did come across people who think that as a boy enters puberty, he should not have a female assistant. That never occurred to us as a potential problem issue.

Our best male assistant came to work on a big Honda motorbike and looked more like a Hell's Angel than a teaching assistant. He was very good with young children. Many children with autism are sensory seekers and they were the ones who enjoyed sitting on his big noisy motorbike.

Often, nobody is quite sure what the teaching assistant is supposed to do. In some cases there is very little teaching going on, it is more about controlling behaviors and making sure the child does not get lost, or have an accident.

In our case the assistants worked for us and so we were the ones that decided what they should be doing. This was a big job in the early years because we had to create a home-schooling program tailored to Monty's needs – call it ABA plus. After personalized medicine, we were later able to just follow the regular school curriculum, with some additions to promote and develop language, plus basic things that were not possible to master earlier, like tying shoelaces, telling time, using money and riding a bike. We never had a formal IEP (Individualized Educational Plan) like you would likely have in the US or Canada.

What's for lunch?

One useful tip I learnt from our original English ABA consultant, was to ask Monty what he had for lunch at school that day. Food really does matter to all of us, autistic or not. Every day the same question should have a different answer and as a parent you should be able to know the correct answer before you ask the question. You can either check on the menu or ask the teaching assistant.

Monty did have some basic words at the age of four, so if he really wanted to reply he could. Most often there would be no reply, or a made-up reply. Then the assistant would intervene and give prompts to hopefully get towards the correct answer.

In January 2013, at the age of nine, all this changed and we have never looked back. Shortly after starting with bumetanide, the fog lifted and Monty would both reliably and enthusiastically tell me what he had for lunch.

I still ask Monty every day what he had for lunch that day. He became an authority at school regarding what is for lunch. He would check the menu in advance and his peers sometimes asked him in the morning what was going to be for lunch.

Food is often a big problem for people with autism. In our family it is Monty's big brother who is the picky eater. Monty eats just about everything, all fruits and vegetables, even fish with all those little bones. His idea of lunch is soup, main course with a salad and then a dessert.

About the only thing he does not like is fizzy drinks. Sorry Coca Cola, Monty really does prefer a glass of cold water.

He has also been to parties with his classmates and will drink a beer. Where we live it is legal.

When Monty was very young, it was still very fashionable to give children fruit juice as a drink. One of his first words was "juice" and people who so happy to hear a spoken word, juice is what he got. Really what he meant by "juice" was "I am thirsty".

People would offer juice and Monty would oblige and drink juice. Unfortunately this is really bad for your teeth, as we discovered. Forget the juice, stick with water.

When we go out for the day, or when we travel abroad, we never have to worry if Monty will eat the food. Food is a focal point of his day and when he writes his diary you can always read what he ate that day.

The diary

Writing a diary was introduced long ago into Monty's routine to help develop more complex speech. Monty talks very little, there is no small talk, he just says what he wants and answers direct questions.

We learned that if you asked him to reply in writing, he could give very detailed answers. So as a therapy we would first ask him to write his reply and then we would repeat the question and ask him to reply verbally. He would then give a full spoken response.

Every Monday he will write an account of what he did over the weekend and then he gets to "retell the story" out loud. He will happily write 200–500 words and later give the out loud version.

It was not always easy to get Monty to write a diary. When we went on a trip, his assistant would casually ask that he keep a diary. Without it being a routine, you then end up trying to write five days of diary in one go, which is no fun for anyone. I think you need to start diary writing slowly and have it be a fun activity, rather than an obligation. I still recall at my own junior school we had to write a diary once a week for homework. This felt like a forced activity; I thought it was none of their business what I did outside school. Monty enjoys making lists and writing a diary.

In a similar way to writing, we have encouraged reading. Learning to read was itself a huge challenge. We had all the books and teaching aides and later I used a great on-line teaching program called Headsprout. What you really need is perseverance and that is what Monty's first assistant had by the bucket-load. There was no way this little boy was going to stay illiterate. I am not surprised many people with severe autism remain functionally illiterate. Somebody needs to have boundless energy to drive the process – a parent, a teacher or an assistant.

Assuming a level of reading is reached, the next big issue for children with severe autism is whether any of what they are "reading" is actually understood.

With a typical child you just give them a list of questions about the chapter and you will soon know how much they understood.

With an autistic child there are other factors in play. Did he understand anything from the chapter? Did he understand the question? Does he actually want to make the effort to give you the correct answer, or just make life easy and ignore the question? If there is doubt that a child is understanding what has been read, with some imagination and effort, rewarding and motivating ways to check comprehension can be found. This all takes time.

Getting your child to read a chapter, or just a few pages a day cannot do any harm. It also becomes a relaxing activity.

ABA

In a small number of countries, like the United States and Canada, great faith is placed in early behavioral intervention using approaches like Applied Behavioral Analysis (ABA). The hope is that you can change the course of autism if you intervene early enough. If you actually dig into the details, as I did in my blog, the reality is usually less rosy.

Where we live there was no ABA, just speech therapy and occupational therapy. I found Tony, an ABA consultant in the United Kingdom who was interested in traveling, and flew him over to teach us all about ABA. We knew another family who had a non-verbal girl of similar age to Monty. They created their ABA home program and we created ours.

In the following years we had Erin, an ABA consultant from the New England Center for Children (NECC), who came to Europe and really struggled to find work, because nobody there wanted to pay for ABA therapy. She moved to Abu Dhabi, where NECC had set up a new business – no shortage of money in the Emirates. She very kindly later helped us find her successor Lilian, our final ABA consultant. Lilian was great, a Greek woman who had spent a decade in the United States, where she completed her PhD. Then she came back to Athens, Greece and established her own ABA center.

Lilian wanted to know the level of Monty's ability across all areas. There is an excellent assessment of skills called ABBLS, or the Assessment of Basic Language and Learning Skills. I had this book hidden away in my all-things-autism sideboard (buffet table, in US English) in the dining room. Using ABBLS is something I do not suppose many parents in the US ever undertake themselves, it is all done for them and paid for by the insurance company. ABBLS is made of many hundreds of incremental skills that you can assess. It covers all domains of learning; you can even use it as a syllabus of what a child with severe autism needs to learn. These are basic skills my elder son had picked up by the time he was three years old. Monty was nearly nine years old and still had huge gaps. It was a painful process to figure out exactly where his level was. I still remember scanning hundreds of pages of the completed assessment and emailing them to Lilian.

It took many hours to update where Monty's level of knowledge was at this stage, but it did force me to read another book with hundreds of pages of tiny print. I guess we finally got our money's worth!

Lilian later told me that Monty was the client she saw the least, but who improved the most. By that time, I had started with personalized medicine. She originally saw the untreated Monty and then later the new and improved treated-Monty. ABA is rather like a religion; you have to be devoted and it is supposed to be exclusive. So, I did not go into the details of personalized medicine with Lilian.

I rather get the impression that ABA goes through a cycle with fresh hopeful energetic young parents coming in at a one end and then they get spun out a few years later, a little broken, downhearted and fatalistic.

For severe autism you need much more than just ABA, or any other learning therapy, you need to start fixing whatever is "broken" in the brain. Fine tuning the brain is a less blunt way to say them same thing. Many medical conditions outside the brain, like gut issues, directly impact behavior, so in the end you have to treat the whole body.

Until the age of 11 Monty would come home after lunch at school to have his home "ABA plus" program till 5pm. During the school holidays he had his home program from 9am to 5pm. It was like a military operation, requiring a lot of input from everyone. He worked very hard and still does, but he genuinely likes it.

At the start of the home program we had classic ABA, with picture cards and also basic exercises to improve things like fine and gross motor skills. Basic things like what to do when a ball is rolled along the grass towards you, or how to catch a ball, all needed to be taught.

People with all levels of autism are known for their bad handwriting. Some kids with severe autism never learn to write, at least not without another person's hand guiding their hand. Handwriting can be improved, but it takes many hours of practice.

I found an excellent program for developing fine motor skills for effective handwriting called *Write from the Start*, you need book 1 and book 2. All these years later and he had the neatest handwriting in his class.

That kind of book you can happily leave out on your coffee table, but some other books you might not want to. The little paperback books that Irena, our first assistant, found really helpful were *Decreasing Behaviors of Persons with Severe Retardation and Autism* and its companion volume *Increasing Behaviors of Persons With Severe Retardation and Autism*. They were written back in 1982 when an autism diagnosis was not something cool and you still could describe someone as being retarded. These two books are all about using ABA (Applied Behavioral Analysis) to improve behavior and compliance. We could never figure out why they could not have put it all in a single book.

Irena moved on ten years ago to work as a teacher, but she still comes to visit.

In the English language, words like retardation are taboo nowadays but not so in other languages. Monty attended a barbecue years ago at a French friend's house and the host casually explained to his French guests, not to worry about Monty and his behavior, he was "retardé" and they should just indulge him. It did not bother me at all. It was information that allowed everyone to enjoy the event. The French use of the word retardé is purely descriptive, it is not offensive as it has become in the English language. It was a surprise nonetheless. I just wanted to get through the event and actually have the chance to sit down and eat something. Monty was, and is, fascinated with fire. Barbecues,

Frenchmen needing their cigar lit with a flashy lighter – all great for Monty. Just watch out in case Monty decides it is time to "turn off" the charcoal glowing in the barbecue.

We have a fireplace at home and in the winter Monty is firelighter-in-chief. He also goes to our big pile of logs and carries them inside. Years ago, I did install smoke alarms all over the house, but to date the only person to set the house on fire was Monty's big brother. I got to play fireman, after a very timely intervention by our neighbour and her garden hose putting most of the flames out. What was most remarkable was the black smoke in the basement, like a solid wall. Since the room on fire has the gas furnace/boiler it could have been much worse. I just turned off the gas supply, got my own garden hose and entered.

Five years of ABA might not look like a good investment when you still get characterized as "retardé". After a few years of personalized medicine, we have left "retardé" behind us. Years later, our French friend actually invited me to meet his wife's relative and her seven-year-old non-verbal son with severe autism and tell her what I had done for Monty, to inspire her to take some action. I do not think anything came of it.

Extreme regression at the age of eight

Life with autism was pretty much under control. We had slow, but steady progress learning with ABA.

Monty had learnt how to read at home, due to the superhuman efforts of Irena, his long-time assistant and buddy, much to the surprise of teachers at school. Irena had become our Mary Poppins, so to speak.

Only now do I fully appreciate just what an achievement it was to teach someone with such severe autism how to read. Many people in these circumstances never learn to read.

Life being life, things change and Irena had to move to another city. How do you replace "Poppins"? There is only one.

Monty understood that he had lost her and it prompted a year long, often violent, regression.

All kinds of never-seen-before negative behaviors emerged, cognitive skills were lost. He started to self-injure and lash out at other people. I would have to stop my car because Monty was smashing his head into the window.

His school report from February 2012 tells the story:

> "The first two weeks of the spring term were extremely difficult for everyone. Monty refused to do any work, even to look at his to-do list. He had tantrums frequently, crying, shouting, hitting his teachers, running from his desk and around the room, often calling Irena's name. Initially, other children were bewildered and considerably distracted by such a radical change in Monty's behavior. Towards the end of the week, though, they started making comments "Oh, Monty misses Irena", although they still twitch at Monty's screams, they try to ignore it and focus on their work."

We now had learnt our lesson and subsequently had two assistants; one in the morning and one for the afternoons.

How do you overcome a situation like this, where violence seems to be stemming from emotional pain?

In some countries you would take a violent child to the local psychiatric unit. In the US some people call the police and have their child taken to the ER, where they may stay for weeks. For such stories just follow the US National Council on Severe Autism (ncsautism on Facebook).

Any clever advice from the ABA consultant? Well, this is a well-known problem when a child gets too attached to their assistant. Best to avoid it happening in the first place. The only thing to do is to endure it and do not change your behavior towards the child, otherwise you may end up reinforcing the new bad behaviors and make them permanent.

So, life went on and over very many months things did gradually settle down, but never quite to where they were.

That summer we were planning to go to Portugal, requiring a connecting flight in Switzerland. On the short flight to Switzerland eight-year-old Monty went completely berserk, with flailing arms, legs and head. I pretty much sat on top of him to restrain him. I would hate to have been a passenger seated nearby. The flight attendant came to investigate and asked if a glass of water would help; perhaps a tranquilizer dart, but spraying water all over the cabin might not be a good idea.

Explosive outbursts continued in Portugal and we could not leave Monty sat in the back of the rental car with his 11-year-old brother, as there would have been a bloody punch up. A decade later and big brother has not forgotten.

The only good thing was that this raging happened when Monty was only eight years old and it did fade away. I would pick him up and hold him upside down, which acted as a reset. This is not in any textbook. I was about the only person he did not hit.

The amazing thing is that he was not expelled from school. Back then I was a parent governor at the school, and they liked me, but everything has limits.

Some people think that this awful year was what triggered my belated interest in personal medicine, but it wasn't, it was purely down to chance.

Enter personalized medicine

In December 2012 I started my trial of bumetanide and there was no turning back thereafter.

Now that Monty's brain was at least partially "fixed", learning became possible at school. I had previously agreed with the school that Monty be held back by two years. In September 2013 he was a ten-year-old in a class of eight-year-olds.

His school report from February 2013, two months after commencing Bumetanide, tells the story:

> "Since the beginning of the school year (September 2012) Monty's behavior has seen a vast improvement. Incidents of hitting peers have ceased and his physical and emotional frustration has significantly decreased. Thus, Monty overall is a lot calmer, more focused member of the class in comparison to early in the school year.
>
> Monty's addition and subtraction skills have shown significant progress. He is able to add and subtract two digit numbers from other two digit numbers up to 50 using the number line. His listening and comprehension skills appear to have made significant improvement since the beginning of the school year as he appears to require less prompting and less paraphrasing."

Back then the teachers thought he would still not be able to keep up with his new peer group and that he would not make it to high school.

I did write in my blog about the delusion of inclusion in schools, where you include pupils who have no possibility of understanding what is going on in the class.

Monty would from now on sit the same tests as his peers and usually got better grades than 30% of them.

ABA therapy

I became a bit of an expert in ABA and a special area called VB (Verbal Behavior) and have a large library of books and teaching resources. I was an early adopter of computer aided learning for children with autism. Before the first iPad, we were using a touch screen at home to teach vocabulary and basic grammar.

ABA, when applied correctly, is a very effective teaching method for many people who do not otherwise know how to learn. If applied badly, or to people who have no need of it, there can be rather disastrous results.

A small number of children with a developmental delay just need a period of intense 1:1 teaching to get their learning back on track. For people with severe autism, the effect of ABA is usually far from dramatic, but any steps forward are highly valued by parents.

ABA was initially oversold by its proponents. The idea was that after a few years of ABA, the person with severe autism would be indistinguishable from his peers. This just is not true, but the idea has somehow stuck, at least with some people. The provision of ABA services, sometimes by minimally trained therapists (now called technicians, for some reason), has become a big business in the US. There has been a boom in private equity investors buying up small firms. The situation in Canada is quite different, because the funding model is different.

Speaking from personal experience ABA or any other 1:1 therapy is very expensive. ABA does not "recover" people from severe autism, but it does help them learn basic life skills.

A decade of home-based therapy

We learnt early on from Lilian, our Greek-American ABA consultant, that older children and adults with severe autism often have no interests and it is a big struggle to fill their time. Related to this, I received an email recently from a US autism Mom who lives at home with her 31-year-old non-verbal daughter. Most of the time, when the Mom can structure some kind of activities, life is OK, but sometimes the daughter gets very aggressive. Mom has to lock herself away for her own safety and call the police. When your child is eight you would never even dream about a future like that. This is why I mention it because it is important people understand the possibility.

I did take heed of Lilian's advice.

Monty's original kindergarten assistant, later to become star ABA therapist, was always very keen to get him interested in music and dance. Dancing is even better than just jumping on a trampoline, though we have two – one small one indoors and a big one in the garden. Dancing while trampolining is also interesting.

I bought a piano when Monty was eight. He went from the "hitting the piano teacher stage", all the way to making recitals in public several years later. He still plays the piano most days, so I think we can say he likes music. He still likes dancing.

Sport is a big part of many children's lives and it does have substantial benefits in terms of socializing and health. Finding a sport for someone with severe autism can be a challenge. They tend to have poor coordination and no understanding of team activity. Some people with autism can run well, but many others do not have enough control over their gait and appear quite clumsy. It all depends what kind of autism they have. A friend has a son with what is called Agenesis of the Corpus Callosum, I had no idea what that was back then. The left and right side of the brain are joined together by a thick bundle of nerve fibers, called the Corpus Callosum. In people with autism the Corpus Callosum is often not quite right, it can be too thick, too thin, or as in the case of Agenesis, it can be completely missing. This teenager was non-verbal, but an excellent runner and his Dad was training him for the Paralympics.

Learning to ride a bicycle is very often possible, although it may take a long struggle. It is not just about riding the bike; parents often wonder what will happen when their child sees a bike coming towards them. Will their child panic and fall off?

We went through all these concerns, but as he became a teenager Monty mastered riding a bicycle, thanks to his then assistant Nela. Now he is really proficient. This reminds me of the years spent learning to tie shoe laces. Some people with autism never learn to tie shoelaces. Is it that people gave up trying to teach this skill, or is it that the person just does not have the motor skills required? Parents do need to prioritize which skills will have the greatest benefits, but at the same time they have to be ambitious and try to expand the comfort zone.

Monty now rides around on his electric scooter, just like his school friends.

High school

In the English school system, high school starts when you are aged 11 or 12, but because I had held Monty back by two years, he was 14 when he entered.

In the junior school they had class teachers whereas in the high school there are just subject teachers. For some children transitioning to high school is difficult, but for Monty there was not such a big difference. It was questioned by some why he was there at all – so much for inclusion! I think some people assumed he would not be able to cope, but cope he did.

As he got older his personalized medicine therapy became more refined. He had long been very diligent with his school work, never missing his homework, albeit having a 1:1 assistant. When it came to sport and any physical activity, he was always a bit of a laggard, a bit lethargic.

The lethargy problem vanished by adding a scoop of Agmatine to his daily polytherapy. This was discovered as much by luck as anything else. There is a lot written about the use of Agmatine in psychiatry, but at that time I knew little about it, and figured out the modes of action only later on. A reader of my blog had mentioned it, but not for lethargy, so I added it to my list of things to investigate. When I present my Polypill therapy at conferences I always include the Energizer/Duracell bunny TV commercial to show the effect of life before and after Agmatine. You do indeed want your little bunny powered with the best alkaline batteries.

Monty got much better at running and could then swim long distances. We swim together most days, usually 500 meters/yards.

The school has an annual poetry and music event at a fancy local hotel. Monty was invited to participate by giving a piano recital. He had played the piano in elementary school, but back then the standard was pretty low and it was more about giving everyone a chance. The poetry night was supposed to be very slick, there were guests and it was all filmed.

Would Monty let the side down? It is a very reasonable concern, because people with autism can get overwhelmed. He came on stage in his smart suit, not giving any signs that he had any degree of autism, played his grown-up piece of music and bowed to the audience. Cue the applause and he came off stage. Mission accomplished and as the Principal told me later, nobody would guess he has autism. Hurrah! That of course is the objective. Some may celebrate it, some may mask it, I just want to banish it.

In elementary school teachers had always wanted Monty to go on their three-day field trip, but back then, before personalized medicine, it had never seemed like a good idea. Where we live even the special schools for kids with severe autism go on short residential trips. I remember getting the gossip from one of our 1:1 assistants, who also used to work at a special school. The children would be dropped off by their parents, each with some kind of supplement they were supposed to take. This was going to be a week when they would not be needing melatonin to fall asleep, they would be worn out by exercise and go to sleep naturally!

We let Monty go on his high school field trip to the mountains, with his assistant. In fact, because she overslept, I ended up driving her half way to the mountains to catch up with the bus. The trip went well of course. The kids all like Monty, his assistant is like a big sister to many of them. Monty and his assistant's twin room was the place to hang out, until Monty declared it was bedtime and he asked everyone to leave. Monty gets up early and goes to bed early.

He never went on the school skiing trips because even though he is very competent at skiing, he could only go if his assistant skied with him. She can ski, but was not confident that she could cope. I actually fully understood, because I started skiing only in middle age and so I am not a natural. If I have to worry about where Monty is, I cannot ski. But it was nice that each year the PE teacher would be pleading with me to let Monty go and I would tell him, it's no problem with me, just try convincing his assistant!

Academic results

Parents are often very interested in the academic results achieved by their children. Nowadays about 20% of children are seen as having some kind of special educational need. The great majority attend mainstream school and sit the same tests and exams as everyone else, perhaps with extra time or some other accommodations. Many children given the right support overcome their early challenges of conditions like dyslexia, or ADHD, and perform well academically by the end of high school.

In our case, in the early years of schooling, teachers did their best to be positive even when not much progress was being made. Most progress was coming from home schooling each afternoon, but it was slow.

With the onset of personalized medicine in 2012, at the age of nine, began the process of catching up all the missing skills and trying to move forward at the same rate as the other children.

In 2022 Monty sat his externally marked final exams (International General Certificate of Secondary Education – IGCSE) and got B in Combined Science (Physics, Chemistry and Biology), C in Mathematics, C in English and C in Geography. The only other subject he was entered for was Art, but the school did not send in the coursework, so no grade was awarded. We dropped History quite a while back. Monty and all his classmates did study ICT, which is like easy computer science, but almost nobody wanted to sit the final exam.

In the kindergarten and elementary school, none of the teachers expected Monty to reach high school, let alone sit an externally marked final exam, or dream of passing one.

I was called into school after the Covid lockdowns and restrictions, when they were not sure whether Monty should be allowed to return to the school. The management got the idea that all that time at home during the pandemic might have rendered him too autistic to be at school. He had to pass a trial period, in case he created any "incidents". When I was asked about my expectations for Monty, my response was that I had no expectations, but I did have aspirations. I wanted him to have the chance to complete what he started and sit his final exams. Whether he passed or failed was of no importance.

Monty went back to school to pick up his final report and his school photo during the summer recess. It was his triumphal moment, when the teachers came up to him and congratulated him. Of course he is no straight-A student, but he did better than some of his classmates.

As Monty would say, "school - done, over and finished!".

Skiing

When Monty was five years old, I thought it was only fair to his big brother that they should both have the chance to ski. Big brother loved it and having mastered skiing both forwards and backwards, later moved on to snowboarding.

For Monty, skiing was a huge challenge. Just putting on the helmet was a problem, let alone all the other gear. Standing in the cable car (gondola) going up the mountain surrounded by other people for ten minutes was not easy.

We found a small ski school in Zell am See, Austria where a very nice lady and her Polish partner taught people with autism to ski. It was still then a very small school. You have to book way in advance and as luck would have it, Monty got an ear infection just before our trip to Austria. This was not a disaster because it meant that the first days were spent off the slope. There was time to prepare to ski, step by step, in a stress-free environment. You see what the ski boots look like and practice putting them on and taking them off. You get used to putting the helmet on. You very importantly get used to the instructor and she gets used to you. The school learnt a lot from this and even now calls it the "Monty method".

In effect, the school has stumbled on ABA for skiing. Break down a complex task into tiny steps, practice the tiny steps before trying to put them together.

In spite of the Monty method, skiing was still a challenge.

All those one-to-one lessons and one broken collar bone later, was it all worth it? At one point I was not really sure. You cannot have a private instructor for ever, just like you cannot have ABA classes for ever. At some point you have to be able to do things for yourself.

The first step to ski independence was to have Monty ski with his brother. Would big brother lose him? Would there be falls and more broken bones?

I told big brother not to worry and just do his best.

Of course, big brother did lose Monty a few times over the years, but nothing bad happened. Monty just skied down the mountain by himself.

Monty is now a slow and steady skier. He can now go down even the steepest black slope and he does not fall.

We have two adult sons who are good skiers; that is not something many would have predicted.

Learning to ski was a good example of stretching your comfort zone and showing to others what you are capable of. People at Monty's school were very surprised that he can ski. It definitely helps inclusion to have some "cool" skills. Something similar was Monty being able to come up to the grand piano at junior school, set up for a teacher to play, and sit down and play himself. One of the in-girls came up to me and said "How can he do that? I've had lessons for years and I still can't play like that". Practice makes perfect.

There are people with non-verbal severe autism who are great skiers and ice skaters, but I think many never get the chance.

Swimming

Swimming is a really important skill for people with autism to master, because drowning is a very common cause of their death. Often children with autism are fascinated by water and it inspires them to wander and then they fall in, fully clothed, panic and drown.

Monty always liked playing in water but until starting personalized medicine it was not possible to teach him to swim properly. He could tread water, but you certainly could not leave him unattended in a pool, let alone a lake or the sea.

Fast forward several years and Monty is a very confident swimmer. He goes to the pool, opens the cover, sprints his 500 meters/yards then has some fun on the pool slide. He closes the pool cover, takes a shower and he is ready to do something else.

Jumping off a jetty into an Italian lake, or jumping into the Greek Aegean Sea, Monty now looks just like a typical teenager.

Theatre and cinema

Going to see performances or films/movies at the theatre is something that is often difficult for young children with severe autism. The sounds can be overwhelming, as can bright lights and then darkness.

The first movie Monty managed to sit through in its entirety was the Simpsons Movie, when he was four years old. Getting to that point involved many less successful attempts.

Children's theatre involving a lot of music and dance was a big hit and a regular event on Saturday afternoons. Later on, we discovered that his current school assistant was in the choir years ago at the same theatre.

Matinees were always better than evening performances, since at the interval in the evening he would just want to go home to bed. He was even able to attend "grown up" ballet performances at Covent Garden in London, without any incidents.

It is easy to give up and exclude your child from these kinds of events, that would be a mistake, especially when many venues now host 'autism-friendly' events with lowered volumes and other accommodations.

Haircuts

Cutting hair and indeed fingernails and toenails is traumatic for young children with severe autism. Perhaps they think you are cutting off a living part of their body, so it is entirely rational to be anxious.

In many families the parents, grandparents or even siblings get involved in cutting hair while the child is sleeping. Over time most people end up at the barber/hairdresser and it may even become a stress-free event.

Monty now loves getting his hair cut. He proudly wet-shaves himself every day and sometimes cuts his own nails. It was not always so easy.

The key, as with most other things, is just perseverance. It is important to stretch boundaries and step out of your comfort zone, otherwise how will you cope with one of life's biggest challenges – the dentist!

Going to the dentist

It used to be that there was nothing worse than thinking your child with severe autism might need the dentist. Where we live few dentists want to even try to treat people with severe autism and I really cannot blame them. The result is that parents put off getting routine dental care until radical interventions are required.

In some countries dental care is easier because it is legal to give full sedation, or even general anesthetic, outside of a hospital environment. In most countries this was made illegal many years ago, because people were dying at the dentist. You really do need a qualified anesthesiologist present.

I found a really good training resource called the D-termined program, by a US dentist called David Tesini. It is a step-by-step guide to build up tolerance to dental interventions and at the end of it, a child with severe autism should be comfortable being treated by any dentist and all with just local anesthetic.

The problem was I could not find any local dentist interested to even watch the DVD – this was back when people still had DVD players.

The only hospital with a special dentistry unit had a three month wait and they focus on what is called radical dentistry, which means pulling teeth out under general anesthetic, not trying to fix teeth.

At the age of five Monty went to a nearby country where you could get general anesthetic at a private dental clinic. They brought in an anesthesiologist from a local hospital, but even injecting the initial sedative involved a lot of screaming and flailing little limbs.

Clearly you do not want to go abroad every time you need the dentist, nor do you want to keep having general anesthetic. Many children and adults with severe autism have all their dentistry under full sedation or general anesthetic. This makes life much simpler, but it is not without risks.

Things did gradually improve and later we found a very nice dentist who got Monty to comply while she checked his teeth, but no actual drilling and filling ever took place. Apparent tooth aches were always a false alarm. She then went on extended maternity leave and then the next thing you know, there was a genuine dental emergency and we had no dentist.

A local dentist, let's call her Mary, had recently started treating her young relative with autism and this then opened a floodgate to other children. She was doing simple fillings, but was wary of starting anything complicated that she could not finish, due to non-compliance by the child.

We ended up back at the special needs dentistry unit at the children's hospital, the one with the three-month waiting list for general anesthetic. This time I was accompanied by Mary, our very committed new dentist. After a quick examination they immediately wanted to do extractions, with a three month wait for the anesthetic. I was not having that; who pulls out teeth in a 16-year-old? At least try and fix them. The hospital dentist told us that the teeth could potentially be repaired, but that this would be a lengthy process involving multiple visits all with anesthetic, this would not be possible in the hospital. She herself would not recommend even trying to do this; all she could do was make an appointment for extractions under general anesthetic.

Now I had a dental dilemma to solve. Our nice new dentist, Mary, did not want to undertake procedures that would require multiple visits, each with an injection of local anesthetic, unless there was an emergency option to go and pull out the tooth the next day under general anesthetic.

Fortunately, I had just had a minor operation under general anesthetic at a small local private hospital. I knew they did a small amount of regular dentistry, so I went to see them to see if they could do dentistry under general anesthetic. I went in to see a new dentist who had come back from working in Brazil for many years. He was very enthusiastic and agreed that unnecessarily pulling out children's teeth was pretty barbaric. He called up one of the anesthesiologists, who said she would be happy to administer anesthetic. Problem solved!

So I called up Mary the dentist and said call the guy from Brazil, who by now had agreed to be our plan B. Then Mary started getting cold feet about the prospect of treating Monty under local anesthetic, because she expected it would take a dozen visits over many months, each time with an injection into the upper or lower rear jaw. "Don't worry Mary", I reassured her, "I will make sure it all goes well and Monty will be fully cooperative. We will practice at home" and practice we did.

A dozen visits and several months later, all the work was completed. Mary has a new favorite patient and Monty likes going to the dentist.

I no longer fear my son getting a toothache.

Even though Mary never watched David Tesini's training videos, she did use many of the ideas in his D-termined program. Everything was done in small steps, was fully explained in advance and she tried to make it as fun as possible.

I had to sit, or stand, by Monty the entire time, making sure he fully complied and didn't hit her, which certainly can happen if you treat someone with autism. During one session the anesthetic did not seem to work, even after a second dose, but Monty endured, although I had to stand directly in front of him the whole time to keep him calm.

When I used to take my elder son to the dentist, I just used to sit in the waiting room and then pay the bill on the way out. Life with autism is not so simple!

I wrote about the dentist in my blog and it was a subject that resonated with readers.

In the United States dentists are allowed to use a restraining device called a papoose board, strapping the child to a board with several wide velcro straps. The end result is the child cannot move and the dentist can proceed without any risk of those flailing arms or legs. You cannot even move your head. I guess the child can still bite the dentist – you certainly cannot scratch your nose. Some parents love papoose boards and some think they are torture.

I was surprised that some dentists see their young autistic patients without the parent physically in the treatment room. You would think the most calming and reassuring thing for any child would be the presence of a familiar face; but I suppose some parents might get upset during the procedure and then make things even worse for the child.

I learned from Mary, our dentist, that autistic children sometimes come with a parent or grandparent and they might just leave the child and go shopping. She then has to somehow control those flailing arms and legs – not an easy task.

Monty is well conditioned to follow my instructions, so he sits still with his hands on his legs. He gets on well with Mary and he has dentistry to music, he tells her what songs to play. They both like

Cyndi Lauper. He followed her instructions, just like he follows mine. Still, nobody likes a big needle being stuck in their rear jaw. I was mainly concerned Monty might bite Mary; Mary was only worried Monty would bite his tongue due to the anesthetic. In the end nobody got bitten.

Going to the doctor

Some people with autism have what I call an over-active immune system. This means they are susceptible to conditions like allergies and asthma.

Monty does have asthma, but it is entirely controlled with a preventative inhaler every morning, so he shows no symptoms.

There were a couple of scary incidents with asthma while traveling abroad when Monty was a young child. The moral of both stories was always double check you have your rescue asthma inhaler and don't be shy about over-using it in an emergency.

We were on holiday in Denmark, to visit the original Legoland, in Billund and also see Copenhagen and other sights. We had taken a short ferry ride to a tourist island which turned out to have an unusual wild grass growing. This prompted an asthma attack, but unfortunately the inhaler was back in the hotel; so get in the car, wait for the next ferry and get to the mainland as fast as possible. Being Scandinavia, the pharmacy will not sell you an inhaler, even if you cannot breathe, because the rule is you must have a prescription. Even the nearby small hospital was completely unhelpful. In the meantime, I had calmed him down, the episode had passed and breathing was normal.

On another trip, this time to Maribor in Slovenia we had the rescue inhaler, but it did not rescue the situation. We were later told by the very helpful local doctor, don't worry about what it says on the instructions, just keep giving more until breathing is normal. If you cannot breathe, you will die and excessive use of the rescue inhaler is not going to kill you.

For the past several years. I have kept a small metal pill box in my pocket, with my autism interventions and indeed my steroid pills to treat an acute asthma attack.

When Monty broke his collarbone skiing, there was no crying, he just held his head leaning over to one side. We drove him to hospital in Zell am See, Austria. The most important first step was to get a credit card imprint, then they quickly strapped him up. It was a very simple process.

However, other than these incidents far in the past, we have little contact with doctors for regular health issues. Monty has had ultrasound examinations, but all precautionary. I arranged for an X-ray of his hand so a helpful endocrinologist could estimate his bone age. You measure the gaps between the small bones to estimate if you have advanced or delayed growth. We have done the panorama X-ray of the jaw for the dentist.

We never visited any kind of DAN! (Defeat Autism Now) or MAPS (Medical Academy of Pediatric Special Needs) doctor; these autism doctors are common in the United States, but not elsewhere.

Via my blog I do have very many contacts with doctors who have a child with autism, but mainly it is them asking me questions.

For children with autism, taking a blood draw is like a parent's worst nightmare in the early days; that is until they have faced a dental emergency. As long as you make a point of mastering blood draws whilst young, by the teen years it should be less of a struggle.

Many children with autism have GI (gastrointestinal) dysfunctions of one kind or another. This can range from reflux and food allergies to various inflammatory diseases. Then you have to find an open-minded gastroenterologist, which for some people is a huge struggle. I discussed this with a mother at a conference in London; she told me how she could not get treatment for her autistic child with GI issues and was told to go abroad. She went to Italy and found a gastroenterologist who did treat her child. Sounds rather crazy, doesn't it?

One condition that seems quite common in autism is Eosinophilic Esophagitis (EoE), I wrote a blog post about it and I thought nobody would read it, but it was very widely read. If you are interested just google "eosinophilic esophagitis epiphanyasd".

Even though Monty had no such GI problems, I certainly did as a child. They were never accurately diagnosed. I even had an operation to remove a so-called Meckel's diverticulum, which is a leftover of the umbilical cord. The only problem was it was a mistake and there was no diverticulum to remove, but there was a grumbling appendix. So, I was never very impressed by gastroenterologists.

We have experienced relatively plain sailing in regard to doctors and dentists. This was in no small part due to taking control of the situation and also not relying on public services.

Many parents do have great struggles with both dental care and broader medical care. People with severe autism and ID are unlikely to receive the same standard of care as the broader public. The comorbidities of severe autism tend to get ignored unless the parents take the initiative. Some parents go to extreme lengths.

Covid shots and the shooting range

Monty's grandfather is a retired career soldier and he shared many military stories with Monty's big brother. From an early age big brother has been going shooting with his grandfather. I think it was assumed that this is one activity Monty would definitely never be able to try.

Over the years Monty became so self-controlled, it seemed only reasonable to show him the shooting range that his brother goes to.

Monty is very diligent about following instructions and so he had no problem with the safety protocols. He also had no problem at all hitting the targets with a variety of weapons, including his grandfather's old army pistol.

Even the loud noises did not bother him.

When it came to getting his Covid shots, there was no drama, I just told Monty that you need two holiday injections before you can go to the beach this summer. The drama came on the way home from Monty's second shot. I had been fulfilling my taxi driving duties, shuttling people around. Monty was in the back with his brother, who was later going to his shooting training; we were stationary in traffic at a busy intersection. Two large men came running through the traffic and one jumped into our car, the door was not locked because someone had recently exited. It was all over in a flash, I shouted to those in the back "get the gun!". By the time big brother had fumbled through the combination lock of his bag, our visitor had wisely decided to make a hasty exit.

Monty was a little agitated and big brother thought we were being carjacked. In retrospect, I think it was just a case of one man chasing the other through the traffic, for whatever reason.

Holidays/Vacations

Holidays are supposed to be a relaxing break from routine, but most people with autism love routine and can struggle with change. Some children with autism find travel by plane very stressful. Cars, trains and boats are often very much appreciated, but planes and airports can be challenging.

Monty's first flight was when he was six months old and since then he has travelled extensively. A baby with autism and a typical baby both cry on planes. It is not much fun for people seated nearby, but I think we all just accept that babies cry on planes. What we do not accept is anyone nearing adult size being disruptive on a plane.

As long as you are still not out of place in a stroller/pushchair, travel is not so hard. Monty got pushed around Euro Disney, outside Paris; he was not so interested. He did neatly line up the toys on the shelf in one of the many gift stores, the only time he really exhibited this classic behavior of autism.

Some children with autism stay in a stroller for many years. The child feels safe and secure and it is hard to lose your child when he is strapped in.

If it is summertime and there are a lot of airborne allergens, Monty is going to be more anxious than normal, but with correct therapy in place, he will be just fine. If you omit these summertime add-on therapies, there will be trouble.

If there is an unexpected and unnoticed autoimmune trigger, like exposure to a food allergen, there can still be pretty wild and aggressive behavior. So far this only happened once and it was treatable.

Monty had his year of rage when he was eight and that might have ended his travels, but that was overcome and then from the age of nine he became much less autistic as a result of personalized medicine. You have a few years to figure out your case of severe autism, before you may find yourself limited to road trips.

From then on, even though he was getting bigger, the gap between his behavior and typical behavior stopped widening. As a result, we can take Monty anywhere, without having to worry if he will cope. There are only a handful of countries in Europe he has not been to.

Some people have a problem with their ears when flying, because their ears do not pop, no matter how much they suck on candy or swallow. They have a problem with the eustachian tube that is meant to balance the pressure in the middle ear with the outside environment. Their ears may only pop many hours later. Monty and one of his cousins have this problem and it can be painful.

This kind of pain is likely to produce disruptive behaviors, particularly if you do not understand what is going on.

It may sound trivial, but imagine trying to take your near adult-sized autistic son through passport control when he has an acute pain in his ears. Some border control staff are extremely understanding and some are truly awful.

The first solution was Monty's own idea – it is to dive into the deep end of a swimming pool. This guarantees to pop your ears.

A pool is often not an option and it takes time to reach it, so I came up with a solution that involves a bottle of water, a straw and squeezing your nose closed. You close your nose and suck water up the straw. Keeping your nose squeezed shut, you then try and swallow. Do this two or three times, during the final 10 minutes of flight and even the most stubborn ears seem to pop as the plane descends. When his ears pop there are sighs of relief all around.

When flying long haul to China, we discovered that Monty has a big issue with the harmonica inward folding toilet doors that some planes have. He thinks he is going to get stuck inside, so he will not use them. I think he probably once got stuck in a toilet, somewhere. For years he would always check the mechanism on the door in an unfamiliar restroom. It actually is very rational, albeit a bit quirky.

Many children with autism are sensory seekers, they like to sit upstairs on an open top bus, ride on roller coasters, or just stand outside on a boat trip. You would think they would like to travel by plane but this is often not the case.

Monty loves an open top bus ride, or a trip of on ferry boat, where he can stand outside on the upper deck in strong wind. When there is violent turbulence during a flight and some passengers are getting anxious, Monty is enjoying the "wobbly airplane".

In the case of some Aspies, with level 1 autism, they worry that the plane is going to crash and that is why they do not want to step on board. Some refuse to fly.

In many airports they now randomly select travelers for more invasive screening, more often than not this has ended up being Monty. Some airports have well trained staff and others do not. We were surprised to find Zurich, Switzerland to be in the latter group.

In China all visitors need to scan their own fingerprints before passport control, Monty managed that just fine, but I think others might struggle.

Once there is no pain or anxiety being in a plane is fun for most children. I always thought the journey was the best part of my childhood holidays. If you are a child you have plenty of space for legs and if it is long-haul they keep feeding you, plus you have all the snacks your parents brought along for you. The inflight TV is great fun for many kids. Some airlines have great services and others do not. We went for a wintertime visit to Israel to see Jerusalem and the coast at Tel Aviv and Jaffa. We took the local bus to visit Bethlehem and meet the Palestinians. The locals in Jerusalem wanted to charge hundreds of dollars for a car ride to Bethlehem; instead we paid about $2 for a local bus and had a Palestinian taxi give us a little tour and drop us off at the barbed wire fence back to Israel. Due to snow back home the flights were cancelled and we had to come back via Istanbul, making it a really long day. Thanks to the inflight TV on Turkish Airlines, Monty had a great time. I think his favourite was the long sandy beach in Tel Aviv.

Wandering and drowning

Wandering is often a problem autism parents have to face, particularly in North America, where missing autistic children often feature in local news. Where we live most people have a fence around their garden/yard and so it is much easier to secure your property.

I made our house and garden/yard escape proof and we never had Monty go AWOL (absent without leave). As he got older, he figured out the combination lock to exit via the garage and which buttons to press to open the electric lock on the gate, but he does not try to wander.

For years he has been going out by himself to take out the garbage. So far, he has always come back.

Often when children with autism wander they end up near water, fall or walk in and drown.

Monty is attracted to water, but he is now a very competent swimmer, so no worry of drowning. All children need to know how to swim, the sooner they start to learn the better.

How parents react to a diagnosis of level 3 autism

Parents of young children with severe, level 3, autism often start out very enthusiastic about how they are going to tackle their child's disability. In some countries the services on offer are substantial and it can become a full-time job just taking your child to all the therapy sessions. Some children quite quickly make considerable progress, the nonverbal child starts to talk, play skills may develop and so on, but for many children progress is painfully slow and sometimes non-existent. Some children even regress. Life is not fair.

In many countries there are very active self-help groups where parents can exchange ideas and avoid feeling isolated.

Some people start their own special school, some people set up a research foundation for their child's sub-type of autism. Other people raise money for autism charities.

One reader of my blog started publishing peer-reviewed research on factors that are linked to autism. One reader started her own biotech firm to try and develop drug therapies aimed at specific types of autism.

Many factors influence the parental response, not least whether the two parents agree what to do. Often, they do not!

What I did initially was to learn all about the best practices in behavioral intervention and then we trained our 1:1 assistants to apply them. Where we live these services did not exist, so we had to bring them. We ended up with a house that looked like a school, with a very extensive library of teaching materials. We had a touch screen monitor for computer aided teaching, before Apple had made its first iPad.

I was very active in supporting the tiny school our children attended, to make sure that it could continue to operate. I ended up helping guide the financial side of the school and recruiting the Principals. The end result was that there was always a lot of goodwill coming back in the other direction. When Monty had a year-long regression at the age of eight, there was never even a mention of excluding him from school. When, at the age of nine, I wanted Monty held back two years, it took just one conversation. The teachers have always been very nice towards Monty, but even nice usually has its limits.

When the school later became a for-profit business things did change. This coincided with when I started to learn about personalized medicine for autism. Quite quickly this evolved into a polytherapy using a handful of interventions.

It seemed a pity not to share this polytherapy and I did present it to the European Medicines Agency (the equivalent of the US FDA) and I discussed it with intellectual property people at the University I graduated from. I took the decision to just share my ideas for free, via my blog.

Later on, I started to get invited to give presentations at autism conferences in Europe and the US. I made some videos for YouTube.

I was often asked about writing a book or other publication. My blog does get quite complicated; after a decade of studying medical science, I can get into quite detailed areas of science.

There is no point writing an autism book that the great majority of parents cannot understand, so I have opted for this science-lite version, with a lot of personal anecdotes of our life with autism.

PETER LLOYD-THOMAS

Part 2

Tips and tricks learnt along the way

Schooling

Choosing how to school a child with autism is a really important decision. In most developed countries, children with severe (called level 3 in DSM5) autism usually get diagnosed when they are about three or four years old. In some other countries it might be five years old, or even later.

Mild autism (called level 1 in DSM5) is usually diagnosed much later and often based on feedback from teachers who report issues at school.

In developed countries there are special schools for children with mild autism, previously called Asperger's Syndrome. This comes as a surprise to parents struggling to find a school for a child with severe autism. Indeed, the UK's only residential school for girls with autism, Limpsfield Grange, which was featured in a TV documentary, serves a group that do not seem disabled at all.

For most people the term special school refers to schools for disabled children. They might be deaf, visually impaired, have intellectual disability (ID), have Down syndrome, have severe autism, or cerebral palsy or many other possible conditions.

About 20% of all children have some kind of special educational need. In years gone by only severe needs were identified and catered for at school; there could be a stigma attached to being in special education.

Across the world there has been a trend towards adapting teaching in mainstream schools to reflect the fact that so many children have some kind of special educational need. This special need is commonly something well known like dyslexia or ADHD (attention deficit hyperactivity disorder) but includes a myriad of conditions. A well-resourced mainstream school can provide support to help children with special needs achieve their full potential.

The question is how great can these special needs be for the mainstream school still to be able to cope, and at the same time for the other pupils to not be disturbed and held back? There is no easy answer to this question.

In some countries very disabled children attend mainstream school with their 1:1 teaching assistant. In some schools there are multiple kids sitting in class with their 1:1 teaching assistant. This tends to result in a class within a class, because the special needs kids cannot follow what the class teacher is doing, but are engaged in some entirely different activity with their assistant. There can be so much distraction in the class that everyone's learning suffers.

In some cases the 1:1 teaching assistant is really there just to supervise the child, minimize disruption and take him out to the toilet.

Special schools vary widely, some have tiny classes and each child has their own 1:1 teaching assistant. With this intense level of staffing, many otherwise entirely non-verbal children can be taught at least basic speech or some alternative method of communication (PECS, sign language, etc).

In parts of the world with much more basic special schools, non-verbal children may get abandoned unless parents are proactive. I gave a presentation at an autism conference in Moscow and I was very pleased to see that the organizer had made great efforts to make the case in Russia that with the right kind of 1:1 teaching, non-verbal children can be taught how to speak, or at least communicate.

Most parents have three choices when it comes to schooling:
1. Mainstream school
2. Special school
3. Home schooling

Home schooling is common in the United States, but is actually illegal in many countries.

There is an excellent book covering the issue of mainstreaming children with autism in the US, by Bryna Siegel, called *The Politics of Autism*. It is quite a heavy read, but full of insights from a lifetime involved in autism and education.

She makes many points and highlights several uncomfortable truths.

You can only include a child in school if they are "includable"; if not, you are really not helping them. Perhaps their parents feel better because their child attends school with regular kids.

I call it the delusion of inclusion. If inclusion works for a child that is great, but if the child learns nothing and is disruptive, then there is no point. You just have to accept the reality and find a better solution.

What do children actually learn in special schools for people with severe autism? Do they learn basic academic skills like reading, writing and basic math? Do they learn valuable life skills? Do any actually gain genuine qualifications, beyond the fact that they attended, until they aged out of the school?

The development of some people with autism plateaus at a very early age. As they get older they become adult sized but cognitively they remain a toddler.

Other children with severe autism continue to learn, but at a much slower rate than typical children, so as they get older the gap becomes wider and wider, to the point where they are not includable.

Home schooling is only as good as the teacher and I guess that is why it is illegal in many countries. Personally, I think home schooling can be a very successful part of the education of a child with severe autism, but it takes a great deal of time and resources.

I could summarize my son's education as having had the following elements.

From the age of three Monty attended a regular Kindergarten initially alone, but shortly thereafter with his own 1:1 assistant. He really did get a socialization benefit from seeing typical children and just getting out of the house for the morning. Did he learn much? Not really.

Every afternoon Monty was back for home-schooling with the same 1:1 assistant, and it continued that way until he was 11 years old.

From the age of nine Monty started personalized medicine and very quickly became academically includable. He could actually learn things from the class teacher, he was no genius, but he was finally learning.

At this point also came the big educational reset when we held him back two years at school.

By the age of 11, Monty was happily following the regular academic curriculum at school and so he started to attend full time.

Home schooling has never stopped. Monty works with his 1:1 assistant during the school holidays. I teach him math/maths at the weekend. He reads a book for about half an hour a day. He has a big collection of drawing materials at home, just like at school. He has a piano to play, a big collection of music and videos and the omnipresent iPad.

The question with Monty and school was always how far he could go. The school had no special needs resources and I think the expectation was that after kindergarten and a few years of junior/primary school he would disappear. As his 19th birthday approached, Monty finished school. Ever since the two-year reset at the age of nine he moved forward with the same peer group. He has not come bottom of the class with this peer group, which is itself a big achievement if you were born with severe autism. Prior to personalized medicine and the two-year reset, Monty could never be assessed using the standard tests/exams at school. He was lost in space and got whatever "pity grades" the teacher chose to give.

By high school, the school management had changed. Special needs were not desirable. The fairy tale was over and we knew that any disruptive behavior, or "autistic incidents" might lead to him being expelled. So, we made sure they did not occur. That is life in the real world, or at least our real world.

For some people writing to me via my blog, their child getting excluded/expelled from school is a constant worry.

Some people tell me, "But oh, this is impossible, it is illegal to discriminate against people with a disability." Welcome to the real world.

When I get questions via my blog asking for advice about schooling, I make it clear that you need to choose a solution based on your own very specific circumstances, there is no cookie cutter answer. Those specific circumstances may change over the coming years and you will then have to modify your plan. As more and more people adopt personalized medicine, more children will become genuinely "includable" and so able to thrive in the mainstream.

Inclusion may then cease to be a delusion, at least for some children born with severe autism.

Why have a blog and why use your real name?

When I discovered in 2012 that at least my son's type autism responded to therapy, my first instinct was to want more, so I looked for other add-on therapies. This proved not so difficult and so I thought I should tell somebody about this.

The developmental pediatrician who had diagnosed my son in 2006 was not terribly interested. I did get a response from the European Medicines Agency, when I presented my Polypill therapy to them. They said it was all very interesting, team up with a doctor and collect more data. I did establish contact with the researchers in France who have been developing bumetanide as a therapy for autism since 2011. We are still in touch and I have kept them informed about my ideas for improving bumetanide as a therapy. They read my blog.

Having a blog connects me with other similarly minded people and I have got useful ideas from all the thousands of comments and emails I receive.

Many people who contact me are actually doctors, or even professors of medicine, who just want to improve the life chances of their own child with autism.

Some readers of my blog adopted virtually the same polytherapy as the one I use and were profoundly affected when they saw life-changing results. So at least I know that while autism is indeed a very varied condition, there are other people out there with a very similar version to the one I am treating.

Of course, most people reading my blog are just lurking. They are not ready or able to make the jump to personalized medicine.

My blog has been criticized for being too much about pharmaceutical drugs, and not the usual OTC (over the counter) supplements and diets. I just follow the evidence and the science and that most often takes you to drugs.

Some elements of my son's therapy are OTC, at least in some countries, so they are easy to try. Some therapies are available in one country and not another.

Bumetanide is impossible to get in Algeria, but easy to get in Egypt. People in the United States either get bumetanide from the local pharmacy, courtesy of a doctor who reads the research, or they buy it from Mexico. People in Poland take a holiday in Spain and buy their bumetanide without prescription.

My sister asked me why I used my real name? If you want to be taken seriously, you can hardly hide behind an avatar.

Helping others?

For some people helping others is a natural reaction, but for many people helping others is not a natural response. In modern life people tend to focus on putting themselves first.

One redeeming feature of being an autism parent is that you get to meet many people who really want to help others and are not just trying to put themselves first. These are the people working as assistants and therapists.

I get frequent requests for financial donations from the business school I paid a lot of money to attend in my early twenties. Back then I paid for it all myself, with no help from anyone, parents included. When I get the "begging emails", I just think to myself "Are you serious? Get real, how about helping some people who really need it?"

Our piano teacher only teaches kids with special needs and has the scratches and bruises to prove it.

Our dentist actually wants to treat special needs kids and even though it takes far more time to treat them than typical kids, she does not charge anything extra. In the US some dentists charge an add-on behavioral management fee, to treat kids with special needs.

We have had a long line of 1:1 assistants, stretching over 15 years. I often thought how I could not do that all day long. It is one thing looking after your own child, who happens to have a disability, but to actively seek out disabled people to work with, knowing the challenges and poor pay, is something very different.

My contribution to helping others comes in the form of fielding questions on my autism blog and answering emails. I always push people towards having a public discussion on my blog, because it might help other readers and also because other readers can chip in with their own ideas.

People have asked me to do personal consultations, but I am not a doctor and do not pretend to be one.

I have learned a great deal about human nature from all these interactions, both virtual and real.

Some parents are completely lost and do very little to help their child. They are still trapped in denial, despair and disappointment. Don't be one of those.

Some parents are the complete opposite and go to extreme lengths to help their child. It has nothing to do with them having a lot of money, or being scientifically educated. They just will not give up and when they encounter a barrier they go over the top, or find a way around it. As you would expect, these are my kind of people and I will always try to help them.

Many parents are dabbling with the idea of going beyond a typical response to autism. They might get involved in nutritional therapies and over the counter supplements. They very likely on principle rule out the idea of using drugs; if you are dealing with a case of severe autism, that is a big mistake.

As their child gets older, most parents have grown to accept the outcome that has befallen their child. Some do have a change a heart; I had an exchange with a father who contacted me on my blog, saying that he was now ready to seek his own epiphany to improve the outcome of his now adult son with autism. Years of DAN! doctor therapy had not helped. He had even paid for genetic testing. He had always ruled out using drug therapies but now he is left with a severely autistic adult son. Could I help? Was it too late? He sent me the genetic testing results, that the DAN! doctor had made no use of. I was amazed to find a long list of potentially treatable genetic mutations, just based on spending a few minutes per gene on the internet. I gave my comments by gene and indicated what potential therapies were suggested from the published research. For me that was a job done. The problem for the father is that where he lives doctors do not treat genetic mutations, they might not even read about them. For them, I am like science fiction. Crazy world.

One striking insight I did learn is that if you have a daughter with severe autism, you really should insist on genetic testing. For boys with severe autism, you are much less likely to find answers from genetic testing, but it is still worth doing it. For girls with severe autism, Whole Exome Sequencing should be automatic.

Females do have more protection against severe idiopathic multiple-hit autism than boys. So, girls are likely to have either very severe autism or just mild Aspie-like symptoms.

I have a group of readers of my blog who have a daughter with a single gene type of autism. Some are extremely rare, quite possibly because other affected girls never had genetic testing.

A little-known fact among lay people is that most single gene autisms are identifiable by variations on the face. There is even a smart phone app (Face2Gene) that can detect many mutations. Unusual hands, feet and even teeth can also be used to identify these syndromes. Fragile X, the most common single gene cause of autism, is really obvious when you see it.

One reader was going through all the myriad of interventions for her young daughter and then learned she had Rett syndrome. This is caused by a mutation in the MECP2 gene. Once you know that you have a specific genetic cause of autism, you can focus on learning about that specific dysfunction and what you can do about it.

Another reader of my blog whose daughter has Rett syndrome has been very proactive in searching out science-based ways to improves his daughter's life. I think he will have an impact.

One reader had a young daughter with severe autism and leukemia – she died. There is an overlap between cancer genes and autism genes and so this is sadly going to happen. It is very rare.

I wrote about a gene called PAK1 in my blog and was contacted a few years later by the father of an adult daughter with severe autism. He had only recently discovered that his daughter had a mutation in this gene and was wondering what he could do to help her.

Some people write to me to ask about their gene mutation that is so rare the associated syndrome has no name. These extremely rare conditions actually do have a name – Syndrome Without a Name (SWAN). Once you know the name of your affected gene, there are numerous free sources available to you on the web which can allow you to become highly knowledgeable. Do not believe for a moment that your doctor is going to do this for you, he is not a medical detective and so that is what you need to become.

I met one family who had spent a great deal of money on the Son Rise program. They also had an ABA consultant, who I know. The mother had dabbled in DAN! type interventions; she had read my blog and I suppose she wanted to know whether she should take it seriously. In my blog I link to thousands of published scientific papers, so it is not really a question of whether I am serious; click on the links and read the research. As a favor, I agreed to meet the family. A few weeks later I got a call from their ABA consultant to say that the boy had responded really well to bumetanide. Son Rise was not a success, by the way.

What I did not expect, when I started my blog, was to be contacted by so many people with mild autism (Asperger's syndrome, or Level 1 autism in DSM5). Such people should also be the ones who are the most treatable, because they have the least severe biological dysfunctions. In reality, the closer you get to "normal", the more differences may stand out. You expect a person who looks normal, dresses normal, walks normal, speaks normal, has normal IQ, to be normal. When they deviate in even a tiny way, it really stands out to other people. We zoom in on any difference or quirk. This becomes a huge challenge for many Aspies from about the age of 10 onwards and hopefully abates when they get into a college/university and meet more people like themselves. Some Aspies have very successful careers, but some do not. I get long emails from people who are just a tiny bit different, but this causes them big problems.

My knowledge is most relevant to the other end of the spectrum, like one mother of a daughter in her 30s. They live together, but all is not well, the daughter self-injures and attacks her mother, who then has to lock herself away and call the police for help. This kind of problem undoubtedly is solvable, but you need to get the entire story, rather than a few snippets of information.

Many readers of my blog have had to deal with self-injury and aggression. A vast amount of money is spent on autism research, much of it painfully trivial. Why doesn't one of the thousands of autism researchers just collate all the knowledge out there on this subject of self-injury and aggression? A hundred possibly effective solutions to self-injurious behavior (SIB) in autism?

Many people blame the doctors for not solving the problem of self-injury. Some complain of the lack of secure psychiatric hospital beds able to take their raging child. Recall that most large psychiatric hospitals were closed down decades ago.

You have the rest of your life to identify the triggers and find effective solutions. Make good use of your time and don't expect miracles from doctors who only prescribe antipsychotic drugs.

There is very often a biological explanation for SIB and by examining the broader health picture of the individual you may find it.

Property damage

Much is written about aggression in autism, either self-injury or injury to others, usually parents or siblings.

Property damage can range from iPads and televisions to walls, doors and windows.

Some people with autism never exhibit any of these challenging behaviors, but for others it is a daily occurrence. I have had mothers writing to me asking how to deal with adult sons and daughters, who are creating havoc at home.

Some parents just keep buying new iPads and TVs, but it is much better to address the underlying causes. There is always going to be a reason, but it may be very difficult to identify it.

We did have our year of raging, but Monty as an eight-year-old was not big enough to do much damage and the last thing he would break would be the TV. He has inherited a huge collection of DVDs and videotapes, mainly with cartoons. One of his favourites is an ancient tape of mine with Greg Norman teaching you how to play golf.

Keeping a daily diary which details behavior, diet, GI symptoms, symptoms of any allergy, the weather and daily routine can often give some clues as to what may be triggering aggression.

I think it is best to consider property damage mainly as collateral damage from self-injurious behavior. There are people who do not understand that you need to recharge your iPad and then just discard it when it does not work; but if you have the cognitive function to use an iPad, I think you can be taught that you need to plug it in after you use it and not throw it out of the window.

Inappropriate behavior

I get asked many things on my blog and I do not ignore any subjects. Inappropriate behavior was one such question.

In my approach to autism, I am trying to make my son as "normal" as possible, so that he will be as includable as possible into real life. As a result, I may have a wider definition of what is inappropriate than many other autism parents. They mainly mean sexually inappropriate behavior and often this results from never having been set rules for any other kind of behavior. If the child is left to do pretty much whatever they want throughout childhood, do not be surprised if when he reaches puberty this continues in ways that may cause problems at school and embarrass the parents.

People with severe autism often do not like wearing clothes and have no sense of embarrassment to be naked in public. Their behavior might not be out of place in Germany or Scandinavia, but in most countries we are all quite prudish.

You start to teach these concepts at a very early age. We had issues at Kindergarten at the age of three with Monty wanting to take his clothes off. It was not an acceptable behavior and it was not allowed. We ended up having to provide a 1:1 assistant to make sure it did not happen. As the head of the kindergarten told me, if she let Monty do it, then all the others would also start doing it. That is how three-year-olds behave.

People with autism can be taught boundaries of what behavior is allowed where, just like you would teach a young child about not picking his nose.

The concept of personal space and touching others has to be taught, but often it is not. The longer you leave it, the harder it will be and the bigger the risks are that the child, or indeed adult, will get into big trouble.

Most parents want their child to be included, but to achieve this they need to make sure their child is includable. Some think the world should change to become more accommodating of their child's behaviors – if only it would.

Public transport

The ability of a person with autism to use public transport is a very good indicator of their real-life status of independence. I met a friend from university who was telling me about his then 14-year-old son, with severe (level 3) autism. He struggled with decoding words while reading, so I suggested the Headsprout reading program. I spoke about our ski school experiences – for his son learning to ski was not yet considered possible, but he travelled to his special school in Paris, by himself, every day, using public transport. That earned a big Wow! It is amazing.

Most parents of a child, or adult, with severe autism are not going to let them out of their sight, for fear of never seeing them again.

There is a small group that lets their child with severe autism roam freely and assume other people are going to watch out for them. You tend to hear about this when it does not end well.

The risk is that some over-protective parents may be holding their child back, who could progress and become more independent.

I remember once taking Monty to a local cinema/movie theatre; of course we had popcorn and so Monty drank lots of water. Since it was not busy, I decided to do an experiment, I told him to go to the restroom by himself and then come back.

For a typical 14-year-old this is a routine task. For someone with severe autism it is not so simple. You have to make your way out without falling over other people's legs or down the stairs. Then you have to find the restrooms and go into the correct one; you have to be not distracted and maybe go back to where they sell the popcorn. You have to return to the correct screen and find your seat, next to your Dad. At least Dad is a navigation point of reference.

I decided to give Monty a head start and then go after him, in case he went back to the wrong screen and watched a different movie.

Somehow, I missed Monty returning and I thought he must have got lost or left the building. When I finally came back to our screen, there he was, sitting in exactly the right seat eating his popcorn, not someone else's. He was totally calm, not at all bothered that Dad was not there. I should not have doubted him.

You will come across adults with Asperger's (level 1 in DSM) who do not work, because they cannot travel independently. They would need to be taken to and from work.

As I said to my friend in Paris, the risk is that someone at the bus stop notices the person with autism and then picks on them, producing a meltdown and then a spiral into a violent confrontation. As I tell autism self-advocates, this is why you want your child with autism to act as normally as possible, no happy-flapping of hands, or random verbalizations. Don't be the one the bullies pick on.

If your child with severe autism grows into an adult who can safely use public transport, unsupported, you have done a remarkable job of parenting.

There are all kinds of options to use technology to track your child, from mobile phones to watches, to devices attached to clothing. Really you just need to have trust in your child and their ability to cope with unexpected situations. Hopefully over the years they will get to this position.

Many children with severe autism love being taken on public transport – buses, trams, metro, trains, ferries and even planes. Monty is one of these people and for him boats are the best.

Many people with Asperger's either refuse to fly, or barely endure it. Perhaps they think the plane is going to crash. It is a rational fear, but such events are extremely unlikely to happen.

Learning to drive is only going to be possible for people with mild autism. In countries that still apply stricter definitions of autism, you cannot even try and learn to drive if you have an autism diagnosis. I think if this applied in all countries you would see a sudden drop in autism diagnoses.

At one point in the UK it was reported in the media that drivers should declare their autism diagnosis to the agency that issues driver's licences. You have to declare any condition that might affect your driving; conditions like insulin-dependent diabetes and schizophrenia are specifically mentioned. The general view was that this was terrible and people said they would not have wanted the autism diagnosis if it meant they might lose their licence to drive. Finally, it was clarified that declaring your autism diagnosis was not required.

In some countries if you have an official autism diagnosis certain professions are closed to you. Where we live, one therapist told me you cannot study medicine if you have autism – no more of the *Good Doctor* on Netflix.

Is there anyone else in there? Autism and the Matryoshka (nesting doll) effect

One question that often occurs to parents of children with severe autism, particularly as they get older, is what is going on inside their child's head. They wonder if there is somebody higher-functioning hidden away inside. It is a very understandable question.

There is a technique called facilitated communication that was popularized in Australia in the 1970s. Various versions still exist today, where a facilitator helps/facilitates a non-verbal child to communicate. One such method is called the Rapid Prompting Method. In all these methods you are very likely to be seeing the facilitator's thoughts rather than that of the child; but it gives hope to the parents. If the child moves forward to the point that the facilitator is no longer required, it ceases to be facilitated communication and you can celebrate. The well-known book *The Reason I Jump* was written by the mother "interpreting inputs from her son". From the book he appears to have a high IQ and you wonder why he cannot write or type his inputs – without his mother's presence. Non-verbal people can be taught to write, type or use an iPad communication app.

Some non-verbal children start with facilitated communication and later learn to type. Bryan Jepson, who used to be an autism doctor, has two non-verbal adult sons. They went to see Soma Mukhopadhyay in Austin, Texas to learn her Rapid Prompting Method. It seems that both can now communicate independently, one types and one uses an iPad – a great end result.

Do not confuse facilitated communication (guided handwriting, supported typing, supported pointing at the letterboard, prompting etc) with augmented communication. In augmented communication, there is no facilitator/parent, the individual uses either low tech picture cards (as in PECS), or a high-tech electronic device, even like that used by the late Stephen Hawking. You cannot fake augmented communication.

Parents clearly do want to believe there is more going on inside their child's head, than is apparent to others.

As their child ages, most parents gradually accept the reality of their child's condition.

The good news is that you can change that reality of your child's condition, by treating the underlying biological dysfunctions. I do receive comments on my blog and emotional emails from parents who have successfully achieved this. They tend to be from the small minority willing and able to use prescription drugs.

You can think of this as the Matryoshka effect. Matryoshka dolls are those Russian dolls that stack inside each other. As you treat each dysfunction, you peel away those negative behaviors to reveal what is underneath.

Remove stereotypy with NAC. Raise IQ with bumetanide. Remove cognitive inhibition with atorvastatin. Banish lethargy with agmatine. Reduce anxiety and halt self-injury with verapamil. Increase speech with leucovorin. The list goes on and is very personalized, depending on what biological dysfunctions are present in your specific case.

Add time, and a big dose of quality teaching, and the result is very different from both what you started with and what would have been.

So, I am pleased to report that, surprisingly, yes! In our case there was someone else in there – just waiting to get out and meet you. It's not crazy, it's called applied science.

Long live the Matryoshka effect!

While on the subject of another child hiding inside a disabled one, I recall an article by Martha Herbert, a pediatric neurologist at Harvard, who had a patient who exhibited an extreme version of the "fever effect", when a person's autism moderates when they have a fever. When this child was sick, the improvement in behavior was so stark that it was like a different child had come to live with her parents. I guess these are the only parents praying their child gets another fever.

Siblings and autism

Most of what you can read about the neurotypical brothers or sisters of a child with severe autism is rather positive, but I think we generally only get to hear the good news. Some boys with severe autism have very understanding sisters and some continue through to adulthood being a very significant caregiver, including happily changing adult diapers.

When it comes to brothers, I very much doubt this is often true, particularly older brothers.

The younger sibling with severe autism usually gets all the attention, which naturally leads to some resentment and this then combines with the "embarrassment" of having a brother at home who is disabled. In olden times the brother would have literally been hidden away at home and kept out of sight.

In our case Monty and his big brother were always at the same school and since it was a small school everyone knew that the two were brothers. I did hold Monty back in elementary school for two extra years, which gave big brother the advantage a few years in high school without his brother there.

Many people seem to have a brother tucked away. In Monty's very small class one boy has a younger brother with cerebral palsy, who sits in his wheelchair, but does attend a special school. One of big brother's best friends turned out to also have an elder brother at home, with very severe cerebral palsy. He was never mentioned and I guess this is why nobody was ever invited to their house. Cerebral palsy is not a genetic condition and the mother went on to have four healthy children. She has to care for her adult son who cannot feed himself, speak or walk. Give her a medal!

All big brother's school friends knew Monty existed and really were not fazed by him. Even though he is disabled by his autism, many people really do seem to like him. That continues to surprise me, given how badly many people treat those with mild autism (level 1 in DSM5).

Some children with severe autism do have behaviors that will cause some embarrassment to siblings. It should be possible to find a way where the neurotypical siblings can have friends come over. They have rights too.

As I discussed with big brother, it is not so bad having a brother with autism. Imagine how your friend feels that he has a non-verbal, wheelchair-bound, adult brother? That really is tough for the entire family. At least you get to ski with your brother.

So, what you may read elsewhere about siblings of those with severe autism (or indeed cerebral palsy) being made more tolerant and accepting of differences, may well apply to many sisters but I seriously doubt it applies to many brothers.

Hopefully in adulthood, male siblings get more accommodating, as in the classic film Rain Man, when autistic savant Dustin Hoffman collides with cool Tom Cruise. This film is criticized by many liberal types and autism self-advocates these days. Of course, it is a film about just one person's autism, but the film's "autism advisor" was Bernie Rimland, one of the most knowledgeable people ever on the subject. He was the one who banished Kanner's idea of the "refrigerator mother" as the cause of autism and showed that autism was caused by biology. He also founded the Autism Society of America and the Autism Research Institute.

It won four Oscars because it was a great film.

The film was based on Kim Peek, an autistic savant who was born with macrocephaly, damage to the cerebellum, and agenesis of the corpus callosum. It is suggested that he may have had FG syndrome. This is usually caused by a mutation on the MED12 gene on the X chromosome. It is another syndrome with very distinctive facial features, which you can see are present on Kim Peek's face. Dustin Hoffman had the mannerisms, even Kim's head leaning over to one side, but he looked pretty good next to Tom Cruise, much more so than Kim would.

Looking good and dressing well is something that can only help a person with autism. We are judged by what we say and how we look. If you are minimally verbal, you can still look good. Some people with severe autism are dressed as if nobody cares about them.

What happens to my child after I am gone?

Many parents of a child with severe autism worry about what will happen after they are no longer present. It is a very valid concern, but you do have to keep it in perspective. Given that average life expectancy in severe autism is less than 40 years, you really need to focus on making the most of the years you are here with your disabled child.

If you maximize the functioning of your child throughout their childhood and early adulthood you are setting them up for the best possible trajectory for the future.

It looks to me that some parents do not do this.

Clearly some people with very severe autism may verge on the untreatable and no matter what you do, the result at the age of 30 is still going to be very challenging.

I have to say that I have never lost sleep wondering what will happen to my son after I am dead. I have invested so much in ensuring that he maximizes his potential, that I sleep very soundly. I do worry about other things, but not that.

The future role of siblings is another question. On the one hand, families are there to support their members for life. In theory friends may come and go, but family should endure. It does not always work out like that.

Some siblings truly hate autism and want nothing to do with it. They have had their fill of autism and they are gone. That is actually completely understandable.

Other siblings take over from their parents, at least in some kind of supervisory role.

Sometimes things end really badly with the parent taking their grown-up child with them. That is really sad, but also understandable.

It is only relatively recently, in the past 40 to 50 years, that severely autistic children are no longer institutionalized shortly after diagnosis; so there is not so much knowledge about caring for large numbers of older adults with severe autism. There are very few such people living today in their 50s and 60s, who were diagnosed with autism at 3 or 4 years of age. By contrast there seem to be many people today in their 50s and even 60s getting diagnosed, or self-diagnosed, with mild autism (Asperger's, or level 1 autism under DSM5).

LGBT+, neurodiversity and the social model of disability

These days you get all sorts of unexpected questions if you apply for a job, or complete a questionnaire on-line. Are you male, female, not sure, thinking about changing any time soon?

Not surprisingly in this environment, confused people are easily led astray.

A few years ago, a boy we know declared he wanted to be a girl. This made him the target of years of teasing at school; but by the time he was a teenager he was happy still to be a boy. Nobody took him to a clinic to transition to a girl, it was just a passing phase. Teachers and classmates wonder if he is gay, he certainly is different to other boys, he has a much wider and more mature vocabulary than his peers and has no real friends at school. If I had to say, I would say he has Asperger's syndrome, not gay at all. He just never identified with regular boy behavior, which he probably sees as inferior and a bit brutish. A few years later and the girls are obsessively posting selfies on Instagram, he probably does not identify with them either, anymore.

Some people with mild autism do have things in common with LGBT+ people. They are nearly all bullied at school, sometimes mercilessly. But autism has absolutely nothing to do with gender/sexuality. Feeling the odd one out does not equal autistic.

The dysfunctions underlying autism are potentially treatable. Autism is connected to other psychiatric disorders like bipolar and schizophrenia. There are well documented genetic overlaps.

LGBT+ behaviors are no longer viewed as psychiatric disorders (they were until not so long ago), but they are almost inevitably genetic/epigenetic conditions. The science has shown that there is no gay gene, rather many genes plus social and environment factors; in many ways a parallel of autism.

Neurodiversity is a very recent idea that arose when the definition of autism was widened to include people who are not disabled by the condition. The idea is to remind typical people that they should not exclude those who are a little bit different from themselves – this is something most people would fully support. Taken to the extreme, it becomes a closed movement of people who were bullied at school for not fitting in, but have now found a unifying common purpose. While neurodiversity is an obsession for some people with mild autism, it drives some parents of severely affected children to a fury. Those parents think their children are excluded from this new rainbow world; severe autism has been pushed aside because there is very little good about it to broadcast to the world on TikTok. The neurodiversity people unfortunately often belittle the challenges faced by severely autistic people and their 24/7 carers; they have just enough autism to lack empathy.

It is often the same people who go on about LGBT+ and neurodiversity. For them autism is just a quirky difference, like the 10-year-old boy wanting to be a girl, before changing his mind later. There already is one advocacy group that combines autistic females and non-binary females. Find another color to add to the rainbow and make it ALGBT+? Finally, a vowel! (A for autism). I hope not.

This leads us to the medical and social models of disability. The medical model focuses on curing or managing illness or disability; so for a deaf child you might insert a cochlear implant, or fit a hearing aid. In the social model the focus is on removing the barriers the person faces and it expects society to adapt to the person with disability – in fact disability does not really exist because the problem is with society. The social model is not very realistic, since the hearing majority are not all going to learn sign language, to help deaf people, for example. The most they would do is to speak a bit louder. Cochlear implants can be highly effective if fitted to a young child. Some deaf parents refuse to allow their child to be treated; by the time the child has any say in the matter, it is too late.

One of Monty's assistants was studying to be a teacher for deaf children, so I know all about cochlear implants and what goes on in schools for the deaf. Surprisingly, some parents send their hearing child with autism to a school for the deaf.

Clearly autism is a medical condition and should be treated as such, but society should make accommodations to help people affected by autism.

The cost of treating autism and not treating it

Depending on where you live and the choices the parents make, autism can become a very expensive drain on the family's resources.

Most people are naturally only concerned with the costs they have to cover personally, but the bigger picture does also matter.

The lost earnings of a stay-at-home parent rarely gets a mention, but in the case of severe autism (level 3 in DSM5), very often one parent will be unable to keep a full-time job.

The cost of special education and therapies like speech, occupational therapy and behavioral therapy is so large that most people could never possibly afford it themselves, on their own. In most countries the government provides some level of free provision, for anything above that, you pay, or in the US your health insurance might pay.

Special education normally costs about three times more than regular schooling. In the case of very severe autism, where the class has six pupils and each one has a dedicated 1:1 teaching assistant, it costs even more.

The handful of private schools in the UK which apply the principles of ABA, charge the equivalent of about $70,000 a year. This is not paid by the parents, it has to be paid by the municipality where they live, which then reduces their budget for their own, much more humble, special schools.

The cost of an ABA program for a young child can be around $50,000 a year. ABA provision in the US has become a big business, because many parents have health insurance that covers ABA. In most other countries parents would have to pay for ABA themselves.

As you can see the cost of treating autism with special education and therapy is enormous when you add up all those years to adulthood.

The cost of genetic testing varies widely across the world. Whole Exome Sequencing (WES) costs between $1,000 and $3,000. Ideally you test the child and both parents. Compared to the lifetime cost of education, the one-off cost of genetic testing looks very small.

The cost of seeing an autism doctor is highly variable. In the US there are many such doctors, in counties like the United Kingdom there are no autism doctors.

Some autism doctors use some very expensive tests and therapies. Therapies like hyperbaric oxygen can cost about $200 per session and so the costs can soon mount up.

Some very expensive therapies, like IVIG (Intravenous Immunoglobulin), are often covered by US health insurance. These therapies would be very difficult to obtain in most other countries, they are just too expensive.

Some autism parents spend tens of thousands of dollars a year on autism therapies, but again this is dwarfed by the real cost of special education.

The cost of the pharmaceuticals actually needed to treat autism is quite low, because they are repurposed existing generic drugs. Any future autism-specific new drug is going to be very expensive, particularly in the US. In a budget I saw, the working assumption was that $50,000 a year is a reasonable cost for a new autism drug.

The cost of treating my son's autism to adulthood were dominated by our cost of providing a 1:1 assistant for 15 years. We probably spent $10,000 on ABA consultants coming to train our assistants.

The cost of medical consultations and testing has been almost nothing, say $200.

The cost of my son's drug therapy has been $3 or $4 a day. It is that low because we live in Europe, where drug prices are much lower than in North America.

The real cost of most generic drugs is much less than the supplements many people buy. Verapamil costs less than $1 for a pack.

You could then ask what is the cost of not treating autism?

I think if you skip all the expensive ABA classes, you usually will end up with a less functional adult. Just how big an impact ABA has, varies widely. People with autism vary widely and ABA does not work for them all. More importantly, the quality and relevance of ABA varies widely. Just how much training/supervision does your $120 an hour therapist have? Some have had very little training.

When I was developing our ABA program and its resources, I came across highly intelligent, communicative and motivated people. These are the people you need to make ABA successful. When today I look at videos of "ABA Technicians" working with children in the US, I see a totally different cadre of people and I am not surprised that the results are very mixed. ABA became a big business, just look who owns the service providers in the US.

What is clear to me is that the huge payback comes from treating the biological dysfunctions with personalized medicine. It costs very little and the return can be game-changing.

I think vast amounts of money allocated to special education and ABA therapy could be saved, by spending money on personal medicine. It would cost much less and the results would be far better.

The argument put forward by ABA enthusiasts is that by spending a lot of money on ABA in the early years, you save money in the long run. I wish this was true, but it often is not. People with severe autism who are treated with ABA are still severely autistic even after two decades of therapy. They are more functional, but they still cannot live independently.

ABA, properly delivered, is good, but it is not enough.

Personalized medicine will have far more impact than ABA and costs a tiny fraction.

Ideally you combine personalized medicine with ABA, or another therapy. First you fine tune the autistic brain and then you apply lots of 1:1 therapy to train it to work better.

Autism/ASD is not a valid biological diagnosis

A key point for readers to remember is that autism is just an observational diagnosis, it is not a biological diagnosis that you normally get from a doctor.

Hundreds of different biological dysfunctions may lead to behaviors, in some shape or form, that will be diagnosed as autism. A behavioral diagnosis of autism is just the start of the process to determine what the biological problems are.

This also means that clinical trials that are based on a group of subjects with completely different biological dysfunctions, but vaguely similar behavioral issues, are doomed to fail.

Fortunately, there are shared pathways affected by many of these numerous biological dysfunctions, so there will be some therapies that apply to clusters of subjects.

In the research jargon they state that an autism diagnosis lacks biological and construct validity. In layman's terms we can say that an autism diagnosis is pretty meaningless.

Wandering and forever young

One reader of my blog suggested I write about wandering. Wandering off and getting lost is a common event for many with more severe autism and while for some it may be an issue only in childhood, for many it will continue to adulthood. US news reports frequently feature this kind of wandering, but it occurs everywhere.

The broader issue here is that many people with severe autism remain child-like their entire lives. So they continue to face many of the same risks as a typical toddler. If you do not pay great attention to your typical two-year-old, they also may have all kinds of accidents. Thankfully they soon figure out that roads are dangerous and falling from a window is going to hurt.

There are lots of clever high tech tracking solutions to help find your child, but the ideal solution must be not to lose him in the first place.

We have a high fence around our garden/yard; we have a cover on our pool that even an adult cannot fall through and a number coded lock on the way out to the garage. It would be hard for any toddler to wander off from our house and hard to fall from an upper window.

Many years ago I used to travel on business to Warsaw, in Poland, and we were fortunate to stay in a smart hotel in the reconstructed old town called the Bristol. You would think this would be a very safe place. Some years later a friend told me how our former colleague was staying there over one weekend with his wife and their typical toddler son. The boy was left unattended and fell to his death from an upper window. Accidents happen and are then forgotten. Lessons are not learnt and then accidents are repeated.

We do not electronically tag all two-year-olds, the idea is that they are given near constant supervision and hopefully things work out well.

The big risks for kids with autism are drowning and seizures. In some cases it is a seizure while in the bath unattended that causes drowning. Drowning should be preventable.

In the US on average 10 people drown each day, of whom two will be under 14 years old. Another 10 children receive emergency department care each day for nonfatal submersion injuries.

Life is a risky business.

Tracking devices

There are numerous types of tracking device, but most have the drawback that they are removable. To be genuinely effective the device would have to be some kind of bracelet that cannot be removed.

Sense of danger

Some people say that their child with autism has no sense of danger, but is that because he has not yet developed one, or he will never have one? I remember being in an outdoor green market with Monty when we met an older boy who was in our mainstream school for a year or two. He was non-verbal, autistic and had seizures. We usually saw him strapped into an oversized pushchair. He could walk, but clearly it was deemed preferable to keep him strapped in.

Monty was used to exploring the stalls in the market and often he would be given something to taste. The other boy was there with his mother and his assistant. I started talking to the mother, Monty started to move to the next stall and then the assistant "pounced", like Monty was about to walk in front of a bus. I explained that it was OK, he was not about to run away; he had already learned a sense of danger from experience.

Clearly people are very different, but you do have to give some space to develop and explore, if you expect them to learn.

Monty likes fire, but rather than hide him from it, he is one who lights our open fire at home. He is now fully aware that you can burn yourself (and your house). We do have several smoke detectors.

I think some people may be over protective and not allowing the child to develop a sense of danger, while some others let their moderately autistic young child roam the street in front of their home and are surprised when trouble occurs.

The tendency to wander has to be matched by the level of supervision.

Dressed to kill

Many people like to be snappy dressers. I think people should be equally attentive to how they dress their adult-sized offspring with severe autism.

I recall a news article a while back when a mother let her adult son with severe non-verbal autism wander from home. He was dressed in green military attire, like a big version of Rambo. He wandered into a neighbour's garden and the occupant saw the intruder and called the police. The police arrived and tackled the non-responsive, threateningly-dressed, intruder to the ground. The mother turned up and was upset that the officer had manhandled her child. I think this was in Canada; a little further south and the officer might have shot him.

Had the youth been dressed in shorts and a Mickey Mouse sweatshirt I doubt the home owner would have called the police in the first place, rather "it's just that boy Jimmy from down the street wandering again, I must call his mother, she did warn the neighbourhood that he wanders".

It does matter how you are dressed and how you behave. I recall another parent commenting that adults with autism are not cute; that sounded odd to me. An eight-year-old with autism banging his head against the wall certainly is not cute. A well-behaved adult-sized person with classic autism can be cute, more than likely he is just a big kid, or a gentle giant. If he is a permanent "big kid", dress him like one and nobody is going to feel threatened by any unexpected behaviours.

Foul!

Some people get very upset when they hear you can actually treat autism.

Sometimes it is a person with mild autism, even self-diagnosed, who thinks using ABA or a drug to help your child to be able to tie his shoe laces or cross a road is some kind of eugenics.

Eugenics is a set of beliefs that aim to improve the genetic quality of a human population, by excluding people judged to be inferior or promoting those judged to be superior. You can argue that human's mating selection process is based on very similar principles. People normally look for winners not losers.

Autism and indeed bipolar disorder have a genetic component and so you would think they should become increasingly rare. In theory the female should reject the "genetically impaired" male, but there is more at stake.

Many of the genetic mutations leading to autism are linked to intelligence and bipolar disorder is linked to creativity. So the male, and indeed female, may have compensating advantages, like a big salary from Google.

I like the endearing comment I heard from genetic specialist Dr Boles, which was that severe autism, in some cases at least, is just too much of a good thing. He finds that many of his patients have parents who are very intelligent or creative. Too many mutations, plus some unfortunate environmental influences tipped the balance and the result is a child with severe autism, rather than the expected whizz kid.

Treating autism or treating its symptoms?

It is actually much better not to use the word autism. You can happily say improving cognition, raising IQ or improving daily living skills.

When you treat autism, you are actually just treating its symptoms or comorbidities, like anxiety, stereotypy, hyperactivity, lethargy, sensory sensitivity, etc. If you take away enough of these troubling symptoms then you would no longer fit the autism label.

I know one boy who was going for his autism assessment with a well-known local Professor. It turned out that when the child was taking the antioxidant, N-acetylcysteine (NAC), the Professor did not want to diagnose autism, but without the NAC he ticked the boxes for severe autism. So if you want the autism diagnosis, skip NAC on assessment day.

In many countries having a low measured IQ opens the door to extra therapies and benefits. In some people with severe autism they have an excitatory-inhibitory (E/I) imbalance, which in layman's terms means that neurons fire too readily and this impairs cognition. Improve the E/I imbalance and you will raise IQ, and then lose your services.

Girls

Girls are diagnosed with autism far less frequently than boys. This is actually a very good thing and is not some kind of sexist discrimination. In multiple sclerosis (MS), those affected are mainly female and nobody is looking for males who mask their MS. It all comes down to biology and when it comes to autism, females have the advantage.

Girls have two copies of all the genes on the X chromosome, boys have only one copy. Many genes on the X chromosome are of critical importance. For example, in Fragile X syndrome, boys will be much more severely affected than girls because while they both have one faulty copy of the gene FMR1 (fragile X mental retardation 1); girls will also have one functioning copy. In Rett syndrome, girls have one faulty copy of the MECP2 gene plus one functioning copy. Boys only have the one faulty copy and they will die prior to birth; you cannot live long without one functioning copy of MECP2.

Girls also are protected by higher levels of female hormones, which are neuroprotective and so allow them to survive environmental insults and shocks to the brain that males cannot endure. The balance between estrogen and testosterone affects an important biological switch called ROR alpha; to minimize autism you want more estrogen and less testosterone.

Girls with Turner syndrome are missing all or part of one of their X chromosomes. They lack growth hormones and critically the female hormone estrogen. They often display the same social difficulties found in autism, although without intellectual disability. They will have masculine features.

Girls with severe autism are very likely to have a single gene type of autism and genetic testing is highly advisable.

Aspie girls likely have polygenic autism; if they have children, they risk having a child with more severe autism or some milder special educational need. Aspie girl plus Aspie boy is risking a severely autistic child.

What causes autism?

Very many things can contribute to autism.

Complications during pregnancy are a risk factor. This can range from gestational diabetes, or an imbalance between male and female hormones, to hypoxia during birth, to sepsis (blood poisoning).

For some people autism really is a visible brain damage. People who lack the Corpus Callosum, the part of the brain that joins the left side to the right side, will fit a diagnosis of autism. The real Rain Man character, played by Dustin Hoffman, had agenesis of the Corpus Callosum.

A non-cancerous brain tumor as a baby can result in an autism diagnosis.

Single gene mutations can cause severe autism and seem to be prominent in girls with severe autism.

Most people have what is called idiopathic autism, this is the "we don't know what caused it" autism. Idiopathic autism is quite likely to be polygenic, meaning that multiple genetic variations combined to produce autism, possibly triggered by an external non-genetic event. This might be maternal immune activation during pregnancy or emotional/oxidative stress during pregnancy.

In addition to the 22,000 genetic codes in our DNA that our bodies need, there is a layer superimposed called the epigenome. Epigenetic markers are like colored post-it tags in your cookbook, that turn on or turn off particular genes. These markers are heritable and we know from the research that this is how the environment affects gene expression. For example, if your grandparents were heavy smokers, their oxidative stress responsive genes were tagged and you likely inherited these tags. Your copies of these genes are not mutated, but if they are tagged to turn them off, they are impaired.

Reversible "autism"

There are some conditions that appear to be autism, but are indeed fully reversible.

Certain products of the digestive system like propionic acid and P-cresol can produce symptoms of autism. Exposure to certain types of fungus/mold can also have this effect.

Many people with autism have highly restricted diets and this leads to a very limited gut microbiome. This then affects what chemicals are fermented in the gut and hence affects behaviors.

An autoimmune reaction within the brain can trigger a variety of symptoms, ranging from hallucinations to tics and obsessive compulsive disorder. Once you treat the immune problem the behavioral/psychiatric symptoms fade away. Examples include NMDA receptor encephalitis and the much better known PANS and PANDAS.

Inborn errors of metabolism

Inborn errors of metabolism are usually genetic conditions that block metabolic pathways involved in the breakdown of nutrients and the generation of energy, a good example is mitochondrial disease.

An interesting, fully treatable disorder relates to biotin metabolism. Biotin is vitamin B7, which is required for a wide range of metabolic processes. You get biotin from food like eggs, and your body cleverly recycles it using an enzyme called biotinidase. Some people have biotinidase deficiency, which is usually considered the reason for low biotin. In a Greek study they found a surprisingly large minority (12 out of 187) of children with autism had low levels of biotin, but had normal levels of the enzyme biotinidase. They were treated with a biotin supplement, which led to a clear benefit in 7 cases.

> "For those benefiting from biotin intervention, the most impressive outcome centered on a 42 month-old boy whose severe ASD was completely ameliorated following biotin intervention. This patient was subsequently followed for 5 years, and cessation of biotin intervention (or placebo replacement) resulted in the rapid return of ASD-like symptomatology. This patient currently attends public school without any clinical sequelae and remains on biotin at 20 mg/d."

Mitochondrial disease is a risk factor because in early life, up to the age of 5, the brain uses a vast percentage of the body's energy supply, making it vulnerable to any interruption in that supply. A viral infection, or similar shock, can trigger a problem that was lying dormant, this then results in what you might consider as a power outage. This causes some neurons to die and some myelin carefully grown to be lost. This all manifests as a loss of skills already mastered, from speech to toileting. Mitochondrial disease does not have a cure, but there are protective therapies. Some children with autism secondary to mitochondrial disease do regain skills they lost and do well; others do not progress well. The current therapy is aimed at avoiding further regressions and hoping for the best. This is a very touchy subject because one possible trigger argued in the US by specialists from Johns Hopkins was multiple vaccinations.

Cerebral folate deficiency (CFD) occurs when there are low levels of folate within the brain. It is essentially a problem with folate metabolism or transport.

The research suggests that 75% of people with autism have antibodies to folate receptors. This would lead to folate deficiency inside the brain and such people may benefit from taking calcium folinate as a supplement.

A how-to guide?

I do get people writing to me asking if I have a "How to Guide" to treat autism. Sadly, I do not. That would require a much longer book; *Game Changer* is an introduction to what is possible. My blog is much more comprehensive.

Many hundreds of things, individually or in combination, can lead to autism.

Ideally there would be a unifying therapy that works in all cases, or at least most cases. Some people see Suramin as such a potential therapy – only time will tell if it is.

The therapies that work for my son do all work for some other people. Some people have just copied all my therapies and had great results – lucky them.

Other people find none of the therapies I use work in their case. In the largest group some of these therapies have a benefit, while others do not. This is exactly what you would expect, if you dig deep into the science. Therapy has to be personalized, but there are few diagnostic tests that are going to help you.

Some parents make huge efforts for their child and do not see much payback. Life is not fair.

How did he do it?

This question is easy to answer. I stumbled upon an article in December 2012 that referred to promising results in a clinical trial of bumetanide in autism. I read the full paper and, suitably impressed, decided that I should make my own trial.

I checked the potential side effects and how to minimize them. I consulted some doctors to see what they thought and then started my trial in late December 2012.

When school started in January 2013, we had a significantly different son. The fog had lifted and he was finally present.

I was called in to school by the head teacher and asked what had happened to Monty. The word she used to describe the new Monty was "joyful". His morning 1:1 assistant described him as "present", as opposed to being lost in space. His friend Chloe described him as "different, but in a good way".

Wow! Is treating autism this easy, I wondered.

I introduced myself to Google Scholar, which just gives you serious grown-up links.

I had several binge sessions reading autism research, that I had not realized existed in such quantity. I discovered that much was known about common features of autism. I decided that I would use a bit of trial and error to treat some of those common features.

My second and third trials were NAC (N-acetyl cysteine) and Atorvastatin. Both trials were successful and so my Polypill therapy was born.

> Bumetanide 1 mg, taken with extra potassium in diet and a supplement
>
> NAC 600mg 4 times a day
>
> Atorvastatin 10mg

The result was a nine-year-old who could now learn at school. He taught himself those tricky preposition words, that I had been trying to teach him for five years. He began to be able to understand basic mathematics. The NAC brought an end to that distracting stereotypy and repetitive nonsense speech. Atorvastatin removed cognitive inhibition and allowed him to apply skills he had mastered but still did not apply.

When summer came, the self-injury and aggression returned. These behaviors vanished when we went to the mountains or the seaside. Antihistamines gave some benefit but not enough.

The solution to this problem was to use verapamil, an L-type calcium channel blocker. By then I had read a vast amount about autism, so I knew all about ion channels and the role of calcium signaling in autism. I made a shortlist of possible therapies and verapamil was at number one. I decided to try it in the middle of an aggressive episode and watch the result. It was amazing to watch the aggression melt away and that bright red angry face turn back to normal.

Monty would later sense he had aggression building up inside and actually ask for his pill.

Self-injury is an acquired behavior. Once you have discovered it, the threshold for it to re-occur is much lower. Something very similar happens with epilepsy, the first seizure is really hard to occur, but thereafter they come much more easily.

Later on, we had some wintertime aggression. This, I figured out, was due to the process of milk teeth dissolving and permanent teeth erupting. This biological process uses inflammatory cytokines as the signal to the teeth. Unfortunately, one common feature of autism is what I call an "over-activated" immune system in both the brain and the wider body. The solution to this wintertime aggression was simple – ibuprofen.

Ten years later Monty caught the mononucleosis (glandular fever) virus and other than a very sore throat, the only symptom was a tendency to raging. The solution to the raging? Ibuprofen three times a day.

One doctor reader of my blog encouraged me to follow up on work done by Professor Catterall in the US. He was using micro-doses of a cheap drug called Clonazepam to modify the excitatory-inhibitory (E/I) balance, which is impaired in much autism and indeed epilepsy. Catterall never went beyond his animal experiments but did share his thoughts about human dosing with my friend. This resulted in low-dose clonazepam therapy which was effective in some children, mainly among my doctor readers.

The effect was not as profound as bumetanide, but still well worth having. The dose is tiny which makes it safe, free of side effects and extremely cheap.

Having written about PANS (Pediatric Acute-onset Neuropsychiatric Syndrome) and PANDAS (Pediatric Auto-immune Neuropsychiatric Disorders Associated with Streptococcal Infections) in my blog, I was familiar with the symptoms and therapies. Just before Christmas in 2016, Monty started to exhibit very loud verbal tics, like some kind of crazy monster in a cartoon. Both PANS and PANDAS become resistant to treatment if there is a delay before diagnosis and can become chronic. I already knew all this, so I treated the tics as a PANS exacerbation with prednisone and over the next two weeks they faded away entirely.

Two years later Monty developed another tic, this time it was a motor tic, rapid eye blinking. At least I knew what to do, five days of prednisone and no more tics.

From being a little hyperactive as a toddler, always jumping around, Monty later became much slower, more lethargic. On a school trip or sporting activity he would tend to lag behind. The fix to the lethargy was a little scoop of agmatine, which is usually sold as a not very effective supplement for bodybuilders. Agmatine increases eNOS, (endothelial Nitric Oxide Synthase), which is a plausible explanation for its effect. It also worked the same way for other lethargic children, whose parents read my blog.

I investigated the ketone BHB in some detail. People on the high fat ketogenic diet produce ketones that fuel their body, rather than the glucose used by the rest of us. The principal ketone is called BHB.

Various new products are being developed because BHB is in effect a super fuel. Army special forces and sportsmen already use BHB.

Some people with autism appear to do well on a ketogenic diet; it has been successfully used to treat epilepsy for 100 years. BHB can be used as an alternative fuel, for example in a person with Alzheimer's, because their brain has reduced capacity to transport glucose across the blood brain barrier. Some people with certain mitochondrial disorders cannot convert enough glucose to ATP (fuel for cells), but they can convert BHB to ATP.

At much lower concentrations than in the ketogenic diet there are some interesting benefits from BHB. BHB has a series of known anti-inflammatory effects and interestingly makes some people feel much better, it reduces anxiety and depression in animal models and in humans. BHB is seen as neuroprotective and in people with low levels of naturally produced BHB it is associated with social impairments, depression and even brain white matter alterations. You clearly need enough BHB, so perhaps a little extra?

At the age of 18 Monty developed extreme sound sensitivity. It gradually increased and then shot up while we were on a visit to Sarajevo. At night he could not sleep because of it. Sound sensitivity is a very common problem in autism, but it usually develops from a very young age. I had already established years earlier that an oral potassium supplement increased Monty's tolerance to annoying sounds. By coincidence, I was corresponding at the time with a US drug firm considering backing Mefenamic Acid (MFA) as an autism therapy. I had written about MFA in my blog and the patent holder has left some interesting comments on the blog. Its possible benefit in autism was suggested to relate its effect on several potassium ion channels. The idea was to give it to very young children diagnosed with autism to protect them from slipping towards severe non-verbal autism. MFA is already sold as a pain relief drug called Ponstan. I had some Ponstan at home.

Would Ponstan overcome our new sound sensitivity crisis? Indeed it did. I mentioned this to a regular reader of my blog, whose daughter has long had the same issue. She later triumphantly sent me a video of her daughter without sound sensitivity.

Low dose Ponstan joined the Polypill.

Autism history

It is useful to put autism in a historical perspective. It does help explain the mess we seem to have today.

Many parents naturally want a treatment today for their child with autism. What has been going on during previous generations, such that autism is so poorly understood today and generally remains untreated?

We will see that autism has been with us for many generations, it just did not have a name. Children would have been diagnosed as feeble minded, separated from their parents and put aside to live a very short life in an institution.

Many people tell me that when they were a child, there were no kids in the neighbourhood with autism, whereas now there are many. There definitely is more autism, but we need to be aware that in the past people with autism, or indeed other disabilities, were hidden away. In some countries they still are.

A couple of years ago we had a family holiday in Stockholm, Sweden. They have an excellent public transport system, but what was most remarkable to me was how many disabled people with wheelchairs there were. Physically disabled people have been integrated and so you see them everywhere. Where we live it is very wheelchair unfriendly, and not surprisingly you never see a disabled person in a wheelchair.

People with severe autism, intellectual impairment, Down syndrome, cerebral palsy etc. have only recently been somewhat included in society. Down syndrome has long been a medical diagnosis and so there is some reliable historic data, take a look at life expectancy for people with this disability.

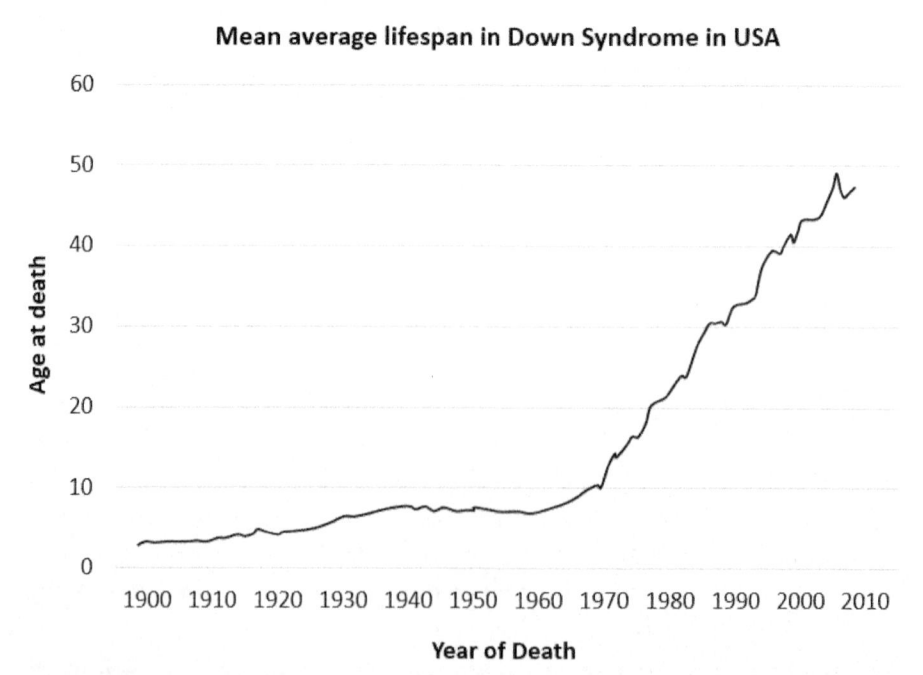

Mean average lifespan in Down Syndrome in USA

Until the mid-1960s, 75% of children with Down Syndrome (DS) were dead before their 10th birthday. 50 years later the average

age at death is getting close to 50 years old. Until very recently children with DS died of neglect.

Before the 1970s, people with DS, autism or intellectual impairment were sent by their parents, on medical advice, to live in large mental institutions. In subsequent decades these institutions have been closed down. Nowadays you will see kids with autism having meltdowns in malls, restaurants, airports and other public places. Back in the 1960s and 70s most of these kids would have been locked out of sight.

People claiming that autism is primarily caused by vaccines tend to ask why are there no old people with autism? The idea being that before mass multiple vaccinations there was no autism. There have been few older people with autism because they generally all died very young, unless their parents insisted on looking after them at home.

A study by the Karolinska Institute in Sweden showed that even today autistic adults with a learning disability were found to die more than 30 years before non-autistic people. At the other end of the spectrum, autistic adults without a learning disability are 9 times more likely to die from suicide.

Grunya Sukhareva, the Soviet; Hans Asperger and Leo Kanner, the Austrians

It appears that the term autism was in casual use by some psychiatrists even as early as the 1910s. Leo Kanner often gets the credit for being the first to identify autism as a condition. Some people credit Swiss psychiatrist Eugen Bleuler. Some people credit Grunya Sukharev as the inventor of modern autism, predating Kanner and Asperger by nearly twenty years. She lived and worked as a psychiatrist in Kiev and Kharkov in Ukraine and also in Moscow.

She published a detailed description of autistic symptoms, in Russian in 1925 and in German in 1926. She initially used the term "schizoid psychopathy" but later replaced it with "autistic psychopathy"

You can read her paper, just search for:

Die schizoiden Psychopathien im Kindesalter

Google translate will do all the hard work for you.

As you will see, the title of Asperger's paper two decades later is remarkably similar, by the time she swapped autistic for schizoid.

History did forget Sukharev, but you have not.

Bleuler is very well known, because he also coined the terms schizophrenia and schizoid.

Hans Asperger and Leo Kanner

Now back to the traditional view of history.

Both Hans Asperger and Leo Kanner were Austrian doctors. Kanner was later educated in Berlin; he was Jewish and had the foresight to emigrate in 1924 to the US. In 1930 he developed the first child psychiatry service in an American pediatric hospital, at Johns Hopkins. He published his research on autism in 1943. His narrowly defined type of autism became known as Kanner's autism, or classic autism.

You can read his paper, just search for:

Autistic Disturbances of Affective Contact, 1943

Kanner clearly made a valuable contribution, but he also had some odd ideas; like autism is just a childhood condition, so adults cannot have autism and that autism is extremely rare. He thought that if a patient had epilepsy, they could not be autistic. He also famously suggested that autism was caused by refrigerator mothers. However, unlike all the doctors who preceded him, at least he wrote down his findings and sought out public attention.

Hans Asperger, not Jewish, eventually became chair of pediatrics at the University of Vienna. In 1943 he published, in German, his paper on autism that focused on gifted children and what would become known in the English-speaking world as Asperger's syndrome, after his death.

You can read his original paper, just search for:

Die Autistischen Psychopathen im Kindesalter 1943

The paper was finally translated and published in English in 1991 by Uta Frith, a German developmental psychologist working at University College London. Thereafter, in the English-speaking world, people would be diagnosed with Asperger's Syndrome. I think it is a very useful, clear diagnosis – no speech delay, no cognitive dysfunction, just the trademark differences of mild autism.

It later became known that while he may have published research on very high functioning people, he also had many patients who were low functioning. The reason Asperger highlighted the gifted children was that during World War 2, the Nazis had a program called Aktion T4, which was set up to kill people with disabilities (and so unable to work). People with Down syndrome, epilepsy, mental retardation etc, were removed from their residential institutions, or even family homes and given a lethal injection, or carbon monoxide poisoning. The family later received a letter that the child had sadly died of pneumonia, or similar.

So not surprisingly, Asperger did not write about those with autism without special gifts and talents.

Is it relevant that Asperger had Nazi connections? It would have been very hard to be an Austrian working in Vienna in 1943 and not have any Nazi connections. For such a prominent figure, Asperger was highly unusual in not being a member of the Nazi party.

On the other hand, Werner von Braun remains a celebrated NASA scientist, but he was a member of the Nazi party and indeed held the rank of Major in the SS, during World War 2. He pioneered the German V2 ballistic missiles that fell on London in World War 2, but was spirited away from Europe in 1945 to work on the United States space program.

Give Hans Asperger a break!

Childhood schizophrenia

The original term for what became autism, was childhood schizophrenia, which started being used in the 1920s.

I mentioned in my blog that I came across an interesting comment written by Michael Baron; back in 1962 he headed the world's first parent organization for autism, the UK's National Autistic Society.

Baron's main point was to highlight how autism has completely morphed in 60 years to a quite different condition. It is not the same autism.

When his organization was originally founded, it was called The Society for Psychotic Children. That was the name the parents came up with themselves, before later substituting the word autistic.

The old name has well and truly been erased from the records. Definitely not politically correct these days.

Autism may now be a cool diagnosis to some people in the 2020s, but being psychotic still is not. Perhaps bipolar will be the next cool diagnosis? (according to Tara, the psychology student, who was proof reading, "it's already cool to be bipolar ... the other one is borderline personality disorder (BPD) which is cute but psycho" – apparently both are fashionable with girls and gay guys")

Note that the only approved drugs for autism are actually antipsychotics!

Great Ormond Street Hospital, London 1870s

Twenty years before Johns Hopkins Hospital had even been founded in Baltimore, children with epilepsy, "autism" and GI problems were being treated in London at Great Ormond Street Hospital, today one of Europe's top children's hospitals.

They were using a very early drug, potassium bromide, to treat epilepsy. Of course, back in the 1870s they did not know why it was effective to treat "autism".

Dr William Dickinson (1832–1913) was a physician at this hospital and left behind detailed case notes, excerpts of which have been published. In particular, a young girl named Ida is notable, she was non-verbal, had epilepsy, GI problems, feeding problems, rocking, screaming and was not engaged with the world.

After treatment with potassium bromide to control her seizures, it was noted that she also exhibited some normal behavior for her age, she started playing with a doll. Today this is called age-appropriate play, something lacking in young children with severe autism.

Today this same hospital would tell you that autism is untreatable and that GI problems are not comorbid with autism, the standard view today in the United Kingdom.

I wrote extensively in my blog about the potential to treat autism with potassium bromide. More recently some French researchers have patented the idea, as their own.

Potassium bromide is still used to treat pediatric epilepsy in German speaking countries and is one of the few effective therapies for Dravet syndrome. Interestingly, low dose clonazepam is effective in the mouse model for Dravet syndrome as well as some human autism.

Homes for the "feeble-minded"

Just as in Austria and Germany in the mid-1940s, in the US being sent to a home for the "feeble minded" was very often a death sentence, albeit a slower one. The Nazi Germans went as far as to financially justify their actions by quoting the cost of keeping a child in an institution for 10 years. Ten years was also the life expectancy of children with Down syndrome in the US up until the mid-1960s.

Given this backdrop, not surprisingly everybody kept quiet about autism, almost nobody was interested in treating it and nobody would dream of using the word autism, for someone who was fully verbal and not mentally retarded/intellectually disabled.

It is hardly surprising that there were very few older people with autism, or indeed Downs syndrome.

There were numerous homes for the feeble-minded in the US and across the world. Here is one example:-

Belchertown State School, Massachusetts

Belchertown state school for the feeble-minded was established in 1922 as part of a movement to institutionalize mentally disabled people. Nobody seemed particularly concerned about conditions inside the school until the 1960s and 70s.

The school housed not only children but adults as well. Families came to visit at weekends and some lucky children went back home for visits, so the conditions inside the facility were well known, if not discussed widely. You might wonder why parents did not remove their children, but at the time people did not think there was any alternative.

Professor Benjamin Ricci, whose six-year-old son entered Belchertown state school in 1953, was so shocked by the conditions he later fought a 20-year battle to close the school. Nonetheless, he left his son Robert there for 27 years.

The horrendous conditions at Belchertown were revealed in 1971 in a newspaper article entitled *The Tragedy of Belchertown*. Ricci and other parents sued the school in 1972 in a class action lawsuit protesting the horrific, medieval and barbaric conditions.

Similar actions were filed at four other state schools and institutions. These five cases were later consolidated. After touring the facilities, the court determined that the level of care at the facilities was indefensible. The school finally ceased operations in 1992.

Ricci recounted his 20-year battle to close the state school in his book, *Crimes against humanity*.

Ruth Sienkiewicz-Mercer was a resident of the same facility for 16 years, she had cerebral palsy and was quadriplegic, but without any mental disability. She left the school in 1978, married and co-wrote an autobiography/exposé called *I raise my eyes to say yes*. She became a campaigner for the rights of the disabled.

A third book was recently published *The Girls and Boys of Belchertown* and you can even read reviews of the book by siblings of those who were sent to live there.

When reading about poor conditions in orphanages in Romania, Ukraine and other countries in recent times, it is important to realize what was common practice in the United States and United Kingdom not so long ago.

Why feeble-minded?

Going back 110 years in the United Kingdom, you can see where terms like feeble minded came from.

In 1904 a Royal Commission was appointed to consider "the existing methods of dealing with idiots and epileptics and with imbeciles and feeble-minded not certified under the lunacy laws."

They disallow the name of "lunatic" and "asylum" and classify the mentally defective as follows:-

- Persons of unsound mind (who require care and control)

- Persons mentally infirm (who are incapable of managing their own affairs)
- Idiots (defective in mind from birth)
- Imbeciles (capable of guarding themselves against common physical dangers, but incapable of earning their own living)
- Feeble-minded (persons who may be capable of earning their own living under favourable conditions, but are incapable of competing with others or managing themselves).
- Moral imbeciles. (persons who display some mental defect with vicious or criminal propensities on which punishment is no deterrent).
- Epileptics
- Inebriates
- Deaf, dumb and blind

Almost all such people were locked up. In the UK at that time there were 149,628 such people deemed to be mentally defective. That is 0.4% of the population at that time.

Modern times

The process of de-institutionalization is complete in most developed countries and large "out of sight, out of mind" institutions are a thing of the past. They still exist in some other countries.

Recently the incentive to hide your disability was replaced by an incentive to promote it. In some countries for each child with a diagnosis, extra money is allocated to the school district and in many countries, families are entitled to weekly or monthly benefits payments.

Changes to diagnosis began to be made such that many children with MR/ID (Mental Retardation/Intellectual Disability) were now diagnosed as having autism, boosting prevalence of autism and reducing prevalence of MR/ID.

Then from the 1990s onwards came the boom in diagnosing Asperger's in children and then later diagnosing Asperger's in adults.

Finally, just to confuse everyone, in the US at least, Asperger's has been merged into autism.

Once a rare condition, autism has become anything but – all over the period of 20 years, but it is not the same autism.

Even though the science is clearly indicating that within autism are numerous separate biological disorders and as many as 1,000 genes are involved, the US psychiatrists, with DSM5, have decided that it is all just "autism". You are ranked on a scale of 1 to 3 for the level of assistance you need.

The key discriminating factors like regressive or not, MR/ID or not, epilepsy or not, speech delay or not, are not seen a relevant.

As a result, the modern diagnosis of autism then just begs the follow-on question "what sort?"

In 2021 the Lancet Commission proposed reintroducing the old term Profound Autism, to describe autistic people with severe intellectual disability and limited communication abilities, who are likely to need 24-hour support throughout their lives. They suggested that the term should not be used for children younger than about 8 years old; it may be appropriate for adolescents and adults.

Bernie Rimland

Bernie Rimland was very well known in US autism circles. He earned his PhD in psychology in 1953; his son Mark was born in 1956 with early onset autism. Rimland then began his research into the cause and treatment of autism. He published his book *Infantile Autism: The Syndrome and Its Implications for a Neural Theory of Behavior* in 1964. He was refuting the widely held view at the time that the traumatized unloved child retreated into autism. That view had originally been put forward by Kanner and was being further promoted at the time by another psychologist, Bruno Bettelheim, yet another Austrian like Kanner and Asperger.

Those Austrians, again!

Rimland took on the task of convincing people that autism had a neurological cause, which is now an accepted fact. Bettelheim ended up committing suicide and was later found to have invented his PhD from Vienna University.

Parents from all over the United States, excited that for the first time a professional in the field did not accuse them of maltreating their autistic child, began to write to Rimland. He called a meeting and this small group of parents became the nucleus that founded the Autism Society of America.

Rimland set up his Autism Research Institute (ARI) in 1967. ARI created the Defeat Autism Now! (DAN!) program in 1995. DAN! promoted the belief that vaccines were a cause of autism and that it could be treated by removing heavy metals from the body.

Rimland parted ways with the medical establishment as he proposed chelation therapy, a myriad of supplements and restrictive diets.

One of his most favored therapies was to use vitamin B6 which he credited, alongside behavioral intervention and other supplements, as the basis of his son's improvement.

Rimland, died in November 2006 and was succeeded at ARI by Steven Edelson, another psychologist. The DAN! program and doctor registry was discontinued in January 2011, but alternative practitioners continue to refer to themselves as DAN and many autism parents in the US consult a DAN doctor. Some have joined an organization called MAPS, set up after DAN was discontinued.

Interestingly, Rimland was employed as the autism technical consultant on the film *Rain Man*. This film is criticized by many autism parents because it does reflect their autism; however when the film was made in 1988 there could have been few other people better acquainted with autism, in all its forms, than Rimland. Dustin Hoffman's character was given savant skills and it is no surprise that Rimland's son, Mark, has some savant skills (a calendar memory).

Even though Rimland was correct that autism is not generally caused by neglect, it is possible. We now know from the Bucharest Early Intervention Project (BEIP), run by Harvard Professor of Neuroscience, Charles Nelson, it actually is possible to create autism-like deficits in a child brought up in a traumatized neglectful environment – a Romanian orphanage in this case.

Andrew Wakefield

Andrew Wakefield is a British gastroenterologist and medical researcher, best known for his 1998 research paper in support of the link between the administration of the MMR vaccine and the appearance of autism and bowel disease. Perhaps if he had been

American the consequences might have been different, but Dr Wakefield was struck off the UK medical register and was later barred from practicing medicine. He went to live in the United States.

Until Dr Wakefield published his paper in 1998, few people were familiar with autism, because nobody spoke about it. Talk of the MMR vaccine and autism created fear among parents.

As the Harvard researcher Dr Martha Herbert pointed out, everything regarded as "Wakefield" became taboo, and research in those areas became un-fundable. The link to GI problems is one area she highlighted.

Jon and his daughter Hannah Poling

Dr Jon Poling, an American neurologist, challenged the medical establishment much more effectively than Wakefield. He received lifetime compensation that reportedly may run to many millions of dollars, for the care of his daughter, Hannah, who developed autism symptoms after multiple vaccinations. The case was very well documented and supported, because Johns Hopkins-trained Poling maintained the goodwill of his medical colleagues. It was judged that a reaction to the vaccines triggered mitochondrial disease, which then resulted in severe regressive autism.

The Hannah Poling case is very interesting and shows what can be achieved playing within the rules and having the right friends/support.

Hannah was born in 1999 and received five vaccines in one day in 2000 at the age of 19 months; this occurred because she had fallen behind on her vaccine schedule as a result of a series of ear infections.

She later developed severe regressive autism. The Poling family filed a case with the US National Vaccine Injury Compensation Program on October 25, 2002.

In the US there is a $0.75 levy on childhood vaccines to fund a compensation scheme.

Her neurologist father, Dr Jon Poling, made the case that children with a latent mitochondrial dysfunction can suffer an inflammatory response to multiple vaccines that can trigger mitochondrial damage leading to profound autism.

It was expected that this case would act as a precedent for further autism cases; it did not.

As Dr Poling pointed out, quite a large minority of people with autism do have mitochondrial disorders. Some MAPS doctors think the majority have mitochondrial disorders.

I think Dr Poling could not have done a better job; he even went on to publish some peer-reviewed research on mitochondrial disease and autism.

On the other side of the argument is the fact that vaccines have saved millions of lives. Vaccines do provide a clear net benefit. Public health knows that sometimes things go wrong and that is why there is a compensation scheme.

This point was also made by Professor Manuel Casanova, an autism researcher, autism grandfather and blogger. He mentions in his blog, corticalchauvinism.com, that his late grandson had an extreme negative reaction to vaccines. Casanova points out though, that vaccines save lives.

In a more rational world, public health authorities would review the way vaccines are given and give at-risk groups the option of single vaccinations. They would publicize the practices used at Johns Hopkins to reduce the chances of a negative reaction to vaccination.

Children who have already suffered one regression into autism are given future vaccines in a different way, in a very small number of leading hospitals. They are given mild immune-modulating drugs like ibuprofen or montelukast for a few days before and after vaccines to try to prevent any damaging inflammatory response.

Perhaps all children should have ibuprofen before and after vaccines?

Paracetamol/acetaminophen should not be given to children because it reduces the level of the antioxidant glutathione (GSH). Paracetamol/acetaminophen use during pregnancy has been shown to increase autism incidence, which is what you would expect.

Children under 12 should not be given aspirin due to the risk of Reye's syndrome, which causes swelling of the liver and brain.

It pays to be careful.

Prognosis

Prognosis is something many parents of a child with autism are interested in.

In the jargon, longitudinal studies are the ones that track outcomes over time.

Catherine Lord in the US has been studying a group as they aged from 2 to 22 years old. Catherine is a good speaker and you can find some of her talks on YouTube.

In France there has been a 15-year longitudinal study called EpiTED.

The results of the two studies are broadly similar and make quite grim reading.

The best predictor of a successful independent life is not IQ (intelligence quotient), it is daily living skills (DLS), which they bizarrely measure in months, not years.

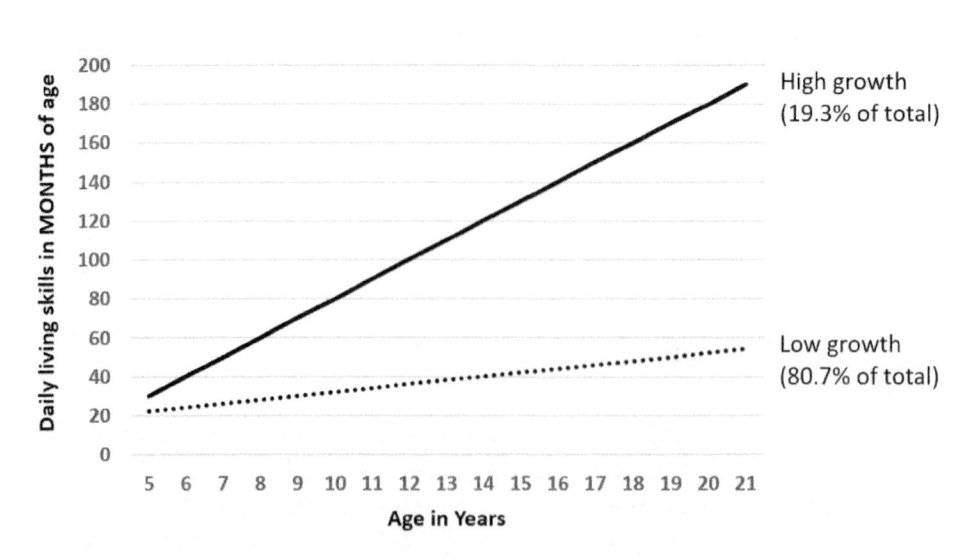

Daily Living Skills (measured in Months)

High growth (19.3% of total)

Low growth (80.7% of total)

Source: Fifteen-Year Prospective Follow-Up Study of Adult Outcomes of Autism Spectrum Disorders Among Children Attending Centers in Five Regional Departments in France: The EpiTED Cohort.

In the French group about 80% of the participants fell into the low growth group. Daily living skills plateaus very early at the level of a three year old.

About 20% of the participants fell into the high growth group and living skills at the age of 22 are like those in a typical 15-year-old.

In the US study there is also a less able group and a more able group. Catherine Lord decided to split out her optimal outcome group from the more able group. These were young adults that typically went to college. Since the US always over diagnose, compared to the French, it would be expected that the US cohort includes some less severe cases.

The less able group is 62%, rather than 80% in the French study. At the age of 19, the less able group end up with a non-verbal IQ of 34 and adaptive skills of a four-year-old.

The more able group end up with an IQ of 105 (i.e. slightly above average) but with daily living skills /adaptive behavior of a seven-year-old

Verbal IQ at Age 2 and 19

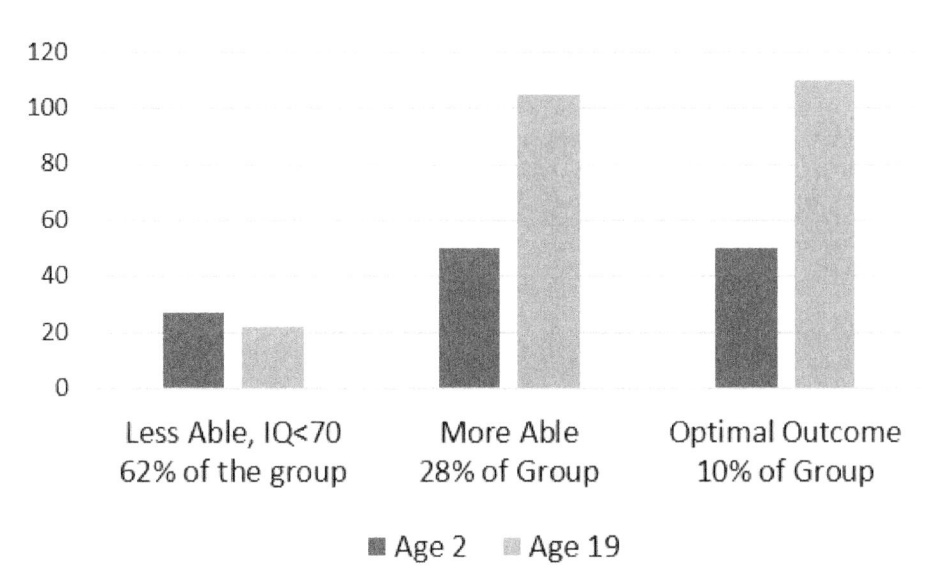

Group	Age 2	Age 19
Less Able, IQ<70, 62% of the group	~28	~22
More Able, 28% of Group	~50	~105
Optimal Outcome, 10% of Group	~50	~110

Source: Longitudinal Studies of ASD from 2 to 22, Catherine Lord, USA

If you read Catherine Lord's work you will see that IQ is not the best predictor of a good outcome, but it is a measure that most people are familiar with. Verbal communication and a good grip on life skills are the most important.

You will note that in the less able group the measured IQ falls as the child becomes an adult. This is because IQ tests get harder as you get older, and people with severe autism add skills at a slower rate compared to typical peers of the same age.

The optimal outcome group did not perform differently in terms of IQ from the more able group, it was on the key issues for independent living where they were differentiated.

Catherin Lord has been following this group for two decades and as she highlights, she is measuring outcomes of those diagnosed with autism at the end of the twentieth century. Back then autism was a severe condition. If she recruited a new random cohort of toddlers diagnosed today with autism, the prognosis over the next 20 years would look much rosier. It is not the same autism.

James Coplan

A retired neurodevelopmental pediatrician called James Coplan has some interesting thoughts.

Coplan wrote a short paper called *Counselling Parents Regarding Prognosis in Autistic Spectrum Disorder*. It is only three pages long and it is free to download. In one of his videos, on his YouTube channel, he comments that autism is 130 years behind most areas of medical science, since it is not diagnosed biologically, merely based on observations relative to an ever-moving benchmark, the US DSM (Diagnostic and Statistical Manual of Mental Disorders).

He points out that back in the 1980s under DSM version 3, the only kind of autism was severe autism with MR/ID. So only a few people were diagnosed. In 1994 version 4 of DSM appeared and it included milder autism, with Asperger's as a sub-type. In 2013 in DSM version 5, Asperger's disappeared as a sub-type.

Coplan went from working with a rare, but severe disorder to a common but generally much milder one.

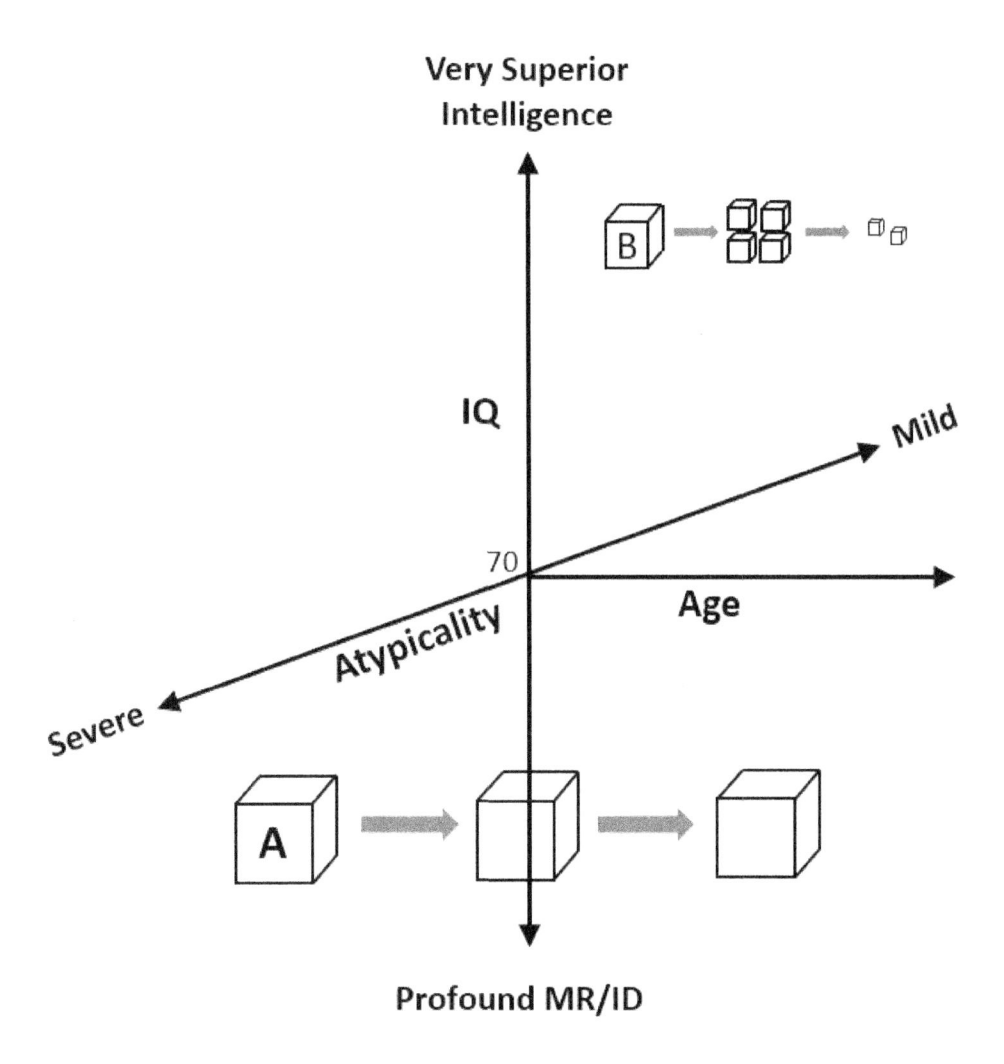

[Figure: Coplan's three-variable model showing axes of IQ (Very Superior Intelligence to Profound MR/ID), Atypicality (Severe to Mild), and Age. Cube A progresses along the lower path; Cube B progresses along the upper path, breaking into smaller pieces over time.]

Coplan considers three variables:

- Atypicality (how autistic you are) occurring along a spectrum from mild to severe.
- Intelligence, with the centre point being an IQ of 70, the boundary of MR/ID
- Age

Autism of any degree of severity can occur with any degree of general intelligence.

The long-term prognosis represents the joint impact of autism severity and cognitive ability; higher IQ leads to better outcome.

The observed severity of autism in the same individual varies with age. Many children with higher IQ do experience significant improvement over time.

The ideal outcome is child B, in the chart, whose atypical symptoms were always mild and whose intelligence is above cut-off for mental retardation/intellectual disability (MR/ID). The core features of ASD break up into fragments, which diminish in severity with the passage of time, until only traces of autism remain.

A less favourable outcome is child A, who has severe autism, plus intellectual disability (ID). As time goes by, he continues to exhibit the same level of autism.

Clearly most children will be somewhere in between child A and child B.

Dr Coplan says that there is little evidence that the prognosis today is different to that in the 1970s or 80s. That suggests little impact from the twenty-year surge in expensive ABA interventions in the US.

Coplan's chart is meant to be in 3D with X, Y and Z axes. This is hard for many people to visualize. I have followed his drawing, but as the engineers/architects among you will have realized, it is not quite right.

Deborah Fein

Deborah Fein is a clinical psychologist who publishes quite a lot of research and you can find interesting videos available of presentations she has given.

Dr Fein also has some nice and simple frameworks, like the one shown opposite.

She highlights that people with autism start to acquire skills much later than typical kids and thereafter add skills at a much lower rate. This means that in any kind of testing, be it of IQ or of adaptive behavior, they are likely to appear to be going backwards.

As you get older, you are supposed to get smarter and have more adaptive skills and so the IQ test for a 9-year-old has a higher standard than the IQ test for a 5 year old.

A typical person's IQ should stay more or less the same; whereas a person with autism is likely to see their IQ fall as they get older.

Fein identifies a small group who against the odds "catch up". She calls this small group optimal outcome, the ones that "recover".

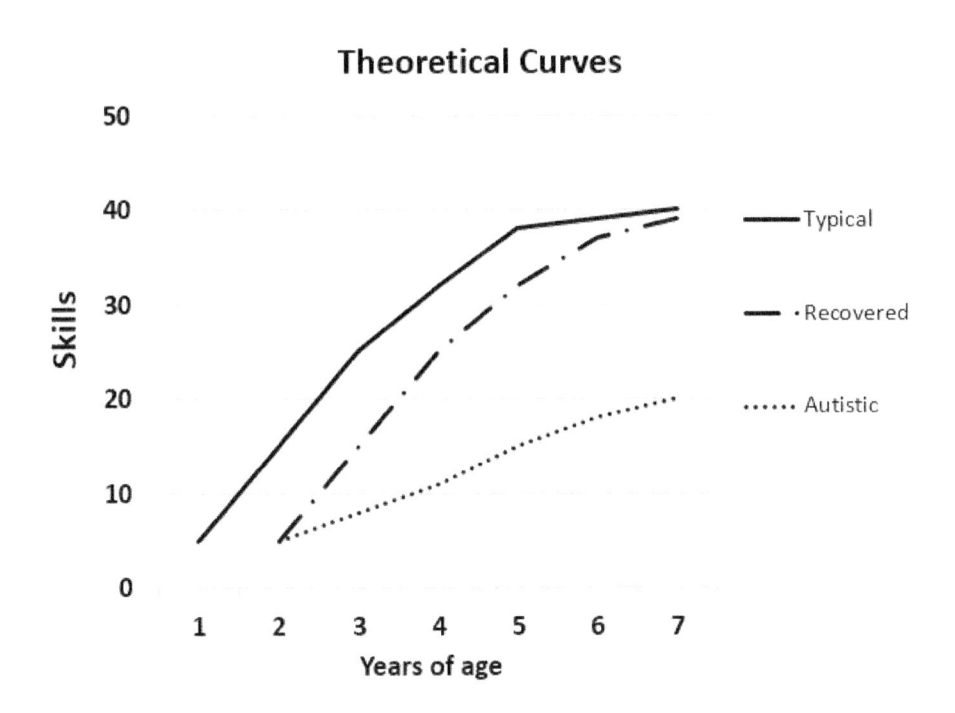

Theoretical Curves

(Graph showing Skills vs Years of age, with three curves: Typical, Recovered, and Autistic)

In the US, children are diagnosed far earlier than in many other countries, two years old and younger is not uncommon. In most other countries it is three, four or five years old. The earlier you diagnose autism the higher your chances are of getting it wrong. Some children have delayed maturation and may seem autistic when very young, but seem very close to typical a couple of years later.

An Italian researcher found that as much as 7% of autism is delayed maturation that fades away to a mild Tourette's (tic) disorder.

Some children develop speech very late, but go on to develop totally normally. So being non-verbal at three years old, does not necessarily point to autism.

In most cases, Asperger-type autism is diagnosed at a much later age in most countries. There was no speech delay, no cognitive impairment and so other differences pass as being quirky, or introverted.

In the past the prognosis for autism was very poor, in great part because only severe cases were diagnosed as autism. Children were taken from their parents and put into institutions before they were strongly emotionally bonded and parents were told to get on with their own lives.

Institutionalization still does happen, but in richer countries it is as a last resort and given a nicer sounding name, like being put "into care".

On receipt of an autism diagnosis, you really need to know what type of autism the clinician is talking about. If the child is non-verbal, with developmental delays in all areas, then he fits the old definition of autism. The majority of what is today defined in the 2020s as autism is something very much milder, with a very different prognosis. Perhaps your child will be the next Elon Musk.

Rather than accepting Dr Coplan's comment that autism is 130 years behind the times, it is important to realize that much can be done to treat many types of autism. The initial behavioral diagnosis is not the end of the matter, it is just the start.

For example, in regressive autism, Dr Kelley, from Johns Hopkins, stresses the importance of not letting things get worse. By taking pharmacological steps to avoid further regressions, over time the expectation is that things will gradually get better. He sees most regressive autism as being a consequence of mitochondrial disease.

In non-regressive autism, where a child is a little different from birth, you may come across the phenomenon I call double-tap. A double tap is when a target is struck twice, and the second strike is the overwhelming one. In these cases, the child has been diagnosed with autism, likely has entered some intensive early intervention program like ABA and responds well. Then something happens and all the progress grinds to a halt and things go backwards. This second strike is too much for the child, who then may switch from being an ABA responder, to a more severe case of autism. I have no doubt there can be many things that can provide such a second hit. It could be a severe emotional shock, it could be a flare-up in an inflammatory condition, mast cell activation; it could even be puberty.

You cannot realistically prevent puberty, but many other strikes, if identified in time, can be treated and the neurological damage minimized. It is best to consider a young autistic child as being in a fragile state and make sure they do not get exposed to further negative shocks.

Dr Kelley's mitochondrial cocktail is like an insurance policy against the second strike, which in this case might deliver a devastating overload of mitochondria in the brain leading to loss of myelination and cell death. This would manifest itself as a profound second regression.

A big risk for someone with severe autism is that they develop epilepsy, often around the time of puberty. An open question is the extent to which you can prevent the onset of epilepsy.

The risk of doing nothing vs the risk of doing something – severe autism

Almost everything we do in life carries some degree of risk, be it crossing a road, or having a drink after work with friends.

We have seen from the work of Catherine Lord, James Coplan and many others that the outcome in severe autism with ID is poor in the majority of cases. You might be one of the lucky ones and have an optimal outcome, but don't count on it. We can say that the risk of doing nothing with this type of autism is huge.

What is the risk of doing something? Even with all the wide range of orthodox and very unorthodox therapies out there, some science-based, but many not, I could only find details on one person coming to grief. Sure, many people waste tens of thousands of dollars on therapies that had no long-term benefit.

Even among the relatively small number of people who correspond with me, children have died from severe autism and its many comorbidities.

I was contacted by a parent wanting to treat his young daughter diagnosed with Rett syndrome, to try and improve her future.

Rett syndrome follows four stages. The early onset stage starts before two years old; stage two is a wide-ranging regression, stage three is a cognitive plateau but with emergence of seizures and sometimes heart problems, stage 4 starts around age 10 and is called the late motor deterioration phase.

He had found a doctor locally in Spain willing to help him, but he was, quite understandably, having some second thoughts. He asked me for advice. I suggested that he compared the risks of allowing Rett syndrome to follow its natural course, with the risk of trying a possibly effective off-label therapy. This therapy is supported by some evidence in Rett syndrome and is supported by his new doctor. I wished him good luck.

The risk of doing nothing vs the risk of doing something – mild autism

If your source of information is that small but vocal group of self-advocates on social media, then you would think that mild autism is no big deal; in fact, it might even be a superpower.

My source of information is all those adults who were diagnosed with Asperger's syndrome and who write to my blog, or me directly. These people tell a very different story: they have their struggles and they are looking for anything that might help overcome them.

The risk of doing nothing is likely to be some combination of depression, anxiety, loneliness, and a general failure to thrive.

The kinds of interventions that may help this group of people are pretty simple – they are basic supplements and some safe old generic drugs. I was going to add, no need for costly IVIG (Intravenous Immunoglobulin) with Aspies, but then I recall an Aspie lady pretty desperate to get hold of Humira, an expensive TNF alpha blocker that you take by injection. An injection of Humira sends her autism symptoms packing for a couple of months and she wants more of it.

The people with mild autism, who contact me, are clearly a self-selecting group, that have chosen to do something about it. They clearly hate their baseline situation and have decided it is worth fine tuning their brains a little to improve their lives. Good for them, but I really never expected them to be contacting me.

Measuring IQ and autism rating scales

The degree of cognitive dysfunction varies widely across the autism spectrum. Cognitive dysfunction is not quite the same thing as having a low IQ (intelligence quotient). People with an

Asperger's diagnosis may be measured as having an above average IQ, but this does not mean they do not have some cognitive dysfunction. Cognitive dysfunction is also present in schizophrenia and bipolar.

Adaptive behavior is measured to indicate your level of practical daily living skills. It is seen as more relevant than IQ for those with more severe autism.

Some cognitive dysfunctions are treatable.

In many advanced countries IQ testing is required to gain maximum access to services and support for autism. There are special tests available to measure the IQ of people who are non-verbal.

Two thirds of the general population score between an IQ of 85 and an IQ of 115, so we can consider that as "normal". About 5 percent of the population scores above 125, and 5 percent below 75. 2.2% of the population have an IQ less than 70 and this is the cut-off point used to determine intellectual disability (ID), formerly known as mental retardation (MR).

By definition, you cannot have Asperger's and ID/MR. Classic autism is associated with ID/MR. Almost all Down syndrome is associated with ID/MR. The middle part of the autistic spectrum that used to be called PDD-NOS (Pervasive Developmental Disorder-Not Otherwise Specified) does include a minority with ID/MR.

Nonverbal IQ assessment is the process of assessing intelligence without placing receptive or expressive language demands on either the examinee or the examiner. Verbal test directions and spoken responses are not required during the administration of a nonverbal test.

For most typical people their measured IQ stays broadly the same as they get older. For people with severe autism, because they add new skills more slowly than their peers, their measured IQ would be expected to fall as they progress through their early school years. For this reason, measuring IQ can be disturbing to some parents. The person with autism is adding new skills, but is nonetheless falling further behind.

When it comes to measuring autism itself, there are numerous rating systems. The best known are CARS (Childhood Autism Rating Scale), ABC (Autism Behavior Checklist) and ADOS

(Autism Diagnostic Observation Schedule). These scales allow the user to differentiate between children in terms of severity and to identify areas of strength and weakness. These scales are used in clinical trials of drugs to see to what extent the drug can improve a specific aspect of autism. They are clearly of great potential value, but will still be somewhat subjective.

Fortunately, at least in Europe, the drug regulator has selected one single rating scale to be used in all clinical trials. They selected CARS (Childhood Autism Rating Scale).

Measuring changes in autistic behavior is the key part in any autism clinical trial. Bernie Rimland's Autism Research Institute (ARI) argued that part of the reason autism clinical trials failed was that the rating scales were not sufficiently sensitive to pick up the changes. So, ARI created its own rating scale to be used to assess the effect of interventions. Their scale is called ATEC (Autism Treatment Evaluation Scale). It is a 77-item assessment tool which is completed by a parent, takes about 10–15 minutes to complete and is designed for use with children ages 5 to 12.

The Childhood Autism Rating Scale (CARS) is a behavior rating scale intended to help diagnose autism. It was designed to help differentiate children with autism from those with other developmental delays, such as intellectual disability (ID/MR). It rates children on a scale from one to four for various criteria, ranging from normal to severe, and yields a composite score ranging from non-autistic to mildly autistic, moderately autistic, or severely autistic. The scale is used to observe and subjectively rate fifteen items. The following is an example:

Relating to People	3
Emotional Response	2
Imitation	3
Body Use	2
Object Use	2
Adaptation to Change	2
Listening Response	2
Taste, Smell, Touch	3
Visual Response	2
Fear or Nervous	1
Verbal Communication	3
Activity Level	2
Nonverbal Communication	3
Level & Consistency of Intellectual Response	3
<u>General Impression</u>	<u>2</u>
Total Score	**35**

A diagnosis of autism is indicated if the score is above 30. The maximum score of 60 would correspond to the most severe autism.

The problem with autism clinical trials

There have been many thousands of research papers published on autism and hundreds of small clinical trials, so how come there are no approved drugs?

To be fair, there has been very little success in treating any neurological disorders, a good example is Alzheimer's disease where even after numerous clinical trials there are just a handful of very partially effective therapies from long ago.

With autism the problem is different because we know there are hundreds of possible dysfunctions that will lead to behaviors that will meet an autism diagnosis. Some of these dysfunctions are diametrical opposites (hypo vs hyper). Yet for decades clinical trials have been based on small groups of people with any biological dysfunction that leaves them with autism symptoms, without any screening into sub-types using biomarkers.

In cancer research, patients are now grouped by small subtypes that describe their specific type of cancer and then therapies are tried on a relatively homogenous group. Then useful conclusions can be drawn from the trials.

Even very simple observations can be confusing. Do people with autism have big heads? Well some do, and that is called macrocephaly, and some have tiny heads, and that is microcephaly. What about data on the average head size? Well that would be completely meaningless. What tells you something is unusual head size, or even muscle tone, in very early childhood.

Meaningful clinical trials will have to be much better constructed, or they have to be much bigger and that would cost much more money. Only then will a therapy effective in one sub-type, which might affect just 10% of those in the trial group, actually make itself stand out in the trial.

Memantine (Namenda) is the most researched drug for autism, but in the large studies carried out by the producer, at the request of the FDA in response to rampant off-label use for autism, the drug failed to meet its target endpoint. The trial was deemed a failure. Was there a small group of genuine responders tucked away in the data? Quite possibly.

A much better use of funds would have been to ask autism clinicians to identify people they had treated who did respond to memantine. You then analyze them as a group to try and find any common biomarkers, hopefully finding something they tend to have in common. Then trial memantine vs a placebo in this group of so-called responders and judge how well they respond to memantine vs the placebo. Are the doctors and parents all imagining the benefit? If not imagined, then you might be able to say that yes, some people do respond, they respond in the following beneficial way(s) and when they received a placebo the good effects were lost. Maybe only 5% of people genuinely do respond to memantine, but even that would be good to know.

In medicine the gold standard is the double blind randomized controlled trial, and anecdotal evidence tends to be ignored. In reality, a clinical trial on subjects with totally different biological dysfunctions, albeit presenting as some kind of autism, is not the Holy Grail. In spite of the fancy statistical analysis, it may be a case of garbage in, garbage out.

Clinical trials on single gene types of autism, like Fragile X or Rett syndrome do not suffer this problem, to the same extent. All the subjects have varying degrees of the same biological dysfunction and so the results should be meaningful. But even in these circumstances, it is important to note that within single gene autism there is a spectrum. Multiple different mutations are possible in the same gene and each specific mutation might be a subtype.

The devil is in the details!

Biomarkers

A biomarker refers to a measurable indicator of some biological condition.

In the world of autism biomarkers you would potentially identify sub-types that could then be treated in very focused, but different, ways.

For example, a common biomarker of inflammation in the body is CRP (C reactive protein). It is a protein produced in the liver that increases following secretion of a pro-inflammatory substance called interleukin-6. An elevated CRP tells your doctor that there is inflammation somewhere in your body, but not where it is.

Ideally, a biomarker would tell you precisely what is going on and what to do about it.

One autism therapy being developed in the US is a combination of pancreatic enzymes. The founder of that company went to great lengths to find a biomarker for those who she thought would respond to her therapy. For that I give her 10 out of 10.

Rather than being a doctor from Harvard, or a scientist from MIT, Joan Fallon trained as a chiropractor at Palmer University. Not surprisingly the scientific community is skeptical of her autism treatment, which is linked to pancreatic enzymes.

In her initial trials, participants needed to have a low fecal chymotrypsin level.

The chymotrypsin test is used to evaluate for pancreatic insufficiency. Pancreatic insufficiency is the inability of the pancreas to produce and/or transport enough digestive enzymes to break down food in the intestine and facilitate absorption of nutrients. It typically occurs as a result of progressive pancreatic damage, such as from cystic fibrosis.

Fallon provided data that showed a correlation between low fecal chymotrypsin level and a positive response to her enzyme cocktail. Based on early results her CM-AT therapy was then fast tracked by the FDA in its approval process, however, later the FDA made her carry out the Phase III trial without the biomarker. They want to know how other types of autism respond.

Biomarkers should remain the goal of anyone trying to implement an intelligent clinical trial in autism. Only trial your drug therapy on the smaller group, most likely to benefit. Once approved as a therapy, anyone can try it.

Off-label autism treatment in the US and elsewhere

The US continues to be the only country where there is widespread off-label treatment of autism, using many drugs and hundreds of supplements. Off-label means using a drug for a purpose other than it was approved for. Most drugs have numerous effects and so a drug approved for one specific purpose might be repurposed for an entirely different purpose. For example, low doses of the painkiller aspirin are given to people at risk of a heart attack.

Healthcare in the US is organized completely differently to other advanced economies. In Europe governments play a much more prescriptive role in how people are treated, in part because the government is directly organizing and paying for that care.

So, whereas you might persuade your family doctor in California to prescribe a drug off-label, because a clinical trial showed a safe old drug can be repurposed for autism, such a request to a family doctor in the UK would be met with a blank stare.

People in more Latin-thinking countries like much of Spain, Greece and Latin America have more access to off-label therapies because pharmacies do not enforce the requirement to have a prescription.

In large countries like Nigeria, Egypt and India pharmacies sell prescription drugs to whoever comes to buy them. It is just a business.

Mainstream science-based therapy for autism

There is a reason why this section is so short. Very little scientific knowledge regarding autism has been translated into practical therapies. This will hopefully change in the next decades.

Mainstream therapy for autism is rather limited and very much depends on where you live. If you live in North America, there is federally funded provision for intensive early intervention starting after diagnosis. Many parents have health insurance that will pay for 1:1 ABA sessions and so many people have access to ABA therapy. In Europe it often takes years longer to get to the autism diagnosis and there is much less in the way of services. In Europe it is not widely accepted that ABA is effective.

The premise is that with intensive behavioral intervention at a very early age you can change the course of autism. I think this is likely true to some degree, particularly in those with apparently severe autism but higher IQ, but the beneficial effect is often greatly exaggerated. Some people have had 20 years of paid ABA therapy and are still at it.

Mainstream therapies

There are no drugs approved yet to treat core autism, but in North America extensive use is made of antipsychotic medications (Risperidone), antidepressants (Prozac, Zoloft) and stimulants (Ritalin). These drugs often produce side effects, one notable one being weight gain, which can lead to type 2 diabetes. Another side effect is tardive dyskinesia, a problem discussed in my blog, when children develop repetitive muscle movements in the face, arms or legs after taking an antipsychotic. These tics may not stop when you discontinue the drug. Boys growing breasts is another side effect.

As yet, no mainstream drug therapies are approved to treat the core features of autism.

The idea of using pharmacological treatment to reduce the symptoms of autism is generally regarded by mainstream clinicians as wishful thinking at best. Even the idea provokes resistance.

Many people with severe autism will develop epilepsy and so take AEDs (anti-epileptic drugs). These fortunately may have the secondary effect of improving autism, Valproate being a common example.

Alternative therapy for autism

About 40 percent of adults in the US report using complementary and alternative medicine, also called CAM for short. In families where autism is present this figure is likely much higher.

There are numerous CAM therapies applied to autism and they all have their advocates.

This book is about science-based therapies for autism that should over time become the mainstream therapies of the future. There is no reason why an effective CAM therapy cannot become a mainstream therapy; all that is required is evidence of effectiveness.

The scientific literature is not just about drugs, it also encompasses research into numerous naturally occurring plant-derived substances. It also looks at why certain plants are used in Chinese traditional medicine, with a view to identifying which chemical in that plant is beneficial.

The extent of published autism scientific research is now substantial. In recent years some highly respected academics have begun to participate. Within this research there is plenty of material on which to develop totally rational therapies that could be mainstreamed. There are some good reasons why this has not happened, but this does not mean it cannot be done.

The goal should be effective mainstream therapy for all types of autism. People with very mild autism can choose for themselves whether they want to be treated; some are vehemently opposed to the idea, but many others are trawling the internet looking for ways to improve their symptoms.

Very many clinical trials have been carried out that concern repurposing existing drugs to treat autism.

Existing drugs already tested in at least one randomised double-blind placebo controlled study

Amantadine	Donepezil	Minocycline
Atomoxetine	Fenfluramine	Naltrexone
BH4	Fluoxetine	Olanzapine
Bumetanide	Fluvoxamine	Oxytocin
Buspirone	Galantamine	Pentoxifylline
Celecoxib	Guanfacine	Pioglitazone
Clomipramine	Haloperidol	Propranolol
Clonidine	Leucovorin	Riluzole
Cyproheptadine	Memantine	Simvastatin
D-cycloserine	Metformin	Topiramate
Dextromethorphan	Methylphenidate	Valproate

There is no shortage of experimental evidence, but there is a lack of interest to read it carefully.

Quacks, charlatans, and who to believe

There undoubtedly are quacks and charlatans involved in treating autism. This is one reason why many mainstream doctors do not even want to discuss the subject of treating autism, or sometimes even its comorbidities.

Deciding what is a genuine therapy is very much a personal matter. There are mainstream medical therapies for other conditions that were originally ridiculed. There is no easy way to know who to believe, because in medicine you can get the right answer for the wrong reason. There are numerous common drugs in use today where the mode of action remains unclear. All the patient cares about is whether it works or not and that there are minimal side effects.

In 2005 Australians Barry Marshall and Robin Warren were awarded the Nobel Prize in Medicine for their work in showing that the bacterium H. pylori causes peptic ulcers and that the condition can be resolved with antibiotics.

The original H. pylori theory was ridiculed by scientists and doctors, who did not believe that any bacteria could live in the acidic environment of the stomach. Marshall decided to take extreme action; having had a baseline endoscopy, he drank a petri dish containing H. pylori. After eight days he had a repeat endoscopy, which showed massive inflammation, and a biopsy confirmed the presence of H. pylori in his stomach. On the fourteenth day, a third endoscopy was done, and Marshall began to take antibiotics to kill the H. pylori.

It is also quite possible in medicine to get a therapy right but for the wrong reason. This happens because many drugs have multiple modes of action. For example, many anti-parasite drugs do some clever things unrelated to parasites; so the alternative practitioner treating kids with autism to get rid of "parasites" may indeed be using an effective drug, regardless of whether there are indeed any parasites. The drug Ivermectin does kill parasites, but it is also a PAK1 inhibitor and a modulator of purinergic receptor P2X subunits. A Nobel Laureate has proposed the use of PAK1 inhibitors to treat some schizophrenia and Professor Naviaux at UC San Diego has spent years on a theory linking purinergic signaling to autism; his therapy involves Suramin, an even more potent anti-parasite drug.

This is also the case with common antibiotics, like penicillin, that do seem to improve some people's autism, but for reasons unrelated to killing bacteria. Penicillin is a beta lactam type antibiotic; this class of antibiotic happens to upregulate the GLT1 gene, which increases the reuptake of the excitatory neurotransmitter glutamate. This shifts the excitatory/inhibitory balance in the brain towards inhibitory. You might expect these antibiotics to also reduce the occurrence of seizures in some people. Many antibiotics, including Penicillin, also have well known immunomodulatory effects, this is why Azithromycin is used to treat cystic fibrosis and non-bacterial prostatitis is treated by an antibiotic like Ciprofloxacin.

Rather than ridiculing bizarre looking therapies it is worth considering whether they might be having a genuine effect, but for an unexpected reason that is far from bizarre.

In writing my blog I keep being surprised how many drugs were just stumbled upon by accident. An example is the original cognitive enhancing drug discovered by the Romanian psychologist and chemist Corneliu Giurgea. He was working in Belgium trying to make a new drug to treat motion sickness, but his drug Piracetam, turned out to have entirely unexpected cognitive enhancing effects. In 1972 Giurgea coined the term nootropic for drugs like Piracetam that can improve cognition.

Correlation, causation, associations, and exceptions

Correlation does not imply causation; what does that mean? It points out that a correlation between two variables does not imply that one causes the other. Smokers tend to drive their car with the window open, this does not mean that driving with your window open means you are a smoker, or that driving with an open window will give you lung cancer.

You can correlate the increase in autism diagnosis in the last 20 years with almost anything linked to modern living, from cellular phone usage, sales of air conditioning units, to vitamin D supplementation in processed food. But do they cause autism?

Associations are also very important. For example, autism is associated with asthma and indeed epilepsy, but they do not cause it. People with severe autism are far more likely to have epilepsy than typical people and they are more likely to have asthma.

We all know the saying, the exception that proves the rule. Just because your neighbour lived to 90 years old, smoking 40 cigarettes a day, does not mean smoking does not cause cancer and COPD; it just means he was very lucky.

Just because Dr Jon Poling received millions of dollars of compensation for proving, beyond reasonable doubt, that his daughter's autism was caused by vaccination, does not mean that your case was. It does however mean that it can happen.

Just because your cousin's friend's next-door neighbour has a child whose autism vanished after an exclusion diet does not guarantee it to be true, nor that the same will automatically happen for your child.

About 10 percent of young children diagnosed today with autism are likely to lose their diagnosis by the time they become a teenager, all without any intervention. It would be unwise to assume you are in that 10 percent.

We will see in this book that numerous things increase the risk of autism, but it does not mean they applied to you. You may know someone who fathered a perfectly healthy child when aged 60, but this does not mean autism is not associated with increasing parental age. Mick Jagger became a Dad for the eighth time at the age of 73, but he is tempting fate.

Treating, healing, curing and recovery from autism

This book is about treating some of the conditions that lead to an autism diagnosis, it is about improving the symptoms. It does appear that the severity of many people's autism can be moderated pharmacologically. A person with severe autism might be shifted towards moderate autism slowly over time, a person with mild autism (Asperger's) might find relief from anxiety and sensory problems, but some differences will likely remain.

There are some metabolic conditions causing autism that can indeed be cured, but even then, if done later in life, there will remain some traits of autism. A good example is Roger, a reader of my blog and indeed many others. Roger has cerebral folate deficiency which was identified and treated in adulthood. He is no longer severely autistic.

In the popular world of autism people talk about healing and recovery. Healing means the process of becoming sound or healthy again. Recovery means a return to a normal state of health, mind, or strength. In the case of severe autism, I think recovery is an unwise word to use and rather cruel to raise expectations so far.

In popular online forums parents will raise questions like "what does recovery with ABA look like?" In other words, if I put my two-year-old into an intensive program using Applied Behavioral Analysis (ABA), what should I expect to happen? Maybe it is a fair question, but it does not really have a meaningful answer.

There are at least 10% of early childhood diagnoses that do not stand the test of time. In some cases, this has been studied.

"Dysmaturational syndrome" was identified and documented by Michele Zappella, an Italian doctor from Siena University, interested in autism and Tourette's syndrome. He identified a sizable subgroup of autism in very young children that was comorbid with the Tourette's syndrome tic disorder. The unusual thing is that by the age of six, these children had "grown out" of their autism entirely. Zappella's study in 2010 suggests that his dysmaturational syndrome applies to about 6% of early childhood autism. In effect, he is saying that 6% of the children diagnosed before five years old with autism, fit his dysmaturational model and recover to have normal IQ, no seizures, and no signs of autism. The tics though do not entirely go away.

There is also the work of Deborah Fein, an American Psychologist, well worth following, who looks at what she calls Optimal Outcome (OO). I have mentioned her previously, but you may have skipped that part. In her optimal outcome group are those children that in effect grow out of their diagnosis, although some mild traits usually remain. She is not a scientist, so she does not get into the biology of autism. Fein suggests that 10 to 20% of children diagnosed with autism will achieve her optimal outcome and she found that people who had early intensive ABA are over represented. If you read her work, she is not saying ABA will lead to optimal outcome, but she does suggest that ABA is a helpful intervention.

You also have the possibility of an overzealous diagnosis of autism in the first place, particularly in countries where they make this diagnosis under two years of age. There still are countries where diagnosis usually waits until the age of five.

It should be noted that there are some children who later develop normally, who do not start to speak before their third birthday. This is used by some doctors as an argument to adopt "the wait and see approach", rather than assuming there is a developmental problem.

Related medical conditions

Most neuropsychiatric disorders are overlapping rather than discrete, so an underlying biological dysfunction that is part of one person's bipolar disorder may also exist in another person's autism. This has now been established beyond doubt in large studies showing which genes are over, or under-expressed in people with different disorders.

This means that someone with autism may share underlying dysfunctions with people who have a different observational diagnosis (ADHD, bipolar, schizophrenia etc).

Going beyond neuropsychiatric disorders we can also look at the well-known and very well studied degenerative disorders like Alzheimer's, Parkinson's, Huntington's and even motor neuron disease (also called ALS). You might wonder what is the point looking at degenerative brain diseases that affect older adults. The reason is that these diseases have been very well studied and many therapies have been put forward, but these are not curative, they are just therapies that tackle dysfunctions that are secondary.

In ALS there are therapies that affect glutamate. They are not very good ALS therapies, but they are very effective in achieving their goal with glutamate. Huntington's disease is caused by a single gene and it is not an autism gene, but one secondary feature of Huntington's disease is a lack of autophagy, the body's intracellular garbage collection service. Autophagy is a secondary feature of autism. So, therapies to upregulate autophagy in Huntington's and also in dementia may also benefit some people with autism.

We know that impaired myelination is a feature of autism, with a special fMRI scan you can actually measure the thickness of the myelin layer. We also know in specific single gene autisms that the genes involved are misexpressed. This means that we can potentially benefit from the research in MS (Multiple Sclerosis) which is caused by the loss of myelin.

Alzheimer's is the most common form of dementia. There are some mildly effective approved therapies and a very long list of identified potential therapies. Some of these may also be relevant to autism. Memantine/Namenda is an Alzheimer's drug widely used off-label to treat autism.

People do not like to hear about cancer, but when you start looking at the molecular level and at the body's complex signaling pathways, you find clear overlaps in the underpinnings of some autism and some cancer. For example, you have RAS-dependent cancers and you have so-called RASopathies, which can be associated with some autism and some MR/ID.

This suggests that in coming years when cancer therapies based on modifying these signaling pathways have been developed, tested and approved, there will be some scope to repurpose some of them to treat some subtypes of autism. This will require a much more sophisticated understanding of autism than exists today, outside a handful of top universities. It will also need the patent on the drug to expire, so its cost drops from $50,000 a year to something affordable for autism, like today's generic drugs for Alzheimer's and ALS.

Schizophrenia

Some adults diagnosed with Asperger's (level 1 autism) exhibit some of the tell-tale symptoms of schizophrenia. This particularly seems to apply to some autism self-advocates who populate social media.

This is only to be expected; both conditions are polygenic and the hundreds of affected genes for the two conditions overlap. You can have Asperger's with a little schizophrenia and even a touch of bipolar.

Schizophrenia is a disorder of the mind that affects how you think, feel and behave. Its symptoms are described as positive or negative.

Positive symptoms

These are unusual experiences. Many people have them from time to time and they need not be a problem. In schizophrenia, they tend to be much more intense, troublesome, pre-occupying and distressing.

Examples are, hallucinations, when you hear, smell, feel or see something that is not there. The commonest one is hearing voices. You may see things that aren't there, or may smell or taste things that aren't there. Some people have uncomfortable or painful feelings in their body, or feelings of being touched or hit.

Delusions are when you believe something and are completely sure of it, but other people think you have misunderstood what has happened. Paranoid delusions are when you feel persecuted or harassed, like someone is spying on you. This seems to apply to some Aspies I have encountered.

Muddled thinking/thought disorder, is when you find it harder to concentrate. You might struggle to complete simple tasks, or cope with studies at university or concentrate at work.

Feelings of being controlled, is when you feel that an external force is controlling your mind and body.

Negative symptoms

Negative symptoms are less dramatic than positive symptoms and there seems to be some overlap.

Negative symptoms concern not really wanting to do things, feel emotions or have normal thoughts. It can appear as not wanting to leave the house or keep yourself clean and tidy.

Schizophrenia affects around 1 in every 100 people, with onset most common between the ages of 15 to 35.

What used to be diagnosed as childhood schizophrenia is now labeled autism.

Like autism, schizophrenia is caused by a combination of genetics and the environment. If you have a parent with a schizophrenia diagnosis you have a 10% chance of being diagnosed with schizophrenia. If your identical twin has a diagnosis, your odds rise to 50%.

As with autism and bipolar disorder, schizophrenia is itself a spectrum. The more mis-expressed schizophrenia genes you have, the more severe your symptoms will be.

At what point does being a little schizophrenic become enough to get the label from a psychiatrist is entirely subjective. The definition of autism was widened and this caused an explosion in diagnoses. The same has happened with ADHD. The same could happen with schizophrenia, if you move the diagnostic threshold.

Bipolar disorder

Bipolar is a mood disorder when someone swings between manic (feeling high) and depressive (feeling low).

Everyone has mood swings, with good days and bad days. In bipolar these extremes are more profound and may be accompanied by some psychotic symptoms.

Within the bipolar spectrum, there is bipolar I and bipolar II, based on an assessment of the types of mood swings. People with bipolar disorder tend to be diagnosed many years after they first exhibit their symptoms.

Estimates of prevalence vary quite widely because it is another polygenic condition with a spectrum with no clear threshold, or cut off point.

An estimated 4.4% of U.S. adults experience bipolar disorder at some time in their lives.

Since the genes that cause bipolar are in all of us, but more so in people with autism, or schizophrenia, it should not be surprising to find mood swings in those diagnoses.

People with bipolar disorder have a tendency to self-harm and suicide, as do people with schizophrenia and mild autism. In autism it is only the Asperger's end of the spectrum who have the suicide risk.

Attention deficit hyperactivity disorder (ADHD)

Attention deficit hyperactivity disorder (ADHD) is another polygenic disorder, so again there is a spectrum. It is also very much affected by nurture/upbringing as the key environmental influence, whereas in some disorders there are many biological influences.

ADHD affects about 7% of children when diagnosed via the American criteria and 1–2% when diagnosed via the World Health Organization criteria.

ADHD is characterized by problems paying attention, excessive activity, or difficulty controlling behavior. In children, problems paying attention may result in poor school performance, and so nowadays lead to a diagnosis. Many children diagnosed with ADHD have a good attention span for tasks they find interesting, which suggests over-diagnosis.

ADHD is diagnosed approximately three times more often in boys than in girls. About 30–50% of people diagnosed in childhood continue to have symptoms into adulthood.

Features of ADHD will very often be present in someone with an autism diagnosis.

Note that there is also ADD, without the H for hyperactive. The H means you have difficulty sitting still. Bizarrely, in DSM5 ADD is now called ADHD-PI (predominantly inattentive). Predominantly hyperactive-impulsive ADHD is now called ADHD-PH.

Niche descriptive disorders

The inability to treat neurological disorders has not stopped psychiatrists from inventing new descriptive observational diagnoses. To the extent that they help describe the issues a person faces they have some relevance, but they are often misused.

Intermittent explosive disorder (IED) describes people who display explosive outbursts of anger and violence. Such behavior is common in severe autism and does occur, although less often, in Asperger's.

In autism, people usually refer to SIB (self-injurious behavior), because most often violence is not directed at others, unless they try to intervene.

Pathological demand avoidance (PDA), was invented in 1980 in England. It is not recognized in the US DSM5 or the World Health Organization's ICD-10, but you will come across people saying they have PDA. PDA might in previous years have been labelled as atypical autism, or PDD-NOS (pervasive developmental disorder-not otherwise specified).

You could easily label many typical teenagers as exhibiting signs of ADHD or PDA, so it is important to maintain a sense of perspective and not over-apply such labels.

Obsessive compulsive disorder (OCD)

If you want to understand the nuances of autism you need to understand the nuances of OCD (obsessive compulsive disorder), tics and stereotypy, which may appear similar at first glance.

Obsessions are thoughts that recur and persist despite efforts to ignore or rationalize them. It could be a preoccupation with the idea of death, or irrational fears like plane crashes, a common feature in Aspies.

Compulsions are things like constantly washing hands for fear of germs. It is quite normal to want to check to see if your front door is locked, but for some people it becomes a compulsive behavior.

Excessive skin picking, hair-pulling (trichotillomania), nail biting, and other body-focused repetitive behavior disorders are all on the obsessive-compulsive spectrum. Interestingly, the antioxidant NAC is a well-established cure for hair-pulling (trichotillomania).

Compulsions are different from tics (such as touching, tapping, rubbing, or blinking) and stereotypy/stereotyped movements (such as hand flapping and body rocking).

Many people diagnosed with OCD are also diagnosed with a tic disorder.

Tourette's

Tourette syndrome (Tourette's), is a common disorder with onset in childhood, characterized by multiple motor tics and at least one vocal tic. These tics are typically preceded by an unwanted urge or sensation in the affected muscles. Some common tics are eye blinking, other facial movements and even coughing, throat clearing or sniffing. Some people are even compulsive joint crackers.

About 1% of children are thought to have Tourette's. Some people have Tourette's and autism, I call it Tourette's-type autism.

Most people with OCD, Tourette's or tic disorders do not have autism. Some very young children with Tourette's and apparent autism, actually may have something termed "Dysmaturational syndrome". I have mentioned this previously, but it is very relevant here.

Dysmaturational syndrome was identified and documented by Dr Michele Zappella, an Italian doctor interested in autism and Tourette's syndrome.

He identified a sizable subgroup of autism in very young children that was comorbid with the Tourette's syndrome tic disorder. The unusual thing is that by the age of six, these children had "grown out" of their autism entirely.

Zappella's study in 2010 suggests that his dysmaturational syndrome applies to about 6% of early childhood autism. In effect, he is saying that 6% of the children diagnosed before 5 years old with autism, fit this dysmaturational syndrome and "recover" to have normal IQ, no seizures, and no signs of autism. The tics though do not go away.

Tics

Some people with autism also have features of Tourette syndrome, particularly the verbal/vocal tics.

Lip biting is considered a motor tic. Hand flapping is a motor tic to some people and a stereotypy to others.

Some people regard head banging as a motor tic. I regard head banging as an acquired behavior, initially it occurred for a good reason, like pain, anger or fear, but it becomes a habit and the threshold for it to occur is reduced, sometimes to a trivial level. One child may engage in headbanging just to gain attention, while in another it is triggered by mild, perhaps undiagnosed, seizures, or intense pain in the head or elsewhere in the body. Rocking side to side is a motor tic; head banging is much more than a tic.

Verbal tics vary from simple grunting noises, to loud exclamations to simple words or even complete sentences. At some point complex verbal tics overlap with scripting.

Scripting

Scripting is very common in autism. It is the repetition of words, phrases, or sounds of the speech of others, sometimes taken from movies, but also sometimes taken from other sources such as favorite books or something someone else has said.

Scripting may or may not have a logical meaningful foundation.

My son, when stressed, used to say "look both ways," which is what he was told when learning to cross a road (a stressful activity). So he associates stress with "look both ways." Totally rational. He also might say "reverse engines," which is what you might do in a cartoon to avoid a crash.

The distinctions between stereotypy, tics and OCD do matter, because the underlying biology is different and so effective therapy will be different.

Stereotypy/Stimming

Stereotypy/stereotyped movements is a classic symptom of autism, where there is often a compulsion for repetition, routine and sameness. There is often heightened anxiety and fear of the unknown. Stimming may also be a form of self-stimulation, which might be pleasurable or a mechanism to deal with anxiety.

Stereotypy in many people with autism responds to treatment with the antioxidant NAC. Interestingly, many people with compulsive hair pulling (trichotillomania) gain complete relief from a similar dose of NAC.

Some people see hand flapping as a stereotypy engaged in when the person is happy or excited.

Irritable bowel syndrome (IBS) and inflammatory bowel disease (IBD)

First of all, we need to differentiate two common conditions with very similar names. IBS is the less serious condition, though it still causes a lot of discomfort.

Irritable bowel syndrome – IBS

Irritable bowel syndrome (IBS) is a common disorder that affects the large intestine. Signs include cramping, abdominal pain, bloating, gas, and diarrhea or constipation, or both.

Irritable bowel syndrome (IBS) sufferers may show no sign of disease or abnormalities when the colon is examined.

IBS does not produce the destructive inflammation found in IBD. It does not result in permanent harm to the intestines, intestinal bleeding, or the harmful complications often occurring with IBD. People with IBS are not at higher risk for colon cancer, nor are they more likely to develop IBD or other gastrointestinal diseases.

The exact cause of IBS is unknown. The most common theory is that IBS is a disorder of the interaction between the brain and the gastrointestinal tract, although there may also be abnormalities in the gut flora and immune system. Stress may be a key factor in how the condition originates and in prompting relapses.

Food allergy and intolerance seems to play a role in making IBS worse, but this is not fully understood.

There are two broad types of IBS, IBS with constipation IBS-C and IBS-D with diarrhea.

Inflammatory bowel disease – IBD

Inflammatory bowel disease is a group of inflammatory conditions of the colon and small intestine. The major types of IBD are Crohn's disease and ulcerative colitis.

Crohn's disease has a strong genetic component and is far more prevalent among smokers. The usual onset is between 15 and 30 years old.

Ulcerative colitis is an autoimmune disease with no known cause. The symptoms are very similar to Crohn's disease, but there are some stark differences. Ulcerative colitis is far less prevalent among smokers; indeed, moderate smoking can even relieve the condition in some people.

Incidence of Ulcerative colitis does seem to be elevated in people with autism, so much so that Wakefield and Krigsman sought to name a sub-type Autistic Enterocolitis.

Dr Krigsman has an informative website (https://autismgi.com/) and has published some interesting research.

If you spend all day looking via the endoscope at children with ASD, you are bound to notice a thing or two. Ignoring what Krigsman observes is rather foolish.

In case you are wondering what Krigsman does, he is going through the mouth to do an upper endoscopy; for the colonoscopy he goes in from below. He does both procedures under general anesthetic. Ulcerative colitis looks like a nasty condition, but Krigsman finds it is generally treatable with some combination of anti-inflammatory medication, antimicrobials, probiotics, digestive enzymes and dietary restriction. Humira, an expensive TNF-alpha inhibitor, is also widely used.

GERD

Gastroesophageal reflux disease (GERD/GORD) is a very common disease. The acid within the stomach rises up into the esophagus and in doing so, damages its lining.

Most children will outgrow their reflux by their first birthday. However, a small but significant number of them will not outgrow the condition. This is particularly true when a family history of GERD is present. It is estimated that 15% of adults are affected by GERD.

In kids with ASD and their siblings, GERD is relatively common.

Mechanisms linking IBD to autism

I have written on my blog about the link between food allergies, autism and behavior. Histamine released from mast cells (along with cytokines and other nasties) was the cause. Treatments included antihistamines and mast cell stabilizers (Ketotifen, Intal etc). I would presume this would fall into the IBS category.

When it comes to IBD, things get interesting. In 1936 the Nobel Prize for Physiology was awarded to Sir Henry Dale and Otto Loewi. One had identified the neurotransmitter acetylcholine and the other had shown how the vagus nerve releases acetylcholine to control heartbeat.

It later became apparent how important the vagus nerve is. The vagus nerve is a modulator of inflammation throughout the body. Acetylcholine, the principal neurotransmitter released by the vagus nerve, can exert its anti-inflammatory effect via binding to nicotinic acetylcholine receptors (nAChRs), which are expressed on macrophages and other immune cells.

Brain samples from people with autism have diminished acetylcholine and nicotinic receptor activity. This can potentially be corrected either by drugs that mimic acetylcholine (e.g. nicotine or acetylcholine), or with an acetylcholinesterase inhibitor (Galantamine or Donepezil).

It is very interesting that ulcerative colitis can be successfully treated by mild smoking (3 cigarettes a day) or with nicotine patches. There are numerous case histories of this.

This then connects various comorbidities in a very useful way and opens up therapeutic directions. The vagus nerve also plays a role in epilepsy. Vagus nerve stimulation is currently used to treat epilepsy and is being developed to treat arthritis.

Experimentally, vagus nerve stimulation is already used in autism. Many people have both epilepsy and autism. One study found that the patients with autism experienced "a number of quality of life improvements, some of which exceed those classically observed following placement of a Vagus Nerve Stimulation device".

From mouse models to mini-brains

One reason why neurological disease and psychiatric disorders are so poorly understood and treated is the great difficulty in seeing what is going on inside the human brain.

There are various types of non-invasive scanning like MRI (magnetic resonance imaging) and the even more clever functional MRI or FMRI, but you cannot just open the skull and take a look inside. Efforts have been made to examine the brains of people who have died; there are so called brain banks where donated brain tissue is stored for research purposes.

One big question is how representative of autism are the people whose brains were donated to science. The total number of autistic brains ever donated to science is tiny.

A problem in autism is that only a couple of hundred human brains have ever been physically studied. This is a tiny number and the same brains are used in numerous studies. Very few parents donate their child's brain for autism research, after a premature death. By contrast, in Alzheimer's very many brains have been donated and studied. It is an open question just how valid the findings are, based on slices of stored brain.

The brain samples in autism are very much skewed to people with severe autism who died young from epileptic seizure, or from a drowning accident – these were not Aspies. The research has to list the cause and age at death. Any analysis resulting from testing these samples should not be generalized to all autism.

Brain scans

For most people with autism, MRI scans do not show physical abnormalities and this is likely why these scans are not automatically offered to people diagnosed with autism. However, in some cases scans can reveal either the cause of the autism or something that aggravates it.

The two sides of the brain are connected by the corpus callosum; in some people this part of the brain was not fully formed and can then result in features that are diagnosed as autism. More generally, the corpus callosum varies from being overgrown to being skinny, across a wide range of autisms.

Autism is very often characterized by extremes of growth-related biological signaling, which results in either an enlarged brain or less often a small brain. Often a small brain comes in a small head (microcephaly) and a big brain comes in a big head (macrocephaly).

Sometimes a big brain does not fit inside its skull and part of the brain is forced down towards the top of the spinal column. This forms what you might consider a brain hernia, which doctors call a Chiari malformation.

Chiari brain hernias are rare in typical people, but not so rare in people with autism. One study suggested that about 6% of people with autism have a Chiari malformation. This hernia can be repaired by surgery and while it will not cure the person's autism, it may well improve it. One reader of my blog decided to have his child's Chiari hernia repaired.

You can also look at the development of myelination on MRI. Some autisms feature a delay in the development of myelin, which is the coating on the axons of neurons that speeds up the electrical signals in your brain. You can use medicines to encourage more myelination. This is covered in some detail in my blog. All posts are indexed by labels, one of which is myelin.

Mouse models

Researchers use animals in place of humans for research purposes, in the case of autism it is usually the unfortunate mouse and sometimes a rat.

The Jackson Laboratory in the US is the source for more than 8,000 strains of genetically defined mice used for research purposes.

SFARIgene has a fascinating online database (search for "animal model module") that lists all the mouse/rat models of autism and the research linked to them. Most importantly it also lists all the "rescue lines", the research showing therapies that improved the mouse's autism.

For example, you can look up the model of human Fragile X, which is called Fmr1, and then see the long list of drugs that helped that particular type of mouse.

There are already well over 200 different mouse/rat genetic models of autism and 1,000 rescue lines.

While no medicine has been approved to treat the core features of human autism, autistic mice appear to be better placed.

There remains the question of how close humans are to mice. They are more closely related than you might think, but there are still big differences.

There are also induced models of autism, where the scientist has not tinkered with a specific single gene. These might more closely relate to most human autism. For example, there is a Maternal Immune Activation (MIA) model, where the immune system is activated during pregnancy, resulting in an autistic-like mouse pup. In the MIA model the pregnant mouse is injected with an immune-stimulant (Polyinosinic:polycytidylic acid, yes that is not a typo) that triggers a big immune response which affects the development of her pup.

There is a similar model where the mother mouse is given an infection rather than induced inflammation.

Depending on the gestational age at which MIA or infection is administered, the offspring can be studied in the context not only of autism, but also schizophrenia. This should not be surprising if you have read the section of this book discussing the overlapping polygenic nature of autism, schizophrenia and bipolar disorder.

You will find a model of advanced paternal age, a model of diesel exhaust particles, and all kinds of other things.

You can even induce temporary autism, using propionic acid. Propionic acid is produced naturally in your intestines when the food you eat reacts with the bacteria that live there. Propionic acid is a SCFA (short chained fatty acid). You need to have some SCFAs, but as is often the case, too much may not be good for you. In the case of a mouse, when injected with a large dose of propionic acid, its behaviors change to those resembling autism. This is entirely reversible over time, or faster still by administering the antioxidant NAC (N-acetyl cysteine).

What some researchers do is to create a mouse model that matches as closely as possible the human condition they are trying to treat. Then they can investigate various drugs that might be of therapeutic benefit. In some cases, a large number of drugs from a library of compounds are tried on the off-chance of stumbling upon one that is effective.

An alternative approach is when a researcher has a theory that a specific drug should be effective, he then tests it in several different mouse models of autism. If the drug is effective in several mouse models that would suggest it might be beneficial in some humans. Human trials might eventually follow, if somebody wants to fund them.

Stem cells and mini-brains

In recent years some very clever people have entered the field of neuroscience. One development they have pioneered is using samples of a person's skin to grow a specific part of their brain using stem cell technology. This is the biological equivalent of growing a biopsy, instead of drilling a hole in the skull and extracting a piece of brain, the scientist can very cleverly grow an identical piece of artificial brain.

The scientist can then experiment with this brain sample, which should be far more relevant than working on a sample from a mouse.

There is an even more surprising development where an entire mini-brain can be grown using similar technology. The mini-brain is not 100% identical to a human brain but is remarkably similar and opens the way to more productive research into complex conditions like autism.

Sensory issues in autism

Entire books have been written about sensory issues in autism. Many people with autism are either overly sensitive (hyper), or under sensitive (hypo) to sensory stimuli.

This might mean being very agitated by touch or being immune to pain when someone steps on your toe. It could be an extreme aversion to some sounds, like a ticking clock, or a baby crying. It might be an aversion to the texture of some or all food, it might be a severe issue with toileting.

Sensory issues often result in varying degrees of difficulty with going to the hairdresser, doctor, dentist, shop, cinema, airport, airplane and the list goes on.

There are numerous therapies used to treat sensory issues ranging from sensory rooms to all kinds of sensory integration therapy.

You may read people saying that cutting their child's finger nails causes him actual physical pain. This is of course not possible, unless his screaming makes you slip and cut his finger. The fear is causing his "pain"; he thinks you are cutting off his fingertips. You have to explain in a way that he understands what you are doing and why. In someone with severe autism you may need to wait several years for him to understand.

Undoubtedly there are biological explanations for many sensory dysfunctions, making them potentially treatable. In most cases the problems reduce over time and what seemed impossible as a toddler becomes less bothersome as a teenager. Normal visits to the dentist and hairdresser do become possible, but you may have to work at it.

Some people do not overcome their early sensory-related issues and they just become a habit. Then you are left with fixed behaviors.

There are known biological causes of sensory overload and sensory gating discussed later in this book. They appear to relate to something called a channelopathy (an ion channel dysfunction). When I was looking to reduce my son's sensory issues I read about hypokalemic sensory overload (HKSO) and its more extreme form, hypokalemic periodic paralysis (HPP). In HKSO the person becomes overwhelmed by sensory stimuli around them and in HPP they even enter a state of paralysis. In both conditions an immediate recovery is produced by drinking a potassium supplement.

There is a section in this book all about channelopathies, but in simple terms the level of certain electrolytes like potassium in your blood influences a wide variety of mechanisms in your brain that are controlled by ion channels (potassium K^+, is one of those ions). Changes in potassium levels affect how some of these ion channels and transporters work. When these ion channels malfunction, all kinds of strange things can happen to your body, from epileptic seizures to sensory overload.

What I did was test the effect of small amounts of potassium on my son's sensitivity to his most hated sound, a baby crying. Over several days we measured the volume he could tolerate of a recording of baby crying, with or without the small potassium supplement. We even tried the same experiment on his typical big brother. In our case it was clear that a spike in potassium levels substantially reduced sensory overload.

Other readers of my blog found similar results. Also, everyone agreed that increasing potassium by diet, for example an extra banana, did not have the same effect as a potassium supplement. A short sharp increase in potassium is required, not a gradual increase from food.

Financial interests

A common concern many people have is that financial interests often get in the way of objectivity; this could be the researcher who holds the patent on a particular therapy, or the clinician who may be making money on very expensive laboratory tests, supplying expensive supplements, or even selling you a hyperbaric oxygen chamber.

In the case of a severe lifelong disorder like severe autism, you might think that everyone would have your best interests at heart- often they do, but sometimes they do not.

I recall consulting a pediatric endocrinologist to discuss central (i.e. brain specific) hormonal dysfunctions and to measure bone age. She was very pleasant and after the initial consultation refused any form of payment. She does though have to live and if all she did was see people like me, she would have to charge something.

Consulting an autism specialist in the US can be extremely expensive. People do write to me complaining about having to pay up to $1,500 for a consultation.

When it comes to published research studies, things cannot always be taken entirely at face value. One medical researcher who follows my blog showed me studies that suggest a substantial amount of research is tainted to favor the author's objective. This is why studies need to be replicated by different researchers; often studies fail this test. This is very common in autism studies.

When it comes to off-label treatments for autism using old generic drugs there is little financial interest for anyone to fund clinical trials. The drug is already available from multiple vendors, so there is no way to recoup the huge cost of clinical trials and approvals.

In the case of naturally occurring products, these cannot be patented. Unless you can modify the molecule slightly, there is no way of patenting your therapy and so creating a future revenue stream to justify developing the therapy.

Drug firms are looking for new molecules that can be patented, even though they very well know that many existing old drugs have interesting effects within the brain and could be repurposed. The old drugs are ignored because the huge cost of proving their secondary effects cannot be recouped.

In my case, I have an autism science blog that you can read for free. I am not selling any kind of therapy to anyone.

I did at one point naively consider bringing my autism Polypill to the market, but that is totally unrealistic; it is now more a catchy metaphor for what could be done. Here is my Polypill, what is in your autism Polypill?

Google scholar and Wikipedia – they're free

Most people know about Wikipedia, the online encyclopedia, that school children plagiarize for their homework. Few realize just how up to date it is in neuroscience. Any medical textbook you might consider buying is already way out of date, but volunteers keep Wikipedia up to date, even in some remarkably specialist areas of science.

The best kept secret is Google Scholar.

In Google, enter "google scholar", click on it and then you enter a very serious version of the internet.

Using Google Scholar you may bypass the pseudoscience and go straight to published scientific papers. To understand any complex terms you cannot follow, you then refer to Wikipedia.

In no time at all you can become a much more proficient reader of autism research.

If you want to read about clinical trials, past and current, almost all of them are registered with www.clinicaltrials.gov

I hope readers are inspired by this book to figure out the nature of the specific subtype that affects their child. Thanks to the internet you can achieve a great deal, even without access to laboratory tests and genetic testing.

Autism in the media

Due to a broadening of the diagnostic criteria over the last decades, a much wider group of people are considered to be autistic. This has had a great impact on how autism is portrayed in the media. The milder forms of autism are ones that tend to get reported on, since people prefer to hear about cute success stories rather than tragedies.

People not surprisingly gather their information from the mass media and so get a rather unbalanced mix of information. Scientists are not usually the most communicative types and journalists rarely understand complex science, so it is very rare that you will read a well-informed newspaper article about the biological basis of autism and often what you read is missing the point. The journalists regularly reporting autism news and particularly writing mass appeal books are no exception.

A very good example is what causes autism. This is a simple question to which there is no simple answer; but there are many clues. Autism in many cases appears to be caused by multiple hits, with each so-called hit increasing the likelihood of triggering neurological changes that lead to autism. Each hit, in itself, does not cause autism, but often it is these hits that are reported in the media as "causes" of autism. You could consider these influences as associations or just risk factors. So, increasing paternal age at conception has been reported as a factor, living close to high voltage power lines and many kinds of environmental and emotional stress are risky. They are not enough in isolation to cause autism, but why live under high voltage cables if you can avoid it?

The case of vaccinations and autism remains a hot potato. It is scientifically partially understood, but is continually misreported. There is a link via damage to the energy producing part of cells, called mitochondria. In some people there is a tendency to be vulnerable to mitochondrial damage. In these people a strong inflammatory response to vaccinations can trigger mitochondrial disease. Mitochondrial disease can quickly lead to changes in the brain that will cause symptoms of autism. At Johns Hopkins this type of autism was given a name – AMD (autism secondary to mitochondrial disease) and Dr Kelley developed a therapy to manage it and they have a therapy given to avoid damage from subsequent vaccinations. Researcher readers of my own blog have asked why Dr Kelley has not published his knowledge in the literature; case reports would prove useful to doctors in other parts of the world. The subject is too controversial.

Viral infections are seen as a common trigger of AMD (autism secondary to mitochondrial disease). Do not assume that all AMD is triggered by vaccines. Dr Kelley does not even mention the word vaccine in his unpublished paper on AMD. Only one case has been proved, beyond reasonable doubt.

You may wonder why you have not heard about this and why so many experts keep telling you that there is no link between vaccination and autism. There is a link, but it is a link between vaccination and some autism, not all autism. How much of autism is "some" autism? That is a good question and one that nobody investigates.

I am repeating an earlier point here, but Dr Jon Poling, a neurologist and graduate from Johns Hopkins, has published research on this subject. He is one of the people who actually received financial compensation when he took his daughter's case to the "vaccine court". He and his wife were perfectly placed to demonstrate the link between their daughter's vaccines and her regression into autism and they won her millions of dollars of compensation.

Dr Poling was interviewed by CNN medical correspondent Dr Sanjay Gupta in 2008 and explained all the facts of the case. The interview can still be found on YouTube. It is probably an interview CNN regrets having made.

What many parents of children with autism are not aware of, is that in the recent past every year thousands of people died from diseases that are now almost entirely prevented by vaccinations. The job of public health officials is to make sure that these diseases do not return and so they feel it necessary to give a clear message "vaccination is good", without any ifs and buts. The reality is that vaccinations are indeed of great benefit and enough people need to participate to make sure that certain diseases do not return. If parents are frightened that giving vaccines might trigger a regression to autism, you will get the certainty that some young children will die from preventable disease.

The intelligent solution would be to try to identify which babies have a potential mitochondrial dysfunction before they are vaccinated. In this group, be it 0.1% of babies or just 0.0001%, you then only give them really critical vaccines, you space them out and you follow John Hopkin's existing use of anti-inflammatory medication before and after vaccination to reduce any potential inflammatory over-reaction to the vaccine.

Vast sums of money have been pledged by the likes of the Bill and Melinda Gates Foundation to reduce preventable deaths in the developing world via vaccination and so there are powerful voices to ensure the message is not confused by talk of a tiny minority that might be damaged along the way.

The sad thing is that many caring parents unknowingly increase the risk of mitochondrial damage in their young child because they give acetaminophen/paracetamol to their child when their child has a reaction to vaccination. The body's own defence to oxidative stress and inflammation is a substance called glutathione (GSH). GSH does you a lot of good, but acetaminophen/paracetamol reacts with GSH, so there is less available to counter an assault on the body. Acetaminophen/paracetamol does reduce fever and pain but is a very bad choice to treat an inflammatory reaction to a vaccination. The good choice is ibuprofen.

People who have already developed autism are highly likely to be in a permanent state of oxidative stress. This can be measured in a lab by looking at the GSH:GCCG ratio, for those who want to check. Such people should always avoid acetaminophen/paracetamol, choose ibuprofen or any other medications that does not further deplete GSH.

My son had all his vaccinations including the Pfizer Covid vaccine three times.

PETER LLOYD-THOMAS

Part 3

Autism 101

A simplified overview of the science and its application to better understand Autism

This book is written like a novel for lay people, so no references and section numbering. Some science is included for those wanting it. If you find something too complex, just skip over it. Most people do look some words up. I have been doing it for a decade!

A few years ago I made a chart to rationalize autism to myself and to help explain classic autism to other parents; at least one autism doctor is using it when talking to her patients. In spite of autism being a very complex and varied condition, it can be simplified. You can choose to go into whatever level of detail you are comfortable with. Some readers of my blog have been very successful without going into any to the complex details.

Central Hormonal Dysfunction

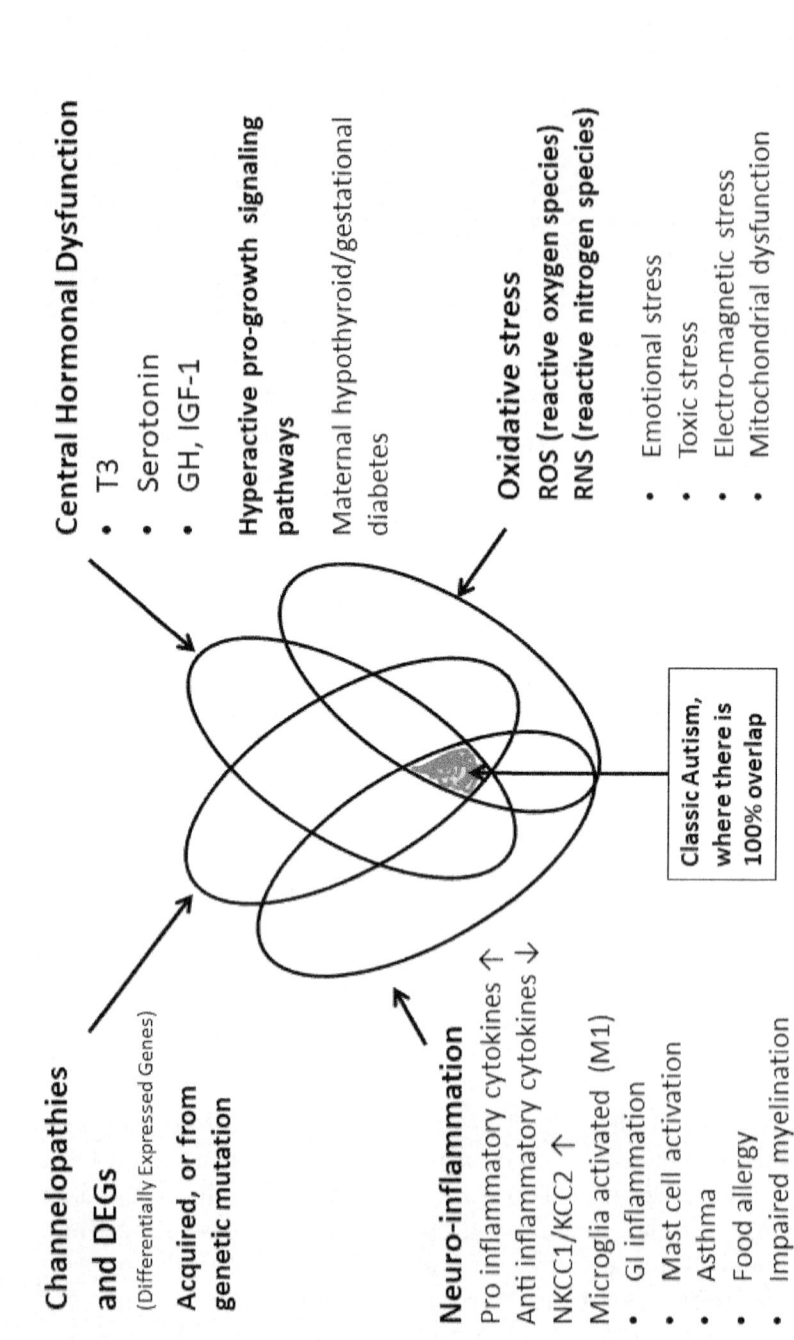

- T3
- Serotonin
- GH, IGF-1

Hyperactive pro-growth signaling pathways

Maternal hypothyroid/gestational diabetes

Oxidative stress

ROS (reactive oxygen species)
RNS (reactive nitrogen species)

- Emotional stress
- Toxic stress
- Electro-magnetic stress
- Mitochondrial dysfunction

Maternal stress

Channelopathies and DEGs

(Differentially Expressed Genes)

Acquired, or from genetic mutation

Neuro-inflammation

Pro inflammatory cytokines ↑
Anti inflammatory cytokines ↓
NKCC1/KCC2 ↑
Microglia activated (M1)

- GI inflammation
- Mast cell activation
- Asthma
- Food allergy
- Impaired myelination
- Impaired synaptic pruning

Maternal Immune Activation

Classic Autism, where there is 100% overlap

Inflammation

Let's start with inflammation. We may think that inflammation is bad, but actually you want there to be an inflammatory response after an injury; it is a protective response and the first step to recovery. Sometimes the body's immune system is a little too eager and it ends up attacking things it should not. The immune system is very complicated and in a way it is not surprising that it gets things wrong from time to time.

In autoimmune diseases, which have seen a great surge in recent decades, the body ends up attacking itself. The immune system has become too sensitive or over-activated. We even know why this is happening – the body has evolved to expect to encounter certain challenges during gestation and shortly after birth, and during this time the immune response should be perfectly calibrated. Unfortunately, in the very sterile modern world the immune response is miscalibrated and it becomes too sensitive. In later life, when it encounters a challenge, the immune system will over respond and may even launch a response when there has been no actual threat. The result is eczema, asthma, irritable bowel syndrome (IBS) and arthritis in later life.

I read of one celebrity autism Dad who developed early onset arthritis, while his wife has PCOS (polycystic ovary syndrome) which is a hormone disorder. All their children have autism.

Neuroinflammation is activation of the brain's immune system. The brain sits inside the protective blood brain barrier and the only immune protection within the brain is provided by the microglia. Microglia have other functions to do within the brain including synaptic pruning, which you can consider like an expert gardener going round pruning the roses and ornamental plants to ensure they develop a perfect shape. Research has shown that in autism these microglia cells are permanently in a state of activation, poised to attack.

Via various mechanisms, including the vagus nerve, there is communication between the brain and the immune system in the rest of the body. It has been suggested that the microglia function like an immunostat reflecting the immune status of the whole body. There certainly is two-way feedback, inflammation in the body does affect the brain and the reverse is also true.

Minimizing any aberrant immune response anywhere in the body should be a treatment goal in autism.

One of the most common animal models of autism is the maternal immune activation (MIA) model. In the MIA model the pregnant mother is given an immune challenge which then results in offspring with autism-like features.

On a practical level for treating autism we want to remove all autoimmune comorbidities that will inevitably make autism worse. Examples would be any kind of allergy, be it food, pollen or anything else; treatment is possible using mainstream medicine. Note that expensive allergy tests are often not scientifically valid. We should recognize the fact that we are dealing with people who may be particularly sensitive to allergies. What might not be troubling for most people might have an impact far more significant in a person with autism.

For example, in my son a pretty trivial looking pollen allergy causes a severe behavioral impact. We found that high levels of nitrates in some home-cured meats and exposure to walnuts produces a similar extreme behavioral deterioration.

Food allergy and food sensitivity is very common in autism. These issues aggravate whatever the baseline of autism really is. In some people with mild autism, when you solve the food related issues there is not much autism left to treat. In people with severe autism, when you solve any dietary issues that were present life will get better, but autism will remain.

Some children with autism are in near constant GI distress, quite possibly of autoimmune origin. This will be a major factor in the severity of their autism. The problem might be reflux, or eosinophilic esophagitis, IBS-D (irritable bowel syndrome with diarrhea) IBS-C (irritable bowel syndrome with constipation), SIBO (small intestinal bacterial overgrowth), poor gut microbiota, or some other type of GI dysbiosis.

Healthy people have both pro-inflammatory cytokines and anti-inflammatory cytokines. These two forces need to be in balance, and when this is not the case there will be problems.

IL-6 and TNF alpha are very important pro-inflammatory cytokines and IL-10 is an important anti-inflammatory one. These can be measured in a blood test to give a profile.

There are special anti-inflammatory drugs developed to inhibit IL-6 or TNF-alpha. These are used to treat a range of conditions from arthritis to Crohn's disease and psoriasis.

I was once contacted by an Aspie woman desperate to get hold of Humira, a drug which blocks the effect of TNF-alpha. She had been prescribed it during fertility treatment, but it had also cured all her debilitating autoimmune problems and also moderated her autism. Her sound sensitivity to her dog barking had vanished. She knew this was an expensive drug and she was happy to pay out of her own pocket; she just wanted a doctor to prescribe it. Being an Aspie, she had done the math and determined that lost income due to ill health was far more than the cost of Humira.

I had wondered in a blogpost about whether etanercept (Enbrel) another TNF-alpha inhibitor should be trialed in autism.

There are expensive drugs that are anti IL-6 receptor antibodies like tocilizumab, while there are also cheap NSAIDs like ibuprofen that reduce the level of IL-6.

Some people use cheap NSAIDs to treat autism and research does support their use to treat schizophrenia, one of autism's two big brothers. The other being bipolar.

Oxidative stress

We all produce free radicals during normal metabolic processes. To counter them we also produce antioxidants to neutralize these free radicals. The net result in young healthy people is the body is able to maintain a balance between antioxidants and free radicals.

Antioxidants are substances that neutralize free radicals by donating an electron.

As we get older, we tend to produce more free radicals and less antioxidants and then our bodies are in some degree of oxidative stress, which then produces negative health effects.

Interestingly, one of the causes of oxidative stress is emotional stress.

Oxidative stress can lead to chronic inflammation which then can lead to conditions like diabetes or heart disease.

The research shows that most children with autism are in oxidative stress, most likely because their metabolic processes are disturbed resulting in an excess of free radicals. Their bodies are unable to compensate by producing more antioxidants.

Whereas healthy young people in their twenties may be wasting their money on detox juices rich in antioxidants, giving antioxidants to a child with autism can be highly beneficial.

The body's main antioxidant is called glutathione (GSH).

When GSH neutralizes a free radical it becomes oxidized and is called GSSG.

The body is very efficient and it has a family of enzymes called glutathione peroxidases (GPx) that act at as a catalyst to help convert GSH to GSSG.

$$2GSH + H_2O_2 \rightarrow GSSG + 2H_2O$$

In the formula above the free radical being neutralized is H_2O_2, hydrogen peroxide. The by-product is water.

These GPx enzymes contain selenium. Without selenium present, glutathione (GSH) cannot do its job.

Some people with poor diet lack selenium and do not produce enough GPx. Selenium comes from the soil into the food chain and in some parts of the world the level in the earth is low, for example in New Zealand. Some people with autism have a mutation in the gene that encodes GPx. People with type 2 diabetes, celiac disease or multiple sclerosis are also known to be at risk from low levels of GPx.

The body then recycles GSSG back to GSH, for use again, as expressed in the formula below:

$$GSSG + NADPH \rightarrow 2GSH + NADP^+$$

Don't worry about what NADPH is.

The above reaction is catalyzed (accelerated) by another clever enzyme called glutathione reductase (GR). The limiting factor with this enzyme is your level of riboflavin, vitamin B2. Most people are not deficient in this vitamin, but if you were then your antioxidant system will not function correctly. If you had a mutation in a gene called GSR you would not make enough glutathione reductase.

How to make more glutathione (GSH)?

One therapeutic strategy I use is to make more glutathione (GSH). To do this you need to provide the body with the precursor chemicals it needs, or increase any missing enzymes.

This does now start to get complicated; NAC (N-acetyl cysteine) provides an immediate precursor to GSH. The amino acids cysteine, glutamate and glycine are natural precursors from the food we eat. It seems that cysteine is the weak link in most people.

You still need an enzyme called glutathione synthetase (GSS) to be the catalyst. For some people GSS is a problem. People with mutations in the GSS gene develop glutathione synthetase (GSS) deficiency. If you carry out whole exome sequencing (WES), keep an eye out for mutations relating to glutathione.

In the very early days of developing my son's therapy I considered whey protein (a rich source of cysteine) and NAC. I choose NAC and this was supported by clinical trials at Stanford University that showed NAC improves autism. My NAC supplement also includes some selenium, which shows somebody else has been doing their homework. As mentioned above selenium is essential for glutathione to function.

Other antioxidants

There are numerous other antioxidants including:
- ALA (alpha lipoic acid), with is similar to NAC
- Coenzyme Q10, which is fat soluble and is good for your brain and its mitochondria. There is a better absorbed variant called ubiquinol
- Vitamin C and vitamin E
- Melatonin and carnosine
- Cocoa, lycopene and cinnamon

You can also activate the redox switch Nrf2, to activate the body's oxidative stress response using sulforaphane (from broccoli) or silibinin.

Nitrosative stress

While you hear about oxidative stress quite widely these days, you tend not to hear about nitrosative stress. The two are very closely related. Without wanting to get too complicated, in oxidative stress you have ROS (reactive oxygen species) whereas in nitrosative stress you have RNS (reactive nitrogen species). The main RNS is the radical/ion peroxynitrite (ONOO·) and it is produced by the mitochondria in our cells that convert glucose into usable fuel (ATP).

Mitochondrial dysfunction, of one kind or another, is seen to play a role in a large minority of autism.

In many diseases you actually have a combination of ROS and RNS, so have both oxidative stress and nitrosative stress.

Peroxynitrite is both an oxidant and nitrating agent and as such it is harmful.

The reasons I looked into the subject of peroxynitrite, dates from when I looked at why so many people with autism seem to benefit from high dose folinic acid. Many autism doctors in the US are prescribing Leucovorin (calcium folinate) to treat a suspected low level of folate inside the brain. I found that this substance has an entirely different benefit, it quenches peroxynitrite and it is about the only known substance to do this.

If you have low levels of folate inside your brain, as opposed to in your blood, your brain cannot function correctly. By taking what seem to be massive doses of an oral supplement you hope to overcome a transport problem across the blood brain barrier and get enough folate into the brain.

But what if the brain is producing too much of the peroxynitrite radical? What if nitosative stress is a factor in your autism? All that folate will sweep up the peroxynitrite and so reduce the damaging nitrosative stress.

Treating oxidative/nitrosative stress has clear health benefits and is easy to do.

Professor Helmut Sies – the redox pioneer

A very thorough overview of oxidative stress was produced in graphical form by Professor Helmut Sies, who first introduced the concept of oxidative stress in 1985.

Do not be put off by any words that you may not understand. The graphic includes a great deal. The simple takeaway is that good diet is extremely important, particularly if you have any kind of chronic condition, be it autism, diabetes or just aging.

On the second version of the graphic I have added where the various supplements/vitamins can be added to perk things up a bit.

Of course Professor Sies includes nitrosative stress.

SOD (Superoxide dismutase) is an important enzyme that you need enough of.

Peroxiredoxins are a family of antioxidant enzymes that also control cytokine-induced peroxide level. You do not want too much peroxide. These enzymes PRDX1, PRDX2, PRDX3, PRDX4, PRDX5, and PRDX6 are really important in neurodegenerative diseases, like Alzheimer's. Researchers in Italy found that plasma levels of PRDX2 and PRDX5 were remarkably increased in ASD compared to healthy controls. They suggest that this is actually a protective mechanism, triggered by neuroinflammation.

Many people know about glutathione (GSH). Working alongside GSH is the thioredoxin (Trx) system, another key antioxidant system defending against oxidative stress. The lesser known Trx system interacts directly with the well known GSH system. You need them both!

The Trx system removes both reactive oxygen and nitrogen species, (ROS and RNS).

Redox switches are clever substances that trigger a response to oxidative stress. The well known one is Nrf-2 and there are plenty of supplments sold as Nrf-2 activators. Thioredoxin (Trx) is also viwed as a redox state sensor, like a switch.

What I noted in my blog is that in some conditions Nrf-2 does not function, because there is a lack of a protein called DJ-1. This is a common problem in smokers, who then develop severe asthma (COPD). You can increase how much DJ-1 you produce using sodium benzoate, which is a cheap food additive but also a metabolite of Ceylon cinnamon. DJ-1 is also a key gene involved in Parkinson's disease, where they choose to call it PARK7, just to confuse us.

Research had shown that elevated DJ-1 expression underlies L-type calcium channel hypoactivity in a type of autism called tuberous sclerosis complex (TSC) and also in Alzheimer's disease. Clearly some people have too much DJ-1 expression and some have too little. Nothing is ever simple!

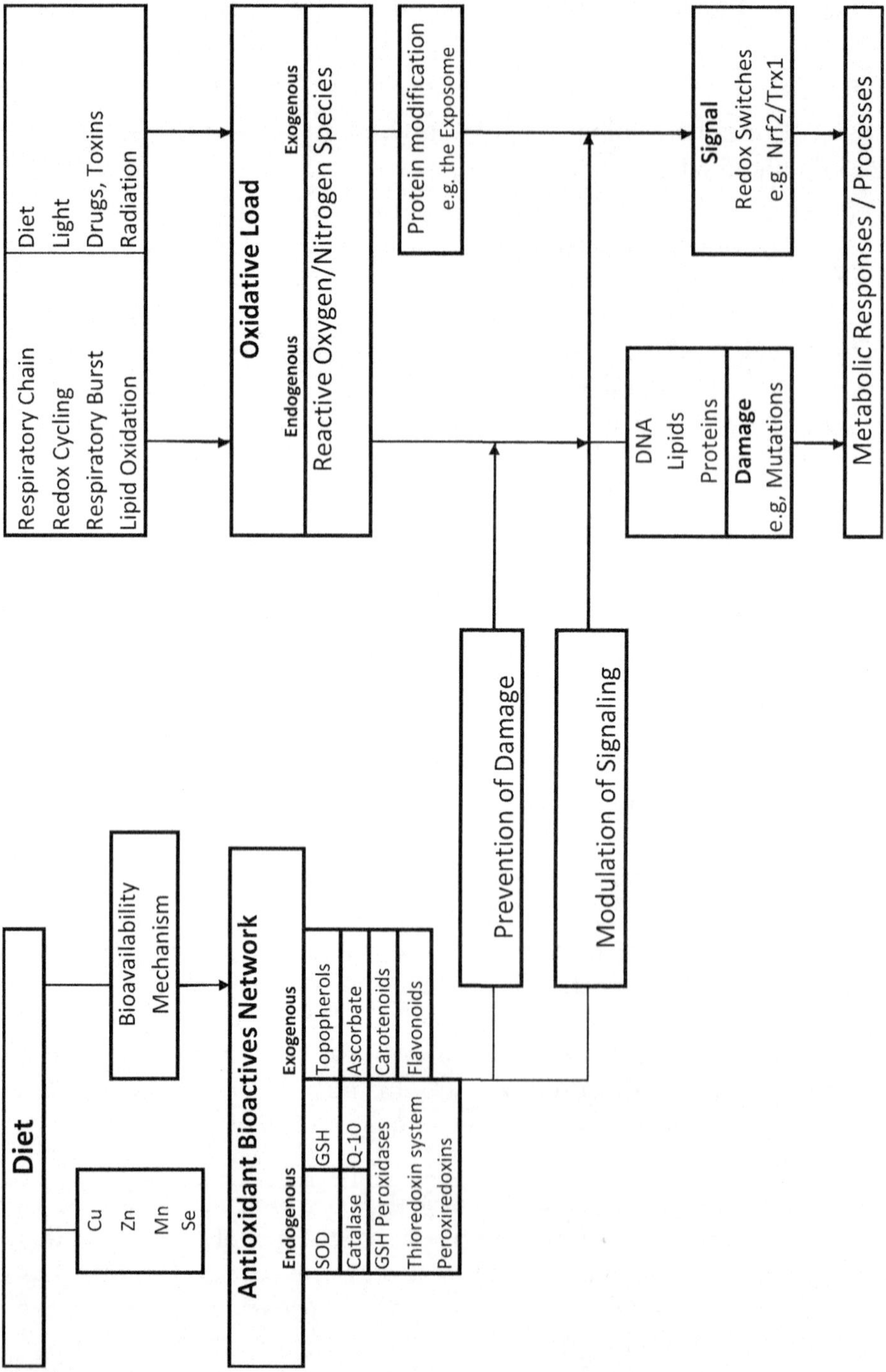
Respiratory Chain
Redox Cycling
Respiratory Burst
Lipid Oxidation
Diet
Light
Drugs, Toxins
Radiation
Oxidative Load
Endogenous
Exogenous
Reactive Oxygen/Nitrogen Species
Protein modification
e.g. the Exposome
DNA
Lipids
Proteins
Damage
e.g, Mutations
Signal
Redox Switches
e.g. Nrf2/Trx1
Metabolic Responses / Processes
Diet
Cu
Zn
Mn
Se
Bioavailability
Mechanism
Antioxidant Bioactives Network
Endogenous
Exogenous
SOD
Catalase
GSH
Q-10
GSH Peroxidases
Thioredoxin system
Peroxiredoxins
Topopherols
Ascorbate
Carotenoids
Flavonoids
Prevention of Damage
Modulation of Signaling

GAME CHANGER

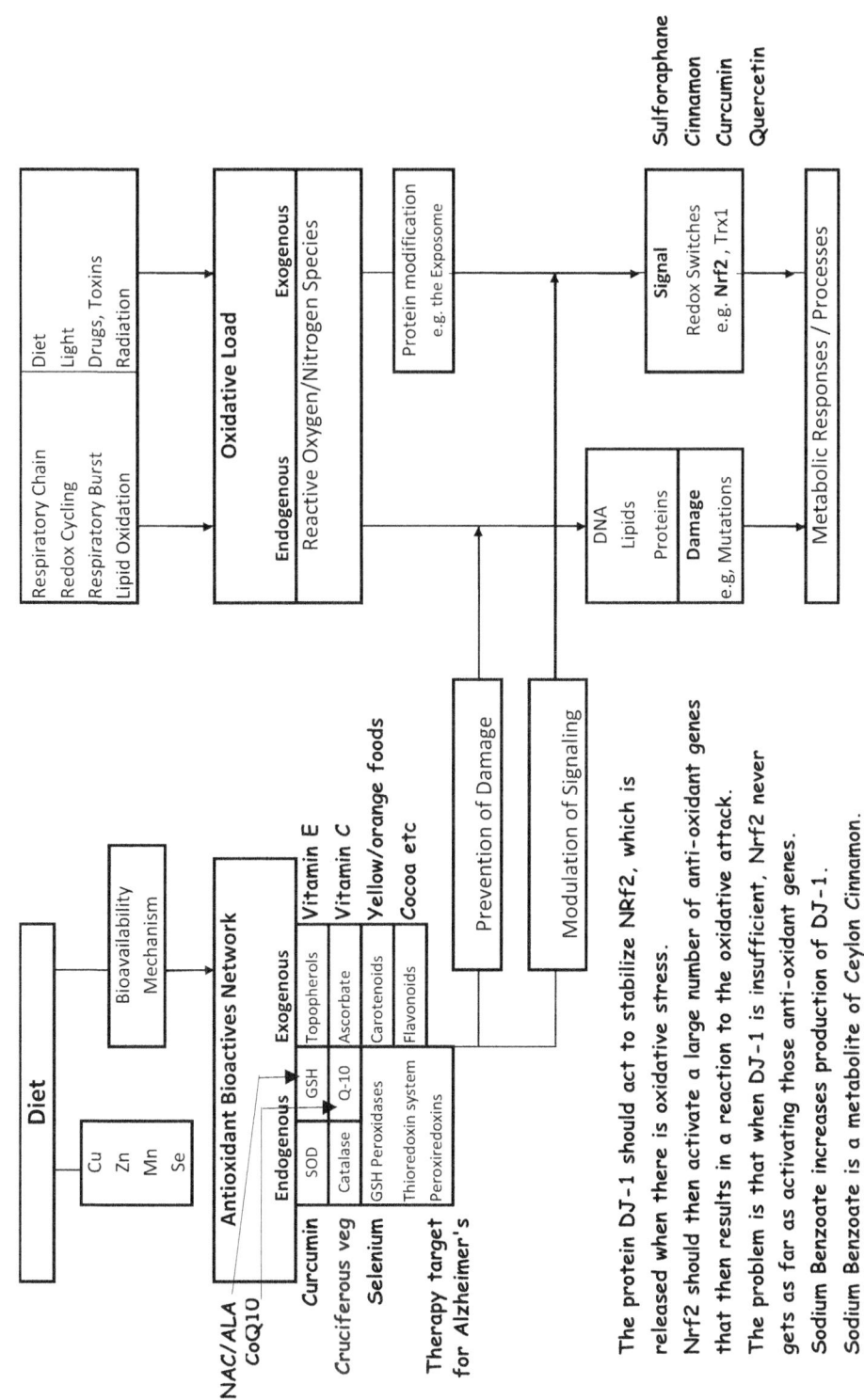

Sulforaphane
Cinnamon
Curcumin
Quercetin

Respiratory Chain	Diet
Redox Cycling	Light
Respiratory Burst	Drugs, Toxins
Lipid Oxidation	Radiation

Oxidative Load

| Endogenous | Exogenous |

Reactive Oxygen/Nitrogen Species

Protein modification e.g. the Exposome

Signal
Redox Switches
e.g. **Nrf2**, Trx1

| DNA |
| Lipids |
| Proteins |
| **Damage** e.g. Mutations |

Metabolic Responses / Processes

Diet

| Cu |
| Zn |
| Mn |
| Se |

Bioavailability Mechanism

Antioxidant Bioactives Network

Endogenous	Exogenous
SOD	Tocopherols	**Vitamin E**
Catalase	Ascorbate	*Vitamin C*
GSH Peroxidases	Carotenoids	*Yellow/orange foods*
Thioredoxin system	Flavonoids	*Cocoa etc*
Peroxiredoxins		

GSH
Q-10

NAC/ALA
CoQ10

Curcumin
Cruciferous veg
Selenium

Therapy target for Alzheimer's

Prevention of Damage

Modulation of Signaling

The protein DJ-1 should act to stabilize NRf2, which is released when there is oxidative stress.

Nrf2 should then activate a large number of anti-oxidant genes that then results in a reaction to the oxidative attack.

The problem is that when DJ-1 is insufficient, Nrf2 never gets as far as activating those anti-oxidant genes.

Sodium Benzoate increases production of DJ-1.

Sodium Benzoate is a metabolite of Ceylon Cinnamon.

Hormonal dysfunction

Hormonal dysfunction is both a possible contributing cause of autism and a factor present in someone with autism.

Gestational diabetes, PCOS (polycystic ovary syndrome) and maternal thyroid disorders are examples of conditions associated with an increased risk of autism in offspring.

When it comes to the child, it is very often growth factors/hormones that are disturbed. This can lead to unusually large bodies/heads at birth or the opposite, small bodies/heads. As the child grows the imbalance can switch the other way.

My son Monty was large and muscular at birth. He was able to support his own head from a very early age – there was no need to stop his head flopping when you picked him up as a baby. An Austrian friend joked that with a son like that I would never need a bodyguard. Within a few years Monty fell down the percentiles from the 90s to the 20s. Still, I can tell my Austrian friend that I will not need a bodyguard because Monty's big brother does competitive shooting.

As an adult Monty is much smaller than me and that is actually a very good thing when it comes to physically dealing with aggressive behaviors.

One interesting framework to consider all autism is to split it into too much growth or too little – that is hyperactive pro-growth signaling pathways vs hypoactive pro-growth signaling pathways.

The key growth factors studied include BDNF (Brain-derived neurotrophic factor), NGF (Nerve growth factor) Insulin-like growth factor-1 (IGF-1), VEGF (Vascular endothelial growth factor), TNFα (a cytokine and growth factor) among many more.

Early research was very crude and hoped to determine if one growth factor or another is elevated in autism. Because there are so many types of autism this approach is not helpful and results from one study are the opposite of the next one.

Growth factors, like all the pro/anti-inflammatory cytokines tend to be disturbed in autism, but in very many different ways depending on the subtype of autism. Indeed you can categorize someone's autism by their levels of these different markers.

It also seems inevitable that each person's levels of these growth factors will change as the disease progresses during early childhood.

At a very simplistic level we can see that male hormones have a negative impact on autism whereas female hormones have a protective influence.

For example, if a female has Turner syndrome, she lacks all or part of one X chromosome. Females normally have two X chromosomes and males have one X and one Y. This is what determines your sex. A female with one and a bit X chromosomes, beyond her many medical problems, will appear masculine and is very likely to exhibit features of autism. These females lack estrogen/estradiol.

Not surprisingly, if you pay a visit to your local school for severe autism you will see that most of the children are boys.

Channelopathies / Differentially Expressed Genes (DEGs)

I have left the hardest of my four categories till last.

Ion channels and transporters are an entire field in science and you may well have no idea what it is about.

It is worth making an effort to understand the basics, because someone with autism almost inevitably has one or more ion channel or transporter dysfunctions (channelopathies) – they just do not know it. If you have epilepsy, it is really just a question of which ion channels are faulty.

When you think about your smartphone or your iPad you know it is a computer and computers are just electrical devices with lots of tiny switches (logic gates) inside microprocessors. It is very clever, but that is all it is.

People mistakenly think their brain is like a computer and that inside everything is fixed/static. People with autism are just wired up differently? Nothing could be further from the truth.

Human brains do indeed use electricity, but they also use ions/electrolytes that are minerals in your body that have an electric charge.

The positively charged ions in your body are sodium, calcium, potassium and magnesium.

The negatively charged ions are chloride, phosphate and bicarbonate.

All of these ions flow through special channels, transporters and exchangers that have specific functions. The concentration of each ion modifies key functions within your body, like your heart beating or whether a neuron fires and sends an electrical signal.

So, in addition to the electric controls of a computer, your body has superimposed on top all these different ions moving around with their own control mechanisms. The human brain is far more complex than any computer and this is why we still do not know that much about it, nor much about curing neurological diseases.

When it comes to autism the following are examples of possible problems:

Calcium channel dysfunctions, for example Cav1.2.

>   Ca stands for calcium
>
>   v means a voltage gated channel
>
>   Cav1.2 is actually the alpha-1 subunit. To make a calcium channel you need several subunits clustered together, any of which can have a mutation.
>
>   Cav1.2 is associated with bipolar, schizophrenia, autism and various heart problems.

When a mutation occurs, Nav1.2 can cause autism, bipolar and/or epilepsy

>   Na stands for sodium
>
>   v means a voltage gated channel
>
>   Nav1.2 is sodium channel protein type 2 subunit alpha. A problem with Nav1.1 will lead to seizures.

The potassium channel family Kv7 may have a problem in its voltage sensor and this can lead to autism.

>   K stands for potassium
>
>   v means a voltage gated channel
>
>   Within the Kv7 family there are 5 members Kv7.1 to Kv7.5

NKCC1 is the key (co)transporter that allow chloride ions Cl^- to enter neurons

N stands of sodium (Na)

K stands for potassium

C stands for chloride

C stands for co-transporter

1 stands for the type 1 that is expressed in the brain, type 2 is in the kidneys

KCC2 is the cotransporter that allows chloride ions Cl⁻ to exit neurons. It proliferates weeks after birth and allows mature neurons to maintain low intracellular Cl⁻ levels that are critical in mediating synaptic inhibition via $GABA_A$ receptors.

K stands for potassium

C stands for chloride

C stands for cotransporter

2 stands for the type 2 that is expressed in the brain and elsewhere in the central nervous system. There is also KCC1 and KCC3. A problem with KCC3 may lead to agenesis of the corpus callosum and intellectual disability. KCC2 and KCC3 are both associated with neuropathic pain. One target of research is to upregulate KCC2 to treat pain. So far this has not been possible, but if such a drug were to be commercialized it could be repurposed for autism.

In bumetanide-responsive autism, an early developmental switch has failed to occur and instead of neurons having a high level of KCC2, they retain the high level of NKCC1 like a new-born. Chloride is elevated, GABA functions as excitatory. Neurons will never mature, unless treated.

Ion channel and transporter problems can be genetic, but do not have to be.

If you do opt to carry out genetic testing and one of the flagged genes is an ion channel, spend some time on Wikipedia understanding what it does. Then move on to the excellent, but more complicated, free resource at www.genecards.org.

Differentially Expressed Genes (DEGs)

If you thought ion channels were complicated, you might want to take a break before this section

We all have about 22,000 genes. They are like the blueprints telling your body how to make each of the matching 22,000 proteins. In the jargon each gene encodes its own protein.

These genes can get turned on and off all the time. The important thing is that the right ones are on/off at the right time. Things can go wrong when this does not happen, then you get Differentially Expressed Genes (DEGs).

For example, we all have various tumor suppressing genes. In men with prostate cancer an important such gene called PTEN is usually stuck turned off, then the cancer is free to grow. Interestingly, PTEN is also an autism gene, as are many cancer genes. This is not strange because as highlighted earlier, much autism is categorized by hyper-active pro-growth signaling pathways. Cancer itself clearly fits that description. In autism the growth mainly applies in the early years and the damage is normally only to the brain and its structure.

Genes can be over-expressed or under-expressed. This can be the result of a mutation in that specific gene or it can be caused by another gene/protein that interacts with it, or it might be an environmental factor. It could even be a bacterium in your gut.

Certain things turn on or off gene expression. There are many examples; the so-called redox switch Nrf2 turns on many of the body's antioxidant defenses. ROR alpha acts like a switch which affects many autism-related genes and it is controlled by the balance between male and female hormones, by moving the balance towards estradiol/estrogen the troubling symptoms may improve. Transcription factors are proteins that control the expression of many other proteins. If you have a mutation in the gene TCF4 that encodes Transcription Factor #4 you will exhibit a severe autism called Pitt Hopkins syndrome. If you have a minor mis-expression of TCF4 you may develop signs of schizophrenia in early adulthood.

The body also has a mechanism for leaving tags on your DNA, I liken these to Post-it stickers. These markers highlight specific genes to be either switched on or silenced. Environment effects like exposure to pesticides, recreational drug use or even smoking can result in one of these tags being attached. These tags are heritable, so if your grandfather was a heavy smoker, his antioxidant genes are not as nimble as they should be. If he or an heir develops asthma of COPD, the steroid drug treatment does not work as well as it should, due to oxidative stress.

Some drug therapies, for example HDAC inhibitors, may be able to remove some of these tags. Not all these tags are bad and some are there for a good reason.

Interaction between proteins is essential to how your body functions. You can think of these as gene-to-gene interactions, or protein-to-protein interactions, it is essentially the same thing.

I recently gave a presentation on the use of genetic testing in personalized medicine for autism. One key part was to show parents whose child has been diagnosed with a genetic autism, how they could investigate treatment options. Free resources exist where you can see maps of all the gene/protein interactions. This shows you what the gene should be doing; in most cases of an autism gene it will be showing you what it is NOT doing. You need to compensate for the loss of gene expression. The loss of one gene has a cascade of downstream effects on many other genes. You want to correct the key DEGs (differentially expressed genes) that have resulted. The human body is pretty clever and has a degree of redundancy built in, you do not need to fix 100% of the DEGs, just the critical ones.

Unless your gene is on the X chromosome and the child is boy, there is a second copy of each gene. You can in theory opt to make the remaining good copy work that bit harder. Sometimes this is possible with an existing drug. In other cases it would require very complicated gene therapy using clever existing technology, now widely used to make some types of vaccine.

Thinking in terms of Differentially Expressed Genes allows you to pretty much understand all disease, not just autism.

In autism, very often the key DEGs will include ion channels. This is great news because very many drugs already exist today to treat ion channels.

For example, in Pitt Hopkins syndrome the gene and so its encoded protein TCF4 (Transcription Factor 4) is greatly reduced.

This causes among other things the genes SCN10A and KCNQ1 to be overexpressed. These genes encode the important ion channels Nav1.8 and Kv7.1.

The next step is to repurpose existing approved drugs as inhibitors of Kv7.1 and Nav1.8. The suggested drug to inhibit Nav1.8 is nicardipine, an existing old drug used to treat high blood pressure and angina.

Dysfunctions that may be present in autism and how to treat them

Mitochondrial disease

The cells in your body are each powered by many tiny mitochondria that convert glucose from your blood to ATP. ATP is the energy currency of the cell. Brain cells are extremely power hungry and so neurons each contain thousands of mitochondria.

The number of mitochondria in each cell varies based on many factors, but they include the level of oxidative stress present and how much power that cell needs.

How effective each mitochondrion is at making this ATP fuel depends on how well your body can make certain special enzymes known as Complex 1 through to Complex 5. The process of producing the ATP fuel is called OXPHOS (Oxidative phosphorylation).

People with a mitochondrial dysfunction typically lack enough mitochondria, or they lack one of more of the five enzyme complexes.

The consequence of mitochondrial dysfunction can be just lethargy, lack of exercise endurance and low body temperature, particularly a cold head, or it can be very severe at the extreme.

Mitochondrial disease occurs when mitochondria in the cells fail to produce enough energy to sustain cell life. When enough cells cease to function properly organs, motor functions, and the neurological system can become impaired.

Mitochondrial disease is often misdiagnosed due to the fact many of the symptoms are synonymous with other, more common, diseases.

Primary mitochondrial disease (PMD) vs secondary mitochondrial dysfunction (SMD)

I received a comment on my blog from a parent who said that tests had ruled out mitochondrial disease. It is actually a very grey area, where it is much easier to rule it in, than out. It looks like most people with autism have some mitochondrial dysfunction, albeit perhaps minor compared to those with an identifiable error in a critical gene, which is easy to diagnose. Note that the genes for your mitochondria come exclusively from the mother.

Primary mitochondrial disease (PMD) is inborn; people with PMD have a genetic variance that makes them vulnerable to a loss of mitochondrial function. This loss may not begin until later in life and may increase in severity.

PMD is extremely rare in the general population, but is thought to occur in about 5% of cases of autism.

Primary mitochondrial disease (PMD) is diagnosed clinically and ideally confirmed by a genetic test. The PMD genes either encode OXPHOS proteins (more about these below) directly, or they affect OXPHOS function by impacting production of the complex machinery needed to run the OXPHOS process.

Secondary mitochondrial dysfunction (SMD) is much more common than PMD. SMD can be caused by genes encoding neither function nor production of the OXPHOS proteins and accompanies many hereditary non-mitochondrial diseases. The cause of SMD need not be genetic; it might be due to environmental factors.

SMD has been documented in a variety of autoimmune conditions including multiple sclerosis and lupus.

Aging contributes to oxidative stress in virtually all organs and tissues in the body and increases the risk for SMD.

Altered mitochondrial fusion/fission dynamics have been found to be a recurring theme in neurodegeneration. There is evidence of mitochondrial dysfunction in neurodegenerative diseases such as Alzheimer's and Parkinson's.

A significant number of metabolic disorders include SMD as a part of their features.

Abnormal biomarkers of mitochondrial function are very common in autism. Depending on whose data you consider, you can say that SMD is present in a substantial minority of cases.

Ideally you would use genetic testing to try to distinguish between PMD and SMD. This is important, since their treatments and prognoses can be quite different. However, even in the absence of the ability to distinguish between PMD and SMD, treating SMD with standard treatments for PMD can be effective.

A good source of information is www.mitoaction.org/diagnosis

Diagnosis of PMD, SMD and specific subtypes

Some researchers/clinicians make the issue of diagnosis sound very clear cut, whereas others see it as a subjective diagnosis associated with some ifs and maybes.

Mitochondrial dysfunction can affect the whole body or can be organ specific. You can take a muscle biopsy for analysis but not a brain biopsy. The latest method being used by some clinicians is to take a buccal swab, which is a sample taken from inside your cheek. www.religendx.com/faq-mitoswab/

There are a small number of well-known specialists who diagnose mitochondrial dysfunction. They all have their own favoured treatments and they do vary; they are often referred to as mito-cocktails, because there are very many ingredients.

Currently the most popular mito-cocktail for autism is SpectrumNeeds. It is recommended by a very serious mainstream mitochondrial specialist, who has no financial interest in it. He suggests it can reduce the symptoms of autism by 20%. I was very surprised he put a figure on it, but he did.

Some readers of my blog who took the buccal swab test which suggested mitochondrial dysfunction, and so started a mito-cocktail, reported there was no benefit. Just how good is the buccal test? What I do know is that nobody seems to take a muscle biopsy and use the mainstream test. Invasive tests are not popular with autism parents, some I know regret this a few years later.

The oxidative phosphorylation pathway

Oxidative phosphorylation (or OXPHOS in short) is the metabolic pathway in which cells use enzymes to oxidize nutrients, thereby releasing energy. This takes place inside mitochondria.

Although oxidative phosphorylation is a vital part of metabolism, it produces reactive oxygen species (ROS) such as superoxide and hydrogen peroxide, which may lead to propagation of free radicals, damaging cells and contributing to disease.

In the mitochondria, converting one molecule of glucose to carbon dioxide and water produces up to 36 units of ATP. This does also require the presence of oxygen. In the absence of oxygen a different, much less efficient process is followed. This is what happens to endurance athletes when they "run out of puff".

When an athlete runs at a pace where the muscles in his legs require more oxygen than his lungs can provide to make the ATP via OXPOS, lactate is produced and rapidly builds up. Eventually lactic acidosis occurs and you feel a burning in your muscles and then cramps and nausea. You have to stop.

When ATP breaks down into ADP (Adenosine diphosphate) and P_i (phosphate), energy is liberated.

By analyzing the level of certain byproducts (pyruvate, lactate etc) of the five major steps between glucose and ATP your specialist doctor can determine which of the five enzyme complexes might be deficient. It is very clever, if done correctly, but it remains subjective.

Many poisons and pesticides target one of the enzyme complexes. Inhibition of any step in this process will halt the rest of the process. One of these poisons, 2,4-Dinitrophenol, was actually used as an anti-obesity drug in the 1930s. Pretty drastic!

The clinicians who like genetic testing look for concrete evidence of primary mitochondrial disease (PMD). Other clinicians look for tell-tale signs in the level of chemicals like lactate and pyruvate to make diagnosis; this might suggest that a specific enzyme complex is deficient.

If you have a diagnosis of say complex 1 deficiency, you can then go into the detail of that step in the process. Here it gets rather complicated because 51 different genes encode components of complex 1. Any one of them being down regulated could impair the level of complex 1.

Complex 1 is seen as the rate limiting enzyme, which means this is the one that you usually have the least reserve capacity. In simple terms this means that for most people you likely want to maximize complex 1.

Therapy

It looks like Dr Kelley, formerly head of department at Johns Hopkins, has the largest following by those treating autism secondary to mitochondrial disease (AMD). Treatment includes augmentation of residual complex I activity with carnitine, thiamine, nicotinamide, and pantothenate, and protection against free radical injury with several antioxidants, including vitamin C, vitamin E, alpha-lipoic acid (ALA), and coenzyme Q10.

Dr Frye is a prolific publisher, unlike Dr Kelley, and their therapies do differ. Dr Frye likes his B vitamins, on his list are B vitamins 1, 2, 3, 5, 6, 7, 9 and 12. Some of these vitamins are at doses 50 times higher than common in supplements.

Dr Kelley is a big believer in the benefit of carnitine. He suggests mutation in one or more subunits of mitochondrial complex I is indicated by the often-immediate response to carnitine, which activates latent complex I.

A problem with carnitine is very low bioavailability. An analog of carnitine, with increased absorption would be useful.

I did suggest in my blog that the Latvian drug Meldonium/Mildronate might be interesting. Mildronate has a similar structure to carnitine.

Research shows that Meldonium protects mitochondrial metabolism that is altered by inhibitors of complex I and that it is effective in the prevention of pathologies associated with mitochondrial dysfunctions.

I wrote a post about Meldonium/Mildronate, a drug that was made famous by the Russian tennis star Maria Sharapova. It is widely used by sportsmen to increase their endurance. This fact was very well known in the old Soviet Union and Meldonium was widely used by their soldiers fighting in Afghanistan. At high altitudes there is less oxygen in the air you breathe and ultimately less in your blood and this compromises the ability of infantry soldiers.

The western world's military have long used acetazolamide/Diamox, which makes your blood more acidic and this fools the body into thinking it has an excess of CO_2, and it excretes this imaginary excess CO_2 by deeper and faster breathing, which in turn increases the amount of oxygen in the blood.

I myself took Diamox when crossing the Himalayas overland in my youth, to avoid altitude sickness. Diamox may have other therapeutic benefits in some autism. It is also used to treat hypokalemic periodic paralysis.

Other than sportswomen and soldiers, Meldonium is used to treat coronary artery disease, where problems may sometimes lead to ischemia, a condition where too little blood flows to the organs in the body, especially the heart. Because this drug is thought to expand the arteries, it helps to increase the blood flow as well as increase the flow of oxygen throughout the body.

Meldonium also appears to have neuroprotective properties particularly relevant to the mitochondria. At one point I thought this was just the Latvian researchers clutching at straws trying to push their drug as a panacea. Rather, I think perhaps its core action may include making the mitochondria work a little better, by increasing complex 1. This might also increase stamina and it might also improve cognition in some.

There have been no trials of Meldonium in autism.

Bypass the need for Complex 1 by ketosis?

Almost all the research on mitochondrial disease assumes that you want to convert glucose to ATP.

If a person has an inability to produce enough complex 1 they might be better off switching from glycolysis (glucose as fuel) to ketosis (ketones from fat as fuel).

There are posts in my blog describing the ketogenic diet, which has been widely used for decades to treat epilepsy.

As I write this section, I recall that I was asked in an online conference by a Russian parent why do I think her child responds better to bumetanide while on the ketogenic diet? It was a really good question. The main ketone is something called BHB and this is then converted by mitochondria to make ATP. But BHB has a long list of other properties, some of which are anti-inflammatory. These properties will themselves help lower chloride within neurons and make bumetanide appear more effective.

There is a case history of a doctor treating her husband with early onset Alzheimer's using high doses of ketones. In Alzheimer's the brain gets starved of fuel because of reduced expression of a glucose transporter called GLUT1 at the blood brain barrier. The wife took the logical step of moving away from glucose as a brain fuel to use ketones. It worked for her and she published a case history.

US special forces reportedly make use of a very expensive BHB supplement as a highly compact source of emergency energy. Some athletes also use BHB supplements. Within the European Union these BHB supplements are banned, but they are widely available in the US.

As is often the case, opinion is mixed on the ketogenic diet and mitochondrial disorders. It seems to make some people better and have no effect on others. This is likely because they do not have precisely the same mitochondrial disorder.

Experimental therapies

My blog looks mainly at experimental therapies.

In the case of mitochondrial disease there really are no approved curative therapies. On the other hand, the scientific literature is full of clues. That would be another story, for another book.

I am pretty sure my son does not have mitochondrial dysfunction, by the way.

Some people's autism does indeed appear to have been solely caused by the lack of mitochondrial enzymes. These dysfunctions can be inherited or acquired.

As Dr Kelley suggests, a baby might be born with a 50% reduction in complex 1 and develop normally. Following a viral infection, or other insult, before the brain has substantially matured a further reduction in complex 1 occurs and this tips the balance to where mitochondria cannot function sufficiently. Siblings may have exactly the same biochemical markers, but continue normal development because they avoided the damaging insult that triggered regression at a critical point in the brain's maturation.

Dr Kelley mainly links mitochondrial dysfunction to regressive autism, as opposed to early onset autism. The data does point to mitochondrial dysfunction being present beyond just those with regressive autism, so a little extra complex 1 may be in order for them too.

Of the five enzyme complexes, complex 1 appears to be the most important because it is "rate limiting", meaning it is usually the enzyme with the least unused capacity. It becomes the bottleneck in the energy production chain. Many other diseases, as well as, aging feature a decline in complex 1, which may account for some people's loss of cognitive function.

Is Mildronate a carnitine analog with better bioavailability? Are its cognitive enhancing effects due to increased blood flow, improved complex 1 availability or perhaps both? We can only wait till the Latvians do some experiments on schizophrenia and autism. The good news is that the dose at which the mitochondrial effects occur is five times less than the anti-ischemia dose.

I can see that the dose for athletes is twice the dose for ischemia. It would seem that tennis players who have used Mildronate for ten years, at ten times the mitochondrial dose, might provide some useful safety information.

To read Dr Kelley's treatment protocol you will not find it in a scientific journal, or on the Johns Hopkins website, but you can find it on the web.

Use google and enter:

> Evaluation and Treatment of Patients with Autism and Mitochondrial Disease, Richard Kelley, MD, PhD

Hopefully you can find it. If not, you can look in my blog under Regressive Autism.

Myelination

There is a great deal written in my blog about myelin, equivalent to 80 pages of this book. So as not to send the reader to sleep, I will give just a very simple overview, but it will include all the actionable steps suggested in the literature.

Your brain is made up of gray/grey matter and white matter. The key difference is a white-coloured, fatty protein called myelin. Myelin is like a coating of insulation that speeds up transmission of electrical signals in the brain.

Only in the third trimester (weeks 28–40) does the brain of the fetus start to make these myelinated networks. In order to control your body and indeed your mind, you need nerve fibers that are myelinated.

Myelin does not last forever and your body is constantly remyelinating.

In multiple sclerosis (MS) the brain's immune cells (microglia) attack both the myelin and the clever cells (oligodendrocytes) that make the myelin.

In autism we know that the myelin layer is not as thick as in typical people and we know that many of the genes involved in the myelination process are mis-expressed. They are DEGs (differentially expressed genes).

We also know that in many diseases, myelin is lost. For example, in the case of hypoxia, when you are starved of oxygen, you can see on an MRI that myelin has been lost. This then causes the person to lose skills they had previously mastered. If you act quickly, the research shows us that you can repair the damage done to the myelin layer.

Anatomy of a neuron

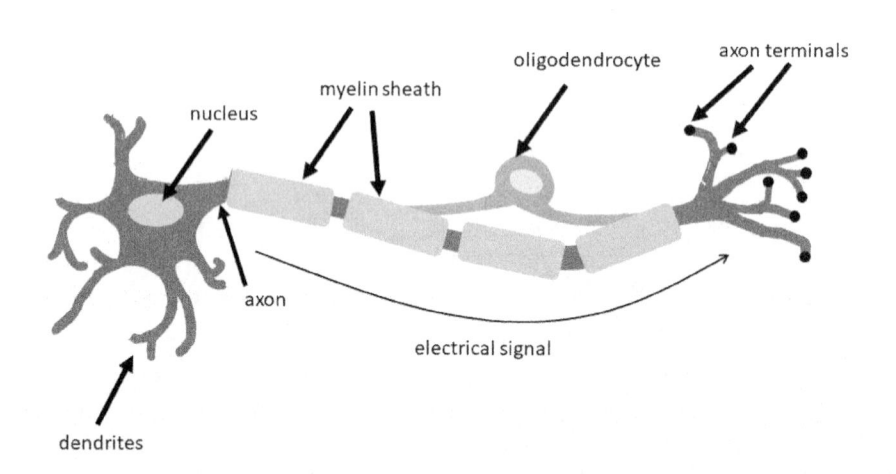

Neurons communicate through synapses – contact points between the axon terminals on one neuron and dendrites on the next neuron. Electrical signals flow across the axon to the next neuron.

In mitochondrial disease, when neurons are unable to fuel themselves, the first consequence is loss of myelin and eventually cell death.

Many things have been shown to affect myelination in the brain. Interestingly, depression is associated with less myelin and when you stimulate more myelination, you improve the symptoms of depression.

One of my favourite studies featured the use of clemastine, a cheap antihistamine, to treat a mouse model of depression. This model also features impaired myelination. Clemastine turned on gene expression in the myelin producing oligodendrocytes; this resulted in more myelin and less depression. This is well illustrated in the graphic below.

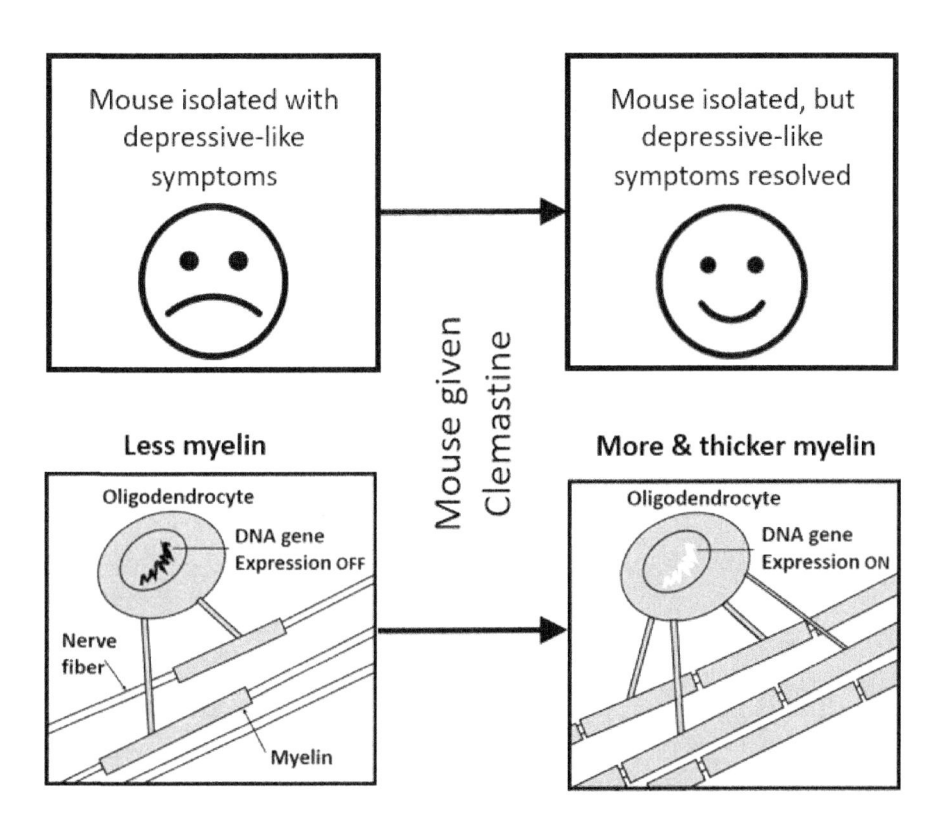

When very young children are put to play in a group, they produce more myelin and when a child is kept isolated, less myelin is produced. Socialization is good.

In order to develop skills like catching a ball, riding a bike, or knowing your times tables, you need myelin.

Not all of your brain needs myelin and that is why you also have gray matter.

In autism we are mainly interested in the brain and the central nervous system. Here the myelin insulation is produced by the rather hard to spell oligodendrocytes. In the peripheral nerve system that extends all round your body the myelin is produced by Schwann cells.

In MS the immune system (microglial cells) attacks the myelin sheaths and the oligodendrocytes cells that produce and maintain it. This attack causes inflammation and injury to the nerve sheath and ultimately to the nerve fibers that it surrounds. The process results in multiple areas of scarring/sclerosis, hence the name multiple sclerosis (MS). A commonly held view is that the myelin produced by the Schwann cells in the peripheral nerve system is not damaged in MS. Research suggests that this is not correct and that the myelin layer in the peripheral nerve system can also be affected. That means that the Schwann cells are relevant to MS.

There is a great deal of research into MS and recently we have started to see clever research looking at myelination defects in multiple types of autism. This autism research is based on mouse models where you can measure the expression of different genes involved in myelination in different types of autism.

MS still does not have a very effective therapy, but the research provides many clues as how it could be treated effectively and cheaply. Many so-called disease changing drugs in MS are extremely expensive, putting them out of reach of many sufferers.

One interesting drug is actually an extremely cheap chemical called DMF (dimethyl fumarate) that was pioneered as a human drug by Walter Schweckendiek, a German chemist, treating himself for psoriasis. He published his results and reported himself cured in 1959. Many people with MS also have psoriasis, so a few decades later it was noticed that in addition to curing their psoriasis these people had also greatly improved their MS. An extremely cheap bulk chemical is today sold as an extremely expensive drug for MS and psoriasis.

DMF has very many other possible applications from neuropathic pain to Huntington's and Parkinson's diseases. It activates Nrf2 and HCA2. At very low doses it seems to help some autism, which is not surprising. In the research DMF is suggested as a treatment for mitochondrial disease because it both increases biogenesis (via Nrf2) and complex 1 expression (via HCA2). At high doses DMF works quite differently and is a potential cancer therapy, by creating a wave of oxidative stress to kill the cancer cells. This is all referenced to the peer-reviewed literature in my blog, for those interested to know more.

The same cells that damage myelin in MS, the microglia, are also dysfunctional in autism. They are "activated". In the absence of any threat to the brain, the microglia should be in their resting state called M0. Classical activation leads to M1, which can lead to depression and other psychiatric disorders. Then we have the M2 activated state, that subdivides into M2a, M2b and M2c.

In the resting state M0, also called ramified, the microglia carrying out their housekeeping duties inside the brain, with a focus on synaptic pruning from week 25 until well into adulthood. Synaptic pruning is the critical task where excess synapses are removed. This is just like pruning an ornamental tree in your garden - you cut off the un-shapely parts and over the years form a beautiful tree.

In much autism it is thought that the microglia are stuck in the M2 state and this results in disordered cortical growth and overgrowth of dendritic spines.

In both autism and MS we want to shift the microglia back to their resting/ramified state M0. Courtesy of the MS research we know how to do this. We can target the P2X7 receptor on the microglia using an old antihistamine drug called clemastine.

We also want to increase the number of those cells that make the myelin, the ones I cannot spell, the oligodendrocytes. We even know how to do that – we go one step backwards to the precursor, the oligodendrocyte progenitor cells (OPC). To get the OPCs to make more oligodendrocyte we can use a PDE4 inhibitor (Ibudilast or Roflumilast, while Pentoxifylline is non selective inhibitor of all types of PDE).

Recent research shows that you can also increase differentiation of OPCs to make more oligodendrocytes using a cheap supplement called NAG or N-acetylglucosamine. NAG is not the same supplement as NAC.

In MS lesions research shows that there are OPCs, but they are blocked from developing into oligodendrocytes by dysregulation of Wnt signaling, leading to a profound delay of both developmental myelination and remyelination. In effect too much Wnt signaling appears to halt myelination. This dysregulation model of remyelination failure requires the Wnt pathway to be active during acute demyelination. You might then think that a Wnt inhibitor might unblock the myelination in MS. In my blog I did suggest the very cheap generic drug mebendazole, used to treat pinworm infections in two-year-olds. Mebendazole kills parasites, but it is also a Wnt inhibitor and as such can be repurposed for many uses, including some cancers.

When it comes to using the microbiome in the gut to modify MS, research has shown that adding the bacteria Prevotella histicola boosts the anti-inflammatory immune responses and inhibits pro-inflammatory immune responses. This is to such an extent that in the mouse model of MS, this probiotic was as effective as the extremely expensive MS drug Copaxone. Interestingly, Prevotella histicola is reduced in people with MS, but when treated with the expensive drug Copaxone, the level of Prevotella histicola increases. So skip the expensive drug and swallow the probiotic bacteria instead!

In my blog we saw something similar with the ketogenic diet long used to treat epilepsy. At UCLA they measured the change in bacteria in the gut following the high fat ketogenic diet and then they replicated the anti-seizure effect of the diet, just by giving those bacteria. Very clever, isn't it?

In autism the anti-inflammatory probiotic bacteria VSL#3/ Viviomixx are very effective in some subtypes.

The common antioxidant ALA (alpha lipoic acid) is protective in MS and actually increases the number of oligodendrocyte progenitor cells (OPCs), the ones that make oligodendrocytes. Very possibly a similar effect might be produced by that other thiol antioxidant, NAC (N-acetylcysteine). I know a lot about ALA.

My father-in-law has been having intravenous ALA (alpha lipoic acid) at his hospital for the last 20 years, to treat his diabetes.

Given intravenously, it is much more potent than a pill you swallow. I think he has benefited from its wide-ranging health effects and it likely added a decade to his life. I remember when the ban on taking liquids on planes was just introduced in 2006, I was carrying boxes of ampules containing liquid ALA (called Thioctacid) in my briefcase, because where we live, they were unavailable. I recall wondering what the inspection at the airport in Romania would make of it. I think they were more interested in my shoes than me exporting these ampules, which all made it home to the fridge.

Back to myelin.

When it comes to autism, we know for sure there is a problem with myelin. To quote Brady Maher, lead investigator at the Lieber Institute for Brain Development in Baltimore, Maryland

"In general, across the whole spectrum, there's a defect in myelination"

What should come next in the medical research is an evaluation of how to improve myelination in autism. Do not raise your hopes!

Reducing cognitive impairment – raising IQ

Neurological and psychiatric disorders are often poorly described and poorly treated, but adult-onset conditions have historically been taken much more seriously and so the research is more advanced. I find myself quite often looking at research on schizophrenia and bipolar; many of the same genes and metabolic dysfunctions common in autism show up in those conditions.

Many people really dislike the old medical term Mental Retardation (MR), which is actually a very accurate descriptive term, meaning that someone is cognitively behind their peers. Most lay people have no idea what Intellectual Disability (ID) means, but ID is the new MR. In the United Kingdom they have their own new politically correct term for Mental Retardation (MR), which is Learning Disability (LD). In the US the term Learning Disability has a different, much broader meaning, it is used to describe conditions like dyslexia.

It is interesting that about 90% of people with schizophrenia and 50% of people with bipolar are cognitively behind their peers. I suspect the figure for autism would also be about 90%, if someone measured it. Most people with Asperger's (mild or level 1 autism)

are not top of the class. I call the people with high IQ "true Aspies" – Elon Musk is a perfect example – these are the ones Hans Asperger wrote about.

Only in extreme cases of being cognitively behind their peers, when their IQ is less than 70, does a person get diagnosed with ID. IQ is based on a bell curve.

The IQ Bell Curve

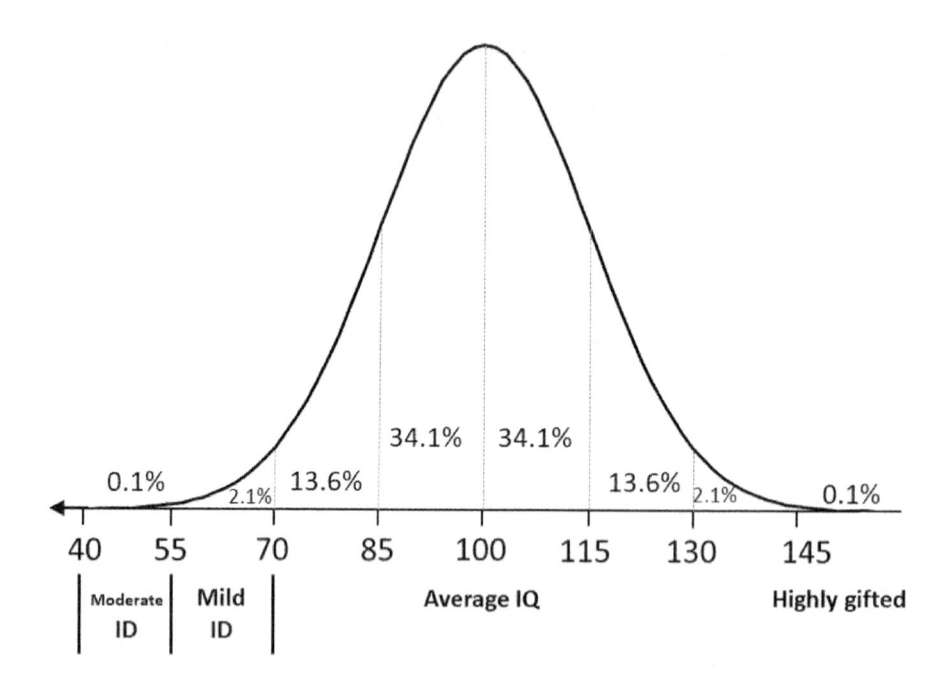

	0.1%	2.1%	13.6%	34.1%	34.1%	13.6%	2.1%	0.1%
	40	55	70	85	100	115	130	145
	Moderate ID	Mild ID			Average IQ			Highly gifted

If your IQ is less than 70 then you would fit the clinical diagnosis of MR/ID. It is just an arbitrary cut-off point for 2.3% of the population. The idea that if IQ is greater than 70 there is no cognitive deficit is entirely flawed.

The cut-off points between the sub-categories of ID are not defined the same by everyone, but here is one view.

Most ID is mild intellectual disability, where IQ is 55 to 70
- Slower than typical in all developmental areas
- Able to learn practical life skills

- Attains reading and math skills up to grade levels 3 to 6
- Able to blend in socially
- Functions in daily life

Moderate intellectual disability is when IQ is 40 to 55
- Noticeable developmental delays (speech, motor skills)
- Can communicate in simple ways
- Able to learn basic health and safety skills
- Can complete self-care activities
- Can travel alone to nearby places

Severe intellectual disability is defined by an IQ between 20 to 39. Most people in this category cannot live an independent life and will need to live in a group home setting.
- Considerable delays in development
- Understands speech but has little ability to communicate
- Able to learn daily routines
- May learn very simple self-care

Fortunately, very few people have profound intellectual disability, which means IQ less than 20
- Significant developmental delays in all areas
- Requires close supervision
- Requires assistance for self-care activities
- May respond to physical and social activities
- Not capable of independent living

For people with lower levels of IQ, times have moved on and the trend is to focus on adaptive functioning rather than IQ. Adaptive functions measures living skills. One common measurement scale is called Vineland.

Autism and cognitive function

It seems that in autism, as in schizophrenia and bipolar, we should assume that cognitive dysfunction is present; the only question is how much and what to do about it. In profound autism, it is the impaired cognition which is the greatest problem.

Today's autism is very broadly defined. There are people with high measured IQ, but they still may have some cognitive issues, like impaired sensory gating.

Having treated their cognitive dysfunction(s), the person will be better able to compensate for any other dysfunctions they might have.

Even though the psychiatrists and psychologists will tell you that autism is all about the triad of impairments, I think they are missing the most important element, which is cognitive dysfunction.

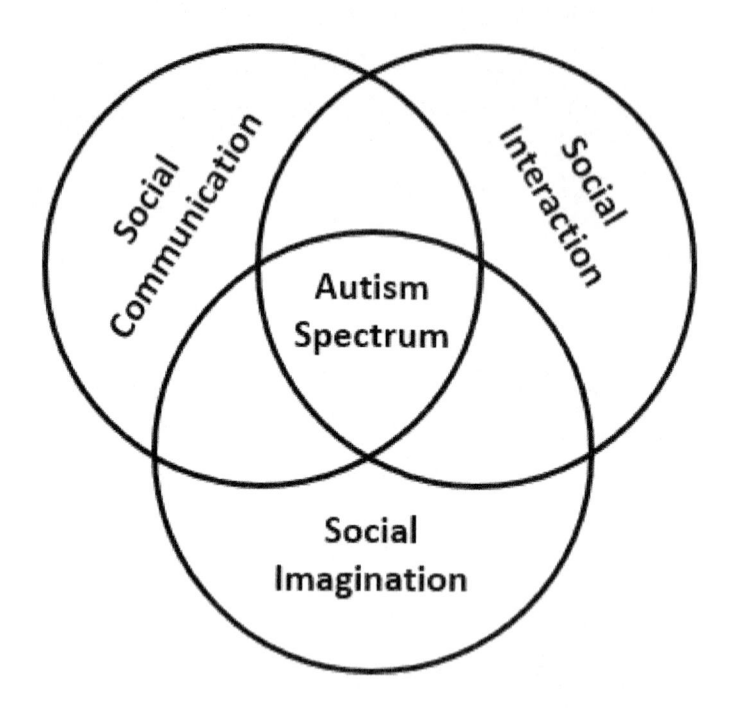

The confusion arises because the definition of autism has changed substantially. In the old DSM3 it would be assumed that a diagnosis of autism usually meant some degree of cognitive impairment. Severe autism usually meant severe ID/MR.

When Asperger's became a diagnosis, this introduced a group with normal to above normal IQ.

When DSM5 appeared all autism types became just plain autism and the diagnosis has been very freely handed out. The result is that very many people diagnosed today with autism will have normal IQ. That does not mean they do not have cognitive dysfunctions.

In my conference presentations and video, I use my own simple framework to discuss the symptoms of autism.

Understanding your specific case of Autism

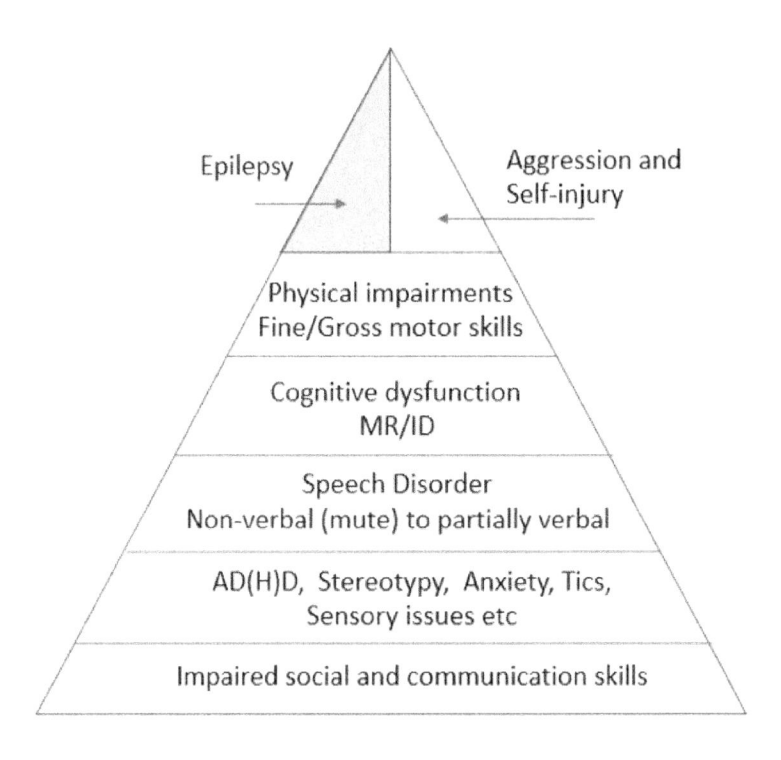

```
                    /\
                   /  \
         Epilepsy /    \  Aggression and
              → /      \ ←  Self-injury
               /────────\
              / Physical impairments \
             /  Fine/Gross motor skills \
            /────────────────────────────\
           /     Cognitive dysfunction     \
          /             MR/ID               \
         /────────────────────────────────────\
        /         Speech Disorder              \
       /  Non-verbal (mute) to partially verbal \
      /──────────────────────────────────────────\
     /     AD(H)D, Stereotypy, Anxiety, Tics,     \
    /              Sensory issues etc              \
   /────────────────────────────────────────────────\
  /      Impaired social and communication skills    \
 /────────────────────────────────────────────────────\
```

How high up you are on the pyramid highlights what kind of autism you are dealing with. There will always be exceptions, like a highly intelligent person diagnosed with Asperger's who self-injures.

Cognitive function as the therapeutic target

Since many children with mild autism do eventually overcome many of their challenges in childhood, perhaps cognitive function really should be given a higher priority in treatment and research.

165

Many caregivers and educators are mainly focused on minimizing bad/disruptive behaviors rather than the emergence of good behaviors and learning.

As the child matures, in many cases these bad/disruptive behaviors may fade without any clever interventions. In other cases, the bad behaviors grow and become a barrier to entering school or a group home later on.

An intervention that stops stereotypy in a toddler, which was blocking learning, may have very much less impact when given to an adolescent. Or at least the impact may be much less obvious.

I remember reading about a parent with two children with Fragile X who was very upset when the arbaclofen clinical trials were halted, since her kids had both responded well. But two years later, she appeared in another article, it was clear that things were going fine without arbaclofen. The son, whose violence towards his mother had been controlled by arbaclofen, was no longer aggressive. The problem had just faded away, without medication. He continued to suffer cognitively, being a male with Fragile X. His sister was naturally very much less affected (females with Fragile X syndrome have two X chromosomes and only one of the chromosomes usually have an abnormal gene, so she had one functioning copy).

The advantage of using cognitive function as a target is that it is much easier to measure than subjective behavioral deficits. For the majority of people, it is likely to be the most important factor in their future success and well-being.

Cognitive deficit in schizophrenia & bipolar

To most lay people, schizophrenia is characterized by abnormal social behavior and failure to recognize what is real. Common symptoms include false beliefs, unclear or confused thinking, hearing voices, reduced social engagement and emotional expression, and a lack of motivation. People often have additional mental health problems such as major depression, anxiety disorders, or substance use disorder. Symptoms typically come on gradually, begin in early adulthood, and last a long time.

Cognitive dysfunction has been reported in about 85% of schizophrenic patients and is negatively associated with the outcome of the disorder. Research indicates that cognitive dysfunction is present in 40-60% of those with bipolar.

Many studies have been carried out looking to improve cognitive function in schizophrenia. It is notable that cognitive impairments are recognized as a major cause of disability in schizophrenia and there really is a genuine search for effective treatments. There is a list of targets.

- H3 histamine antagonists
- The HDAC inhibitor and inflammatory response modifier sodium butyrate
- α7 nAChR agonists, like nicotine
- multiple classes of serotonin (5HT) receptor
- $GABA_A$ α2 agonists
- NMDA receptors modulators
- mGluR2/3/5 the metabotropic glutamate receptors
- D_1 selective dopamine agonists

The fact that trials are yet to find a single universal therapy to improve cognition in schizophrenia perhaps should not be a surprise; it is a polygenic heterogeneous condition just like autism. Some individuals do indeed respond to some of the above therapies.

Cognitive function in Down syndrome

Down syndrome (DS) is caused by the person having an extra copy of all or part of chromosome 21. This results in over-expression of 300–500 genes.

One result of this over-expression of these genes is cognitive impairment, with an IQ nearly always less than 70, meaning ID.

The sub-unit expression of the $GABA_A$ is of great importance for cognitive function. It appears that in both Down syndrome and some autism there is a problem with the α-type subunits. In some autism increasing the effect of the α3 subunit has positive cognitive effects. In Down syndrome Roche was targeting a reduction in the effect of the α5 subunit using a new drug called basmisanil. It is a negative allosteric modulator at $GABA_A$ α5.

I think it is quite possible that basmisanil would have a positive cognitive effect in some autism. Roche has given up on Down syndrome and is trying basmisanil on schizophrenia.

It also appears that people with Down syndrome may have the same faulty GABA switch found in autism. Mouse models of Down syndrome respond positively to the bumetanide treatment developed for autism. I have seen one published case history detailing a child with Down syndrome who responded very well to bumetanide.

Learning from dementia and mild cognitive impairment

Before I started my investigation, I had never considered dementia, or mild cognitive impairment (MCI), as having any relevance to autism. I learned that by understanding mechanisms that impair cognitive function in old age we can learn about mechanism that may be active in some autism, as well as schizophrenia and bipolar.

There are very many causes of age-related loss of cognitive function. Some are called dementia, but everyone is going to lose some cognitive function during aging.

- Alzheimer's disease and tauopathies
- Vascular dementia
- Loss of autophagy
- Loss of mitochondrial function
- Lack of Nerve Growth Factor (NGF)
- High levels of homocysteine
- Oxidative stress

The big question is what lessons can be learnt from these conditions and applied to young people who have reduced cognitive function.

Alzheimer's disease and tauopathies

By far the most common form of dementia in older people is Alzheimer's disease (AD). Alzheimer's often affects people with Down syndrome from middle age.

Alzheimer's disease (AD), is characterized by the accumulation of the β-amyloid peptide (Aβ) within the brain along with protein tau. It is thought that the first step in the development of Alzheimer's is production of neurotoxic Aβ from something called amyloid precursor protein (APP). So high levels of APP would not be good.

High levels of APP are common in severe autism and Fragile X, but not mild autism.

Plaques and tangles are seen as the likely cause of cell death and tissue loss in the Alzheimer brain.

Plaques are clusters of chemically sticky proteins called beta-amyloid that build up between nerve cells. Small clumps of plaque may block cell-to-cell signaling at synapses. They may also activate immune system cells to devour these disabled cells.

Tangles form inside dying cells. Tangles are twisted fibers of a protein tau. In areas where tangles are forming, the twisted strands of tau block nutrients from moving through the cells, causing cell death.

Most people develop some plaques and tangles as they get older, but people with Alzheimer's tend to develop far more. Plaques and tangles tend to form in a pattern, starting in areas related to learning and memory and then spreading to other regions of the brain.

APP is present in everyone and it has numerous functions unrelated to Alzheimer's. There is research looking at the connection between Fragile X and Alzheimer's. It is suggested that some Alzheimer's therapies might be effective in Fragile X.

By the age of 40 years, virtually all people with Down syndrome have sufficient plaques and tangles in their brains for a diagnosis of AD.

It is not clear if anyone has looked for plaques and tangles in 40-year-olds with Fragile X or severe autism.

Most research in the last quarter century has focused on the role of amyloid rather than tau protein.

Tau is implicated in Parkinson's as well as Alzheimer's. Tau is present in all humans but it can dysfunction (hyper-phosphorylation) and form tangles. When tau behaves like this it leads to so-called tauopathies, like Alzheimer's.

The question is to what extent are infantile tauopathies present in autism. This is debated in the research.

Tuberous sclerosis (TSC) is a widely used research model of autism. TSC is a genetic disorder that is usually caused by the TSC2 gene, but can be caused by TSC1. Both TSC1 and TSC2 are growth suppressors and dysfunction leads to the growth of benign tumors. TSC is associated with seizures, autism, MR/ID and other issues. TSC is a tauopathy.

It is unknown to what extent tauopathy may be present in autism or those with intellectual disability (ID). In autism one study of people with severe autism found they had low levels of tau protein. But what appears to be relevant is not the amount of tau, but rather its behavior.

A very expensive drug called everolimus, is being used to treat TSC. Everolimus is a potent mTOR inhibitor, with mTOR being part of a key constellation of signaling pathways implicated in cancer and autism.

A gene called ADNP with encodes a protein of the same name is one possible link between Alzheimer's and autism. Mutations of this gene can cause both autism and Alzheimer's. It is suggested by Israeli scientists that activity-dependent neuroprotective protein (ADNP) is a master regulator of key ASD and AD risk genes. If true this would have profound implications.

In the case of autism, ADNP connects to something with a long name called eukaryotic translation initiation factor 4E (elF4E). The role elF4E plays in autism is discussed in detail elsewhere in the book, because inhibiting it could be a successful autism therapy.

Loss of autophagy

Autophagy is the process by which the body disposes of intracellular garbage. If it does not function properly bits of junk will accumulate and impede cellular function.

The kind of autophagy that clears up in the mitochondria is called mitophagy.

Impaired autophagy occurs in old age, but is a key feature of Parkinson disease and Huntington's disease. Autophagy plays a role is conditions as varied as cancer and arthritis.

Impaired autophagy appears to be a feature of some autism and the over activation of mTOR is put forward as the reason. Much autophagy is "mTOR-dependent" and this will be down regulated in many people with autism.

In benign aging, loss of autophagy causes gradual cognitive decline, that can be reversed by intervening to stimulate more autophagy. Fasting is the simplest way to trigger autophagy.

There is a case that interventions might help people with autism who have down regulated mTOR-dependent autophagy. Also of interest are the pro-autophagy experimental therapies being considered, for example at Stanford researchers working on Huntington's disease suggest the calcium channel blocker verapamil.

There are natural substances that can increase autophagy. One such substance is a substance called spermidine, found in wheat seedlings. A clinical trial is underway in Germany to treat cognitive decline in older adults, a study called Polyamine-enriched Diet in Healthy Older Adults With Subjective Cognitive Decline (preSmartAge).

There are also mTOR-independent inducers of autophagy. Intracellular inositol 1,4,5-trisphosphate (IP3) levels negatively regulate autophagy. Pharmacological inhibition of IP3 receptor (IP3R) induces autophagy.

IP3 is interesting in autism and has been highlighted by one of the few top-class researchers with an interest in autism Jay Gargus, from University of California at Irvine.

> "we propose dysregulated IP3R signaling as a nexus where genes altered in ASD converge to exert their deleterious effect...
>
> deficits in IP3-mediated Ca2+ signaling may not be limited to neurological correlates of ASD, but may also explain other characteristic ASD-associated heterogeneous symptoms, such as those of the gastrointestinal tract and immune system"

Loss of mitochondrial function

There is a section in this book that explains mitochondria and their possible kinds of dysfunction. If your mitochondria lose function your cells lose their source of energy.

Mitochondrial dysfunction, and indeed oxidative stress, are key features of early-stage Alzheimer's disease.

It has been suggested that there should be a category called mitochondrial dementia.

Mitochondrial disease is seen by Dr Kelley, from Johns Hopkins, as the prime cause of regressive autism. He calls it AMD (autism secondary to mitochondrial disease).

A key feature of AMD is a severe loss of cognitive function and previously acquired learning.

Lack of nerve growth factor (NGF)

In the brain there are various different growth factors, one of which is nerve growth factor (NGF).

It is known that serum nerve growth factor (NGF) level is reduced in mild cognitive impairment and Alzheimer's disease. In Sweden they are experimenting with an implant that releases NGF inside the brain. They placed NGF-producing capsules in the basal forebrain. These capsules, which can easily be removed, then released NGF to the surrounding cells in order to prevent their degradation.

There was a ten year long trial that used gene therapy to upregulate NGF in Alzheimer's brains.

A simpler NGF therapy was developed by an Italian Professor, Rita Levi-Montalcini. In 1986 she received the Nobel Prize in Physiology or Medicine for the discovery of NGF. She died in 2012 at the age of 103, having had a remarkable life. She was also a pioneer in the area of mast cells, which it turns out are closely linked to NGF. She spent much of her very long life researching the brain and concluded that to preserve her own mental capacity in old age she would need a little help. For her final 30 years she treated herself with home-made NGF eye drops, which she claimed restored her brain function to that of her youth. It is notable that she outlived her twin sister by 12 years. She never retired and in her 90s founded the European Brain Research Institute. It seems many people have tried to copy her, but NGF is not so easy to obtain.

NGF is critical for the survival and maintenance of sympathetic and sensory neurons. Without it, these neurons will die. There is evidence that NGF circulates throughout the entire body and is important for maintaining homeostasis.

When researchers compared the level of NGF in spinal fluid in children with autism and Rett syndrome they found normal levels in autism but near negligible values in Rett syndrome; they even suggest that NGF be used as a test to discriminate autism and Rett syndrome.

This finding is confirmed when postmortem brain tissue from Rett children was analyzed.

No studies have actually looked at NGF over time in autism and indeed the picture is far from simple. Research in 2013 looked at links between non-verbal communication deficits in people with autism and the gene that controls NGF. The conclusion of the study was that NGF is a promising risk gene for non-verbal communication deficits.

High levels of homocysteine

Of over a hundred clinical trials to treat Alzheimer's over a 13-year period since 2000, only three reached market, each with minimal therapeutic effects.

Homocysteine seems to be consistently elevated in both Alzheimer's and heart disease, so it is a risk factor, but does lowering homocysteine improve outcomes?

Certain B vitamins are known to be able to reduce levels of homocysteine (B2, B6, B9 and B12).

Recent data show that B-vitamin supplementation virtually halts grey matter atrophy in areas of the brain related to Alzheimer's disease while slowing some cognitive decline.

So lowering homocysteine with B vitamins and indeed NAC would seem a wise idea.

Homocysteine has been shown in studies to be elevated in autism and correlates significantly with the severity of the communication deficit. That would suggest people with Asperger's might not need to worry, but people with severe autism might benefit from less homocysteine.

Oxidative stress

There is a lot in this book about oxidative stress. Oxidative stress is a feature of aging and most disease, including all types of dementia. High levels of homocysteine are a good indicator of oxidative stress.

Oxidative stress, and the closely related nitrosative stress, are almost inevitably present in autism. Lab tests exist, so this is easy to check.

Antioxidants are a wise preventative measure to delay age-related loss of cognitive function. Some older people lack B12 because they take medication to lower stomach acid, which blocks absorption of B12 from food. Products exist that combine the antioxidant NAC with B12 and folic acid (B9).

Treatable ID masquerading as autism?

There is a big overlap between the causes of some ID (intellectual disability) and the causes of some autism.

If you have a case of autism, it is worth reviewing the treatable forms of ID, just in case you have one, even a mild version causing minimal ID.

These are mainly inborn errors of metabolism, most but not all are genetic.

A small group of mainly Canadian and Dutch clinicians have been collaborating on a website and smartphone app that brings together all the treatable types of intellectual disabilities (ID). In 2012 the number was 81, increasing to 89 in 2014, and by 2021, they had identified 116 types of treatable intellectual disabilities.

The web site can be found at **www.treatable-id.org**

You will see on the site how to diagnose and treat all these conditions.

There definitely is an overlap between these conditions and some types of autism.

A good example is cerebral folate transport deficiency, one of several causes of ID that relates to folate – all of which are treatable. Roger, a regular reader of my blog, used to have cerebral folate deficiency, but now it is treated. He is a new Roger.

Another example I like is biotin deficiency, because I wrote a post in 2014 called Biotin/Biotinidase Deficiency in Autism and perhaps Autistic Partial Biotin Deficiency (APBD)?

Biotin is vitamin B7 and is very important for your brain. Biotinidase is an enzyme that helps recycle biotin to be reused by the body, so it does not just rely on fresh biotin from what you eat every day.

I referred to a study on the Greek island of Crete, where the researchers studied 187 children and identified 13 whose lab results suggested something strange was going on with biotin. When they did the further tests for biotin deficiency, which is usually caused by deficiency in biotinidase, they could find nothing unusual with biotinidase.

Nonetheless, they implemented the standard therapy for biotin/biotinidase deficiency. This involved large doses of oral biotin, which is very cheap and seemingly harmless.

The researchers found that 7 of the 13 made clear advances. This indicates that they suffered from a biotin deficiency, but not a biotinidase deficiency.

The part that still remains is my mind is patient #1.

> "For those benefiting from biotin intervention, the most impressive outcome centered on a 42 month-old boy whose severe ASD was completely ameliorated following biotin intervention. This patient was subsequently followed for 5 years, and cessation of biotin intervention (or placebo replacement) resulted in the rapid return of ASD-like symptomatology. This patient currently attends public school without any clinical sequelae and remains on biotin at 20 mg/d."

How cool is that?

Some of the doctor readers of my blog have pondered the question as to why all children with intellectual disability, or indeed severe autism, are not routinely screened for these 116 types of treatable-ID.

Sadly it comes down to money. The diagnostic yield is just too low to make it worth the bother. Tell that to the parents of the little boy in Crete, whose severe autism was made to vanish.

Vascular resistance and hypoperfusion in some autism

People with vascular dementia exhibit progressive loss of cognitive function; this can develop acutely, sub-acutely and frequently step-wise, after multiple strokes. Vascular dementia is caused by reduced blood supply to the brain due to diseased blood vessels.

Increasing cerebral blood flow and indeed increasing the amount of oxygen in the blood supply are potential methods to improve cognitive function in the elderly and potentially in others.

There are no medications approved specifically for prevention or treatment of vascular dementia, but often partially effective Alzheimer's drugs are used.

More broadly in people who have not had a stroke but for some reason have reduced cerebral blood flow there are many possible therapies. In essence you want to reduce vascular resistance to the blood, so it is able to flow more freely.

Very extensive research has been carried out at Harvard to look at the benefit from the flavanols found in cocoa. Trials have shown that dietary cocoa flavanols reverse age-related memory decline and Mars have already commercialized a product called CocoaVia. It is well known that cocoa has antioxidant properties and that oxidative stress is a feature of both aging and most neurological disease. Cocoa flavanols were originally targeted because they are associated with good cardiovascular health.

It has been shown that coca flavanols induce vasodilation by activation of the nitric oxide (NO) system.

The subject of nitric oxide is dealt with more fully elsewhere in this book. The subject is not yet fully understood in the literature. Drugs like nitroglycerin are used in people with serious heart conditions because if taken during a heart attack they very quickly produce nitric oxide (NO), which will widen the blood vessels to ease the flow of blood and improve the outcome.

It is possible to affect the nitric oxide (NO) system without actually producing more NO. In effect, you just make better use of the existing NO, which seems to be the case with cocoa flavanols. This subject is not fully understood.

Another food that works via the nitric oxide system is beetroot juice, widely used to improve exercise endurance in sportsmen. In endurance sports like cycling a limiting factor on performance is how much oxygen you can get into your blood. You either want the volume flow rate of blood being circulated to increase or increase the amount of oxygen in a given volume of blood. A glass of beetroot juice increases the amount of nitric oxide in your blood and so reduces vascular resistance. It produces a measurable drop in blood pressure.

In medical terminology reduced blood flow to the brain is called hypoperfusion; it is measurable by MRI. Hypoperfusion is a feature of Alzheimer's and also some autism.

In a Rotterdam study that looked at cerebral blood flow (CBF) velocity and dementia, it was found that the greater the velocity the lower the risk of dementia. Low velocity was associated with both those with dementia and those about to develop it.

Researchers have measured the effect of cocoa consumption of cerebral blood flow (CBF) and it peaks in just under two hours post consumption.

In autism, studies have shown cerebral perfusion abnormalities that are region-specific. It has been suggested that this is related to cognitive dysfunction and underlying abnormal behavior patterns. It has also been found that unlike in neurotypical brains where blood vessels are stable, thereby ensuring a stable distribution of blood, "in the autism brain, the cellular structure of blood vessels continually fluctuates, which results in circulation that is fluctuating and, ultimately, neurologically limiting," according to Professor Patricia Whitaker-Azmitia.

In my therapy I did include agmatine, which will increase endothelial NOS (eNOS), the enzyme that increases the release of nitric oxide, which will increase blood flow through blood vessels. Agmatine is already present in your body and has long been considered as a possible therapy in psychiatry. Other readers of my blog reported good effects ranging from self-treating Aspies to doctors treating their child with autism. I found it very effective against lethargy, both physical and intellectual.

Some nootropic drugs, the ones supposed to make you more clever, work by reducing vascular resistance and so improving cerebral blood flow (CBF). One such is vinpocetine, sold as both a supplement and a drug.

Types of autism

People do try and classify autism by type. There are many terms and often they are used inconsistently.

Classic "Kanner's" Autism

We have already come across Kanner. In 1943 Leo Kanner, an Austrian-born psychiatrist working at Johns Hopkins University in Baltimore, published a paper called *Autistic Disturbances of Affective Contact* in which he described eight boys and three girls with what he called autism.

Even though Kanner's 11 cases from 1943 included some that could not be described as severe, when people today refer to Kanner's autism they mean severe autism.

For all practical purposes, today:

Classic autism = Kanner's Autism = Early onset severe autism

For the record, from his landmark paper in 1943, Kanner's subject #1, later identified as Donald Triplet, grew up, went to college, learned to drive and was a keen golfer. Not really a case of what today we would call Classic or Kanner's autism.

Regressive or not

Early onset autism is the name given when a child appears different from birth. His autism may well appear to get more severe during early childhood, but differences were always there.

Many people's autism has cycles bringing good days and more challenging days.

Regressive autism is something more pronounced; it is used to describe young children who have achieved their early developmental milestones and then, perhaps after a viral infection, begin to lose key skills. They might lose language skills, social skills and even toileting skills. After a few months they are quite different; they developed regressive autism

A small number of children are late-regressive, when they are three to five years old before the regression takes place.

Childhood disintegrative disorder (CDD), also known as Heller's syndrome, is the extreme regressive autism. It typically occurs after three years of normal development and the child may even notice the regression himself. CDD is very rare and is also not a biological diagnosis. As with most other types of autism, CDD mainly affects boys, rather than girls.

It can be very difficult for some parents to judge whether their child has regressive autism or not. For others it can be obvious.

By syndrome

Numerous genetic syndromes have been identified that can have autism among their symptoms, the most common ones being Fragile X, Rett syndrome and Down syndrome. There are also extremely rare conditions like Pitt Hopkins syndrome.

There are syndromes yet to be given a name, they can be called SWANs (Syndrome Without A Name). Undoubtedly there are also yet to be identified syndromes.

The syndromes that have been identified tend to be genetic and commonly also have noticeable physical features. Before the era of genetic testing, the physical features alone were used for diagnosis.

Facial recognition software (Face2Gene) developed in Israel can accurately identify many single gene autisms, using a smartphone.

In some advanced countries, clinicians will seek to rule out Fragile X in every case of severe autism. The test is widely available. In most countries little testing is carried out.

Children with Rett syndrome will invariably be girls because male fetuses with the disorder rarely survive to term.

Fragile X syndrome is twice as prevalent in males as females, and males are much more severely affected. Fragile X is a disorder which occurs as a result of a mutation of the fragile X mental retardation 1 (FMR1) gene on the X chromosome. We all have 46 chromosomes in our cells, two of which are sex chromosomes. In females, there are two Xs; in males there is one X and one Y. Females therefore have two copies of the FMR1 gene and so at least one is likely to be fully functional. This explains the protection females have and why if a brother and sister both have Fragile X, the boy will be much more disabled than his sister.

Down syndrome (DS) is caused by the presence of all, or part, of a third copy of chromosome 21. This leads to the over-expression of 300–500 genes (you only have 22,000 genes in total). Down syndrome is far more common in the US than in Europe; this is because in the US two thirds of DS pregnancies are terminated, whereas in Europe often more than 90% are terminated. Screening the fetus for DS is standard practice.

Some children with DS can be non-verbal and exhibit many features of autism. DS is itself a wide spectrum. DS is a biological diagnosis whereas autism is just an observational diagnosis.

Autism can be caused by both over-expression and under-expression of certain genes.

Smith Lemli Opitz syndrome (SLOS) is caused by a mutation in an enzyme involved in cholesterol synthesis usually leading to very low cholesterol levels. SLOS is characterized by physical differences, mild MR/ID and features of autism. It can be treated by dietary cholesterol, antioxidants and statins. Yes, statins – the ones older people take to lower cholesterol. Simvastatin increases the expression of the DHCR7 gene, which has lost its function in SLOS.

SLOS is caused by having a mutation in both copies of the DHCR7 gene. This causes lack of an enzyme which is needed to make cholesterol.

One parent sent me the results of his son's whole exome sequencing and this raised a question. What happens if you have a mutation in just one copy of DHCR7? Can you have partial SLOS? Is this a factor in his son's severe autism? I would check cholesterol levels, for a start.

By single gene dysfunction

When a single gene causes autism it tends to become a syndrome; but there are a growing number of so-called "autism genes" where it is known that dysfunctions can lead to autism.

Tuberous sclerosis complex (TSC) is a condition caused by one of two dysfunctional genes TSC1 or TSC2. TSC is associated with autism.

Shank3 is a gene widely studied by autism researchers. It plays a key role in synapse formation and dendritic spine maturation; this is basically where brain cells form connections with each other. Mutations in this gene are not surprisingly associated with autism.

By physical abnormality

Autism is not normally thought of as something you can identify using an MRI scan of the brain, although in most countries people receiving an autism diagnosis never receive an MRI investigation.

One physical abnormality that will very likely cause autistic behaviors, is when all or part of the corpus callosum is missing, a condition called agenesis of the corpus callosum (AgCC). The corpus callosum is a thick tract of nerve fibers that link the left and right side of the brain.

AgCC varies from mild to severe depending on how much damage there is. Without an MRI it would usually be diagnosed as classic autism. AgCC is rare, affecting about 1 in 4,000 people. In theory you can diagnose AgCC before birth by ultrasound.

A friend of mine from business school has a son with agenesis of the corpus callosum.

By channelopathy

There is a section dedicated to channelopathies in this book. If you have autism, you very likely have a channelopathy – you just do not know which one(s). Channelopathies cause many conditions ranging from epilepsy to cystic fibrosis. This is a somewhat daunting area of science and it involves both ion channels and transporters; when they go wrong it is called a channelopathy.

The pleasant-sounding Timothy syndrome causes autism, among other symptoms. It is a syndrome caused by mutations in a single gene called CACNA1C. This gene produces part of an ion channel, in this case the calcium channel $Ca_v1.2\ \alpha\ 1$ subunit. The mutations cause delayed channel closing and result in increased cellular excitability. The prognosis is very poor, but the logical treatment is to block/close that special ion channel.

Italian researchers from the beautiful city of Perugia have suggested classifying people with autism and/or epilepsy by their channelopathies. (e.g., K_vx.y-channelASD and likewise Na_vx.y-channelASD, Ca_vx.y-channelASD; etc.)

So, somebody with Dravet syndrome (epilepsy and autism caused by a sodium ion channel dysfunction), would become $Na_v1.1$ channelASD-channelepsy.

Somebody with Timothy syndrome but without epilepsy would be $Ca_v1.2$ channelASD.

By affected signaling pathway

Signaling pathways are another very complex area that can be simplified. These pathways are key to understanding and treating many biological dysfunctions, resulting in anything from cancer to diabetes, to autism.

For example, over active mTOR pathway is very much implicated in some autism and epilepsy.

PAK1 signaling is implicated in some autism and schizophrenia, but also in prostate cancer. So, a future prostate cancer drug could be re-purposed for PAK1 autism.

RASopathies are a group of conditions where mutations in genes that alter the RAS subfamily of proteins. RAS disorders can lead to autism and intellectual disability but also to RAS-dependent cancer.

Noonan syndrome is one RASopathy. It is associated with autism and learning difficulties. It has some tell-tale physical signs such as a short stature, large head and wide set eyes. Unfortunately, it is associated with congenital heart defects.

My favourite unifying framework

Some researchers from Johns Hopkins came up with a simplifying view that an imbalance of signaling pathways activity leads to autism. They split autism into two groups: hyperactive pro-growth signaling pathways (big babies with big heads) and hypoactive pro-growth signaling pathways (small babies with small heads).

The paper is called *Characterizing Autism Spectrum Disorders by Key Biochemical Pathways*. It is easy to find.

Imbalance of Signaling Pathway Activity Leads to Autism

	HYPER-ACTIVE PRO-GROWTH SIGNALING PATHWAYS	**HYPO-ACTIVE PRO-GROWTH SIGNALING PATHWAYS**
	BDNF mTOR ERK wnt	BDNF mTOR ERK wnt
	⬇	⬇
BRAIN	Macrocephaly	Microcephaly
NETWORK	Overconnectivity Too many synapses	Underconnectivity Too few synapses
CELLULAR	Increased proliferation and survival	Decreased proliferation and survival
SUB-CELLULAR	Increased dendritic spine growth	Decreased dendritic spine growth
PROTEOMIC	Excessive protein synthesis	Decreased protein synthesis
	⬇	⬇

AUTISM SPECTRUM DISORDERS

I think it is quite a useful framework to at least start the process of a biological diagnosis.

Neglect – institutional autism

One surprising cause of autistic behaviors, is perhaps the worst of all, since it is entirely avoidable. Research took place as to why so many children brought up in Romanian orphanages in the 1990s and the later adopted by families in Western Europe and North America, exhibited autistic behaviors. One study in the UK found that 25% of adoptees exhibited ADHD and 12% had autistic behaviors.

A more rigorous long-term study was later carried out by Charles Nelson, a professor of neuroscience and psychiatry at Harvard Medical School. He set up a project to study the effect of neglect on a child's development. He believed that significant neglect can be profoundly harmful to a young child's development. He has proved this through his Bucharest Early Intervention Project (BEIP) which compared the effect of living in an orphanage compared to high quality foster care.

BEIP was not studying autism, but Nelson showed that long term neglect can affect physical brain development leading to permanent damage, visible on MRI brain scans years later.

I have been to Romania many times. You might wonder why there seem to have been so many Romanian orphans. In 1966 Nicolae Ceausescu, the Communist Dictator, outlawed access to abortion and contraception in a bid to boost the country's population. In 1981 he banned further foreign debt and insisted on repaying all the country's existing foreign debts, achieved by 1989, but at a great cost to the economy and people's level of income. Now it is clear why so many children ended up abandoned in orphanages.

Institutional autism unfortunately is a genuine condition and has to be a consideration for those adopting internationally.

Polygenic disorders that overlap – autism(s), schizophrenia(s), bipolar(s) and ADHD(s)

One clear message from the more sophisticated research into neuropsychiatric disorders is that they are generally associated with variances in the expression of numerous different genes, making them polygenic.

What I find interesting is that there is a substantial overlap in the genes that are mis-expressed across different neuropsychiatric disorders. This is further proof, if it was needed, that the observational diagnoses used by psychiatrists are rather primitive.

Individual people will have a near unique set of genetic variances that make their symptoms slightly different to everyone else. However, it is highly likely that discrete biological dysfunctions will exist across the diagnoses. So, for example, elevated intracellular chloride will be found in some autism, some schizophrenia and was recently identified even in Parkinson's disease. A calcium channelopathy affecting the channel $Ca_v1.2$ would be found in some autism and some bipolar.

Eventually you would dispose of the old observational diagnoses like bipolar and give the biological diagnosis. Then you might have the same drugs being used in a person with "bipolar" and another with "autism". When all this will happen is no time soon.

In the meantime, people interested in autism can benefit from the research into the other neuropsychiatric disorders. These other disorders can be much better researched, partly because they usually concern adults who are fully verbal and have typical IQ. In many cases there are both hypo and hyper cases (both too much and too little of some biological factor) in these disorders.

Also of interest is that the same unusual gene expression in schizophrenia/bipolar is linked to creativity and the autism genes are linked to intelligence. This is put forward as an explanation as to why evolution has conserved rather than erased neuropsychiatric disorders. Girl finds creative actor charming, in spite of his mood disorder. Girl finds quirky, but wealthy, computer programmer attractive. These are examples of natural selection.

Assortative mating is when Aspie girl choses Aspie boy to then produce Aspie kids and more likely than non-Aspie couples, kids with classic autism.

Genes vs the environment

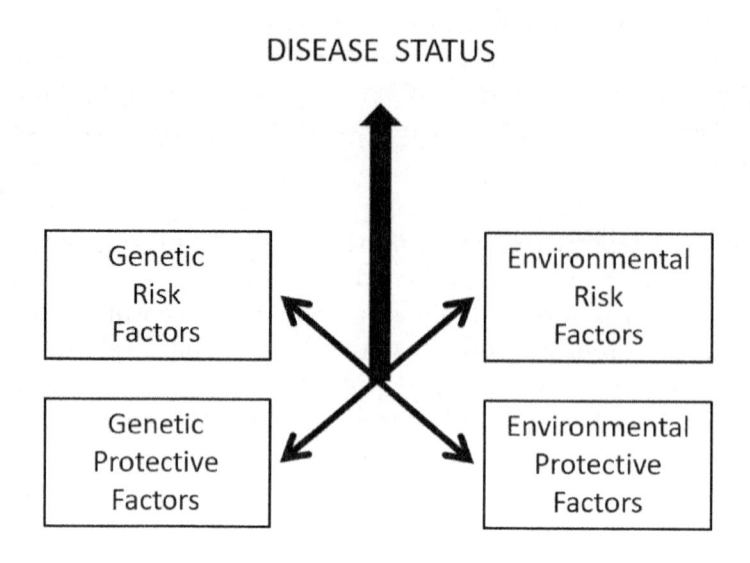

DISEASE STATUS

```
┌─────────────┐         ┌─────────────┐
│   Genetic   │         │Environmental│
│    Risk     │         │    Risk     │
│   Factors   │         │   Factors   │
└─────────────┘         └─────────────┘

┌─────────────┐         ┌─────────────┐
│   Genetic   │         │Environmental│
│  Protective │         │  Protective │
│   Factors   │         │   Factors   │
└─────────────┘         └─────────────┘
```

The spectrum of human diseases is caused by a multitude of genetic and environmental factors acting together. In certain conditions such as Down syndrome, genetic factors predominate, while in infections, for example, environmental factors predominate.

Some apparently entirely genetic conditions may require a trigger.

A mother wrote to me about her son with 16p11.2 microdeletion, which just means he is missing a bit of his DNA on chromosome 16. This can cause autism, MR/ID and epilepsy. Some people have this same 16p11.2 microdeletion, but are entirely unaffected. In the mouse model of 16p11.2 microdeletion the mouse has normal behavior until given a stressor, at which point it behaves like an "autistic" mouse.

Most chronic non-communicable conditions such as autism, schizophrenia and cancer are caused by an interaction of both genetic and environmental factors.

Some genetic and environmental factors are protective.

The environment and epigenetic change

Some environmental influences, like smoking or pollution, can also become genetic in that heritable epigenetic markers can become tagged to a specific gene. This impacts whether the gene is turned on or off, at any point in time.

Multifactorial vs polygenic inheritance

Multifactorial inheritance diseases show familial clustering, but do not conform to any recognized pattern of single gene inheritance. They are determined by the cumulative effects of many genes together with the effect of environmental factors.

These conditions show a definite familial tendency but the incidence in close relatives of affected individuals is usually around 2-4%, instead of the much higher figures that would be seen if these conditions were caused by mutations in single genes (25–50%).

Examples of disorders of multifactorial inheritance are asthma, autism, schizophrenia and diabetes.

Polygenic inheritance involves the inheritance of the disorder being determined by many genes, with each gene exerting a small additive effect. No single gene is enough to trigger the disorder.

The biggest future autism risk is likely to be a previous occurrence.

There are ways to actively promote protective factors, but a risk will remain.

So what is autism?

Most people's autism is of unknown cause (idiopathic) and this is most likely to be polygenic, but highly likely to have some environmental influences making it multifactorial.

What is interesting and potentially relevant to therapy is that the polygenic footprint of autism overlaps with those causing other neuropsychiatric diseases like bipolar, schizophrenia and even ADHD.

As you broaden the definition of autism and so move the threshold you will eventually diagnose everyone as having autism; because we all have some autism genes.

If you then consider all these overlapping diagnoses, you find that you are looking at more than ten percent of the population, depending on where you get the data from.

Autism at the center of a cloud of genetically-related observation diagnoses

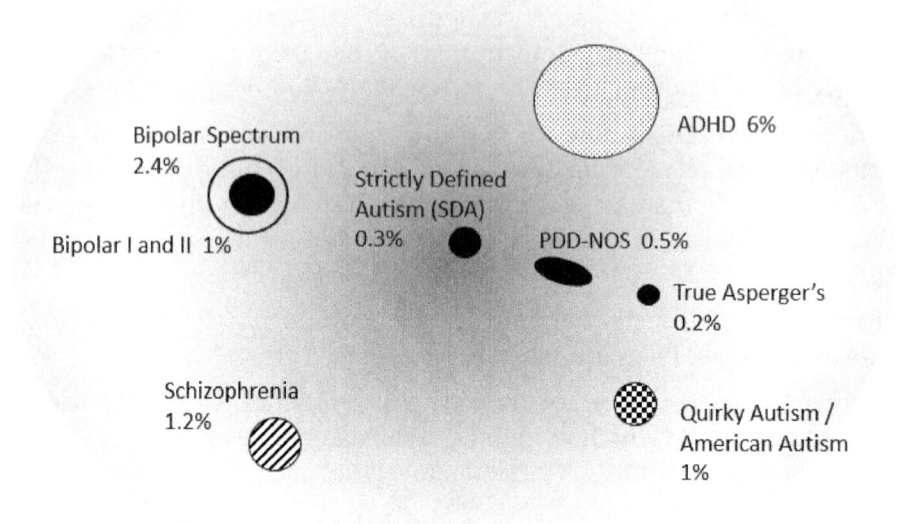

Bipolar Spectrum 2.4%

Bipolar I and II 1%

Strictly Defined Autism (SDA) 0.3%

ADHD 6%

PDD-NOS 0.5%

True Asperger's 0.2%

Schizophrenia 1.2%

Quirky Autism / American Autism 1%

Percent of the population affected by various disorders genetically overlapping to strictly define autism (SDA). Estimates of prevalence vary widely by country and study.

If you start with autism from the 1970s and call this Strictly Defined Autism (SDA) you can then move along the bell-shaped liability curve. This brings you to what used to be called PDD-NOS (Pervasive Developmental Disorder-Not Otherwise Specified) and then true Asperger's syndrome (those with a high IQ). Finally, you will arrive at what might be called Quirky Autism; these people have some of the characteristics used to define autism, but not to the degree that they are disabling.

Condition	Prevalence
Strictly Defined Autism	0.3%
True Asperger's	0.2%
Old PDD-NOS	0.5%
Quirky Autism	1.0%
Total modern ASD	**2.0%**
ADHD in children	6.0%
Schizophrenia in adults	1.2%
Bipolar I	0.6%
Bipolar II	0.4%
Subthreshold BP	1.4%
Bipolar Spectrum	2.4%
Total all above conditions	**11.6%**

People with SDA, PDD-NOS, Asperger's and Quirky Autism may have signs of ADHD, schizophrenia or bipolar. They may be below the current threshold for a diagnosis of say schizophrenia, but have tendencies nonetheless.

Autism prevalence

Autism prevalence matters because it then lets you put your case of autism into perspective.

Everyone who has a genuine autism diagnosis is a serious case, whether they have mild or severe autism. People ever so slightly different to the norm are the ones who can feel most different. The kids who get bullied at school are not usually the non-verbal ones sitting with an assistant, they are the ones who are just a tiny bit different. A person with non-verbal autism and intellectual disability can be very happy and not bothered in the slightest about his autism; most likely he does not understand what the word autism means.

If your child with severe autism gets bullied at school, something is seriously wrong with the school. Find a different school.

The person with high IQ and Asperger's-type autism may suffer from acute anxiety and be deeply troubled that he does not seem to fit into the wider world.

Once you begin to see where your case fits in, then you can accept it and deal with it. If you choose to, you can even treat it.

The quality of autism statistics is woeful, in great part due to how the diagnosis has been changed over the years. What was called autism in 1970s and 80s is quite different to that of the early 2020s.

A very well-known researcher in this area is Dr Éric Fombonne a French psychiatrist and epidemiologist formerly at McGill University. He carried out some high-quality studies that give a useful insight into what lies within the Autistic Spectrum.

Within the bounds of fairly tightly defined ASD it looked like about 30% have actual strictly defined autism, 20% have Asperger's and the remaining 50% have something in between them that used to be called PDD-NOS (Pervasive Development Disorder Not Otherwise Specified).

When it comes to Mental Retardation/Intellectual Disability (MR/ID), it is 0% in Asperger's, 10% in PDD-NOS and 70% in autism. Fombonne's studies were done in 2001 and 2005. In my blog I combined the study data into a single set of results.

What has happened, particularly in the United States, is that what was called autism is now called severe autism, to make space for all the new milder variants. In older times, and even today in less developed countries, SDA (strictly defined autism) was the only kind of autism.

Since Fombonne's studies, ever more people have been diagnosed with milder and milder forms of ASD. I think Fombonne's data correspond to 1% of the population having ASD. In the US, in children, they are now way above this rate, but they are including such mild forms to the extent that some people diagnosed with the "disability" of autism are themselves saying they are not disabled; rather it is their super-power. Clearly there is a now a degree of over-diagnosis and this is the "quirky/nerdy" autism variant. It may result in eating disorders and getting mercilessly teased at school, so it is a serious problem.

I even get comments on my blog from people saying their child has very mild, American-type, autism.

What is concerning is that not all of the increase in autism diagnosis can be explained by ever widening definition of autism. Something else is going on.

Given the biological underpinnings of autism, is not surprising that the prevalence of more severe autism is increasing. The same mechanisms that apply to autoimmune disease like asthma and also many types of cancer mean that modern living will increase prevalence. There is too much cumulative damage from environmental effects, much mediated by epigenetic changes passed down the generation.

There is also the impact of the hologenome concept of evolution; this considers a human as a community with all the symbiotic microbes in the environment that he has evolved with. This means that changes in the microbiota inside your body are now affecting your immunologic, hormonal and metabolic homeostasis. So due to the lack of certain gut bacteria that you were never exposed to, in your super clean farm animal-free modern life, your immune system is no longer as well tuned as that of your great grandparents.

If you live in polluted city, smoke cigarettes or marijuana, or work in a chemical plant you are accumulating significant damage to your DNA that will be passed down through the generations, via epigenetic tags.

Then you add incremental risk factors like the rise in cesarian delivery (missing out on oxytocin from the mother and her bacteria, during birthing), older parents, use of formula milk, stress during pregnancy etc, the net effect means more autism.

If you overload the fetus with genetic damage and remove the protection accumulated over generations from the hologenome/microbiome there will be consequences, autism is just one.

Strictly defined autism (SDA) and mild autism

Many carers of those with Strictly Defined Autism (SDA) get upset by people with mild autism saying they too have autism. This was never an issue when the term Asperger's was always used. The two extremes of this spectrum can appear so very different and the problems people face are completely different.

However, you will see that many people have both extremes of autism in their wider family and this is not a coincidence. The two ends of the spectrum are indeed biologically related. In the media you can read about a man in his 40s saying how his life now makes sense after his recent autism diagnosis and then he almost casually refers to the fact that his late son had severe autism. Apparently, he did not make the connection, or he needed a psychiatrist to make it for him. Autism is no more than a label; you are still the same person you were before you were labelled.

You will also come across people who have a child with Strictly Defined Autism and in their extended family there have been suicides, where an intelligent, but quirky, person completed university and got a job, but never felt they fitted in and opted for an early exit.

Mild autism can have dire consequences, but most often does not. Most of the current and future generations with mild autism will be going to college, getting a job and having a family just like everyone else.

Severe autism is quite different; no college, no job, no driving a car, not having a family and it usually means a life-long struggle for whoever is doing the caring. This is sometimes not appreciated by people affected by mild autism, who may struggle with empathy at the best of times, without ever realizing it. In the days of the internet, where people can very publicly express thoughts and opinions, some comments can really upset the carers of those with severe autism. It is not a debate, because that requires informed open-minded participants on both sides. It is best to avoid reading the comments on articles in the mass media regarding autism, whichever side you are on – it will just drive you crazy.

GAME CHANGER

PETER LLOYD-THOMAS

Part 4

Treating Autism Using Personalized Medicine

Our gamechanger was bumetanide,
but yours may be something quite different.
How to find it?

Before getting into the details, there are some important points to emphasize.

There is no single cause of all autism; it is a very broad observational diagnosis that encompasses hundreds of different biological dysfunctions. There will likely never be a single treatment that works for everybody. Therapy needs to be personalized.

Science is far ahead of the medicine. Scientific journals contain thousands of research papers into autism and potential treatment; this is not reflected in what your doctor learnt at medical school.

Science shows autism is treatable, medicine still thinks it is not. Medicine seeks to apply treatments to well defined conditions; you run some tests and out pops the answer. Testing inside the brain is very limited. Blood tests do not necessarily reflect what is happening inside the brain and can give an entirely false picture. Testing spinal fluid would be much more insightful, but it requires a difficult procedure.

Polytherapy is the key. Find therapies that genuinely improve your specific type of autism; the combined effect of these multiple therapies can be impressive.

Treat individual features of autism. The research shows that there are many common features shares across different types of autism.

- Oxidative stress
- Neuroinflammation and activated microglia
- Impaired myelination
- Ion channel and transporter dysfunctions

Many other diseases share some of these features and so therapies from these conditions can be re-purposed for some types of autism.

The sooner you start the better the result will be. It is never too late to start treating troubling symptoms of autism, but the younger you start, the more profound the benefit is likely to be.

Parents avoid invasive testing. Taking samples of central spinal fluid, which do reflect what is happening inside the brain, and even having an MRI scan, rarely occurs. Some parents regret this when their child is much older and wonder what might have been. Some parents want invasive testing but cannot access it.

Genetic testing is still emerging. Whole Exome Sequencing and Whole Genome Sequencing can reveal the cause, or at least contributing factors, in about 30% of autism. Most typical people have 20–30 mutations in their DNA and when interpreting the results in someone with autism, great care is needed to understand which might be relevant. This interpretation is often poor. Having identified any possibly relevant genes, there is generally a reluctance to do anything about it, beyond diagnosis. The idea of targeting the affected gene using therapies suggested in the research literature is seen as fanciful, though it may well be possible.

I gave a 40-minute presentation on this subject, talking about the potential use of genetic testing in personalized medicine for autism. It is on my YouTube channel.

Insights from actually treating autism

One doctor/autism parent mentioned to me that readers need to be made aware that drug interventions for autism can take time to show effect and that since parents see their child every day, they may not notice such gradual changes and potentially throw away a drug that actually is effective in their case.

Some parents do not value small improvements, but if you combine five therapies, each providing a small improvement, the net effect can be substantial.

If you stop the therapy, is the effect lost? Albeit possibly gradually, and does the same benefit return when you restart the therapy?

As the child gets older, does the therapy continue to have value? I recall being asked by Dr Ben Ari, how do I know after eight years that my son still benefits from bumetanide? Every now and again we make a pause from bumetanide and see how he responds. How would you measure the response? I use how good my son is at his online math tutoring program as an objective measure of cognitive status. I also ask him in the afternoon what he had for lunch that day; without bumetanide he usually cannot answer.

Another doctor who was treating his own son with bumetanide and also low dose clonazepam for some years, told me that he ran out of clonazepam and decided to see if it still provided a benefit. He concluded that clonazepam was no longer needed. It is important to check; there is no point using drugs for the sake of it.

Some people find a positive effect is lost and they need to readjust their dosage. This seems quite common with sulforaphane.

As some readers have found, interactions between drugs and supplements mean that dosages may need to be adjusted. Low-dose clonazepam in particular has only a very narrow effective dosage range. Very many drugs, including verapamil, reduce the excretion rate of clonazepam and so increase the level in your blood. Vitamin E increases the metabolism of clonazepam.

An even more fundamental issue is whose interventions should you consider trying and where is the line between potentially helpful therapies and crank therapies.

I am surprised how different clinicians react to other people's therapies. For example, one US neurologist when introduced to my idea of potassium bromide as a therapy for autism and indeed its current use in Germany for pediatric epilepsy, thought the idea was very interesting and lamented not being able to try it. Another US neurologist's immediate reaction was "call child protective services". Both neurologists are well known autism doctors.

A few years after I raised the idea of potassium bromide as a therapy for autism, some French researchers patented the idea and started tests in mouse models of autism.

Navigating "Medical" Approaches to Treating Autism

Science-driven
  Open-minded
  Stumbled-upon is fine
  Nothing ruled in/out
  Bold but not foolish

Progressive
Mainstream Medicine
  Dr Chez, Dr Frye etc
  Kennedy Krieger Institute

Conservative
Mainstream Medicine
  FDA approved drugs, no off-label
  Behavioral therapy

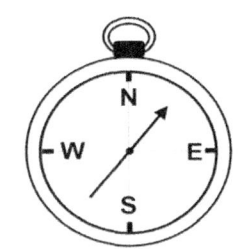

Complementary and
Alternative Medicine
  Naturopathy
  Homeopathy
  Traditional Chinese medicine
  Some dieticians

Protocols
  Nemecheck
  DAN!
  Yasko
  Klinghardt
  Culter (chelation)
  Neubrander (B12)
  Yu (parasites)
  Goldberg (SSRI +)
  etc ...

There are many widely shared approaches to treating autism, some are dietary like the gluten and casein free diet, the ketogenic diet or the popular GAPS diet. Some use dietary supplements like fish oil and vitamins. All approaches have their committed followers.

Most medical doctors are critical of any therapy claiming to treat autism. The few progressive mainstream doctors who do attempt to treat autism can be very disparaging about the methods used by others.

Some "protocols" that are put forward are presented as treating a very wide range of conditions (chronic pain, Alzheimer's etc), far beyond just autism and this does naturally raise suspicions. We should note that some conditions, with very different symptoms, do share similar underlying biology. You have to keep an open mind.

Mainstream medicine is by its very nature extremely conservative, cautious and slow moving. Different countries may practice very different mainstream therapies and some techniques take 20 years to become adopted from one continent to another. There is no single mainstream, even that varies.

Progressive mainstream medicine gradually pushes the boundaries. In the world of autism such practitioners are mainly in the United States and surprisingly in Italy.

Science driven autism therapy stretches beyond progressive mainstream medicine. It takes many years for ideas in the scientific research to become part of medicine. If you do not have a couple of decades to wait, you can choose to look at the science and identify what might eventually become medicine.

Applying an open mind to what might seem far-fetched alternative therapies can reveal alternative modes of action which are very much science based. Dr Yu has therapies for autism based on drugs normally used for treating parasites. It turns out that some anti-parasite drugs like ivermectin, mebendazole and suramin have modes of action that really should benefit some types of autism, but may have nothing to do with parasites.

If someone finds their Alpha Lipoic Acid (ALA) chelation therapy beneficial, this is not a surprise, because ALA is a potent antioxidant and will benefit those with oxidative stress (autism, mitochondrial disease, cardiovascular disease etc). It might have nothing to do with chelating metals from your brain. Antioxidants are widely used in German-based medicine and ALA is seen as standard treatment for diabetics in many countries. It increases insulin sensitivity and reduces neuropathy. In the English-speaking world, doctors are totally unaware of this and see ALA as some supplement placebo.

The DAN! (Defeat Autism Now) protocol was very popular and many people in the US still have a "DAN Doctor" who is applying the ideas of Sidney Baker, Jon Pangborn and others. DAN! was a project of the Autism Research Institute (ARI). DAN! used mainly dietary supplements rather than prescription drugs. DAN! closed down in 2011, but ARI still exists. Some DAN! doctors rebranded and became MAPS (Medical Academy of Pediatric Special Needs) doctors.

In North America there are doctors of functional medicine, integrative medicine and holistic medicine. There are naturopaths, homeopaths, doctors of osteopathic medicine (look for the DO after the name and not MD) and doctors of chiropractic medicine (DC after their name).

What is clear is that most autism parents prefer the idea of special diets, supplements and the simple protocols like that promoted by

Nemechek, which are often claimed to work for everyone. I do not think many turn to Dr Chez and his book on medically managing autism; he does not claim to offer a simple answer and that is what parents want and are able to handle.

I am surprised how popular Nemechek is and that people have even informally translated his book into different languages, which then get shared virally. It is like the new DAN! protocol. Based on feedback on my blog, I should note that his ideas do indeed seem to work for some people, but others report a negative effect and many no effect at all.

You would think that having a doctor of medicine (MD) is best, but then nothing much about autism is taught at medical school. Nemechek is a DO (Doctor of Osteopathy), not an MD.

A common feature of many autism doctors who have their special protocol is that they can get quite upset with parents for whom their approach is not successful. Some then blame the parents for the failure.

Autism is so heterogeneous that there can never be a single approach that works for everyone. When you read that a doctor says that his therapy works in 90+% of cases, you really should beware. The prolific Memantine/Namenda prescribing doctor was one of these.

I would have thought a clever neurologist like Dr Chez would be best, but I take note that many people have found an open-minded psychiatrist who helps them trial off-label therapies is best. This seems to be particularly true of adults with mild autism/Asperger's.

There is no one-stop-shop for treating autism, no matter how big your budget is. You have to navigate your own path, rather than just hoping for the best.

Do no harm vs do some good

Most doctors take some form of the Hippocratic Oath.

Primum non nocere (first do no harm) is actually still a guiding principle for physicians.

When it comes to treating autism, the balance is so far towards risk aversion and fear of doing any harm, that they often do not even try to do some good.

My autism treatment goal is to do some good, but without doing any harm.

It has to be understood that the biggest risk is likely the risk of doing nothing. Go and visit some adults with untreated severe non-verbal autism and intellectual disability.

In many countries the fear of doing harm is actually harm to the doctor's reputation and indeed license, rather than harm to their patient.

Doctors actually report their colleagues who try and treat autism to the regulator to try and force them to stop. This is why in the United Kingdom you will struggle to find a single doctor who now attempts to treat autism. Even finding doctors willing to treat those with severe autism for any comorbid medical condition can be extremely difficult.

In the United States many autism doctors are not MDs (doctors of medicine), they are a DO (doctor of osteopathy) or an ND (doctor of naturopathy).

Autism is medical, but behavioral strategies can be very useful

This book is mainly about treating the symptoms of autism and intellectual disability (ID) using personalized medicine. For five years prior to embarking on that mission, our house looked like an early intervention centre using behavioral methods. A very good example to show the benefit of the behavioral approach vs the biological approach is the subject of compulsive behaviors.

A hallmark feature of autism is inflexible thinking and ritualistic behavior, which affects people across breadth of the spectrum. It can appear as a cute behavior, especially in young children, but it may build into quite a disruptive one.

When I was studying engineering at university there were no people with Asperger's syndrome (now called Level 1 autism), because they had not started to diagnose it. Today I expect that 10% of the class might be able to get the diagnosis.

A ritualistic behavior of an undiagnosed Aspie that sticks in my mind from back then concerned Anchor brand butter from New Zealand. I lived in a large apartment for eight students. One of the girls came up to me and said "Do you know that Ian will only eat

Anchor butter?" This really bugged her. To most students, butter is butter and margarine is margarine; most often neither would be in the fridge anyway! This behavior harms no one, but it can be much worse.

I was recently told about a young adult with autism, sometimes living with his Dad. Among his obsessions to satisfy is to park the car in exactly the same spot near where they live. If the spot is not available, they drive around in the hope that someone comes back to take their car and vacate the special place.

You regularly hear about young children with autism who will only drink from a specific novelty cup, or eat a specific brand of processed food. Disaster strikes and the novelty cup has got lost, the five spares ones in the cupboard have been used up. Then the appeal goes out on social media for help. We are told that without the magic cup the child will not drink at all.

You will hear stories from autism mothers about how they must always drive to the park the same way, or their toddler will have a meltdown in the car. I am thinking big mistake; you are taking the easy option now but building up a huge problem for the future.

I remember we had exactly the same issue with Monty, then aged three. From where we lived, he went to the park by pushchair. You could turn left from the house or right, it did not matter, you could still get to the park. Monty started to insist on a specific direction and his very caring assistant would completely ignore his request. This was exactly the right response and by applying this method throughout early childhood, we have an adult without these rigid inflexible behaviors.

Once you get to adulthood it is very difficult to change obsessive behaviors that have been allowed to develop throughout childhood.

These behaviors might seem trivial at the time when they first emerge, but over the years they can become a burden for both the individual and the whole family. I recall one family where they always have to go on holiday to exactly the same place every year, nothing can vary. It did not have to be this way.

There are many types of compulsion and I recall discussing this with one autism mother/doctor. She told me she never thought she would have to be thinking about whether something was a tic or a stereotypy and how to treat it. It is important to recognise a tic early on, because you can usually treat it and if you do not, it can become problem. A good example of a common repetitive behavior is compulsive hair pulling, called trichotillomania. Then there is also hair twirling. In the world of autism this would be called stimming. People develop unique stims, my son wanted to pick all the wild flowers growing in cracks in the pavement/side walk. Stims can get in the way of whatever the task at hand is. It could be walking down the hill to the park, or it could be trying to learn something at school.

Many people's trichotillomania disappears when then they take the antioxidant NAC and many autistic kids stims dramatically reduce when they take NAC.

For some people the problem is a tic, not stereotypy. NAC is not going to do anything for a tic. As my doctor friend told me, you need to know your tics from your stims.

Some compulsive behaviors respond well to a behavioral therapy while others need a biological fix. A degree of common sense is required. If your little boy with severe autism gets obsessed with hair twirling, cut his hair short. By the time it grows long enough to twirl, he will have forgotten all about this desire.

Tics are important because they can be a sign of an underlying problem. In the US people with autism are quite often prescribed an antipsychotic drug like Abilify or Risperidone. One side effect of these drugs can be tardive dyskinesia, which can appear as facial tics like lip-smacking, tongue thrusting and rapid blinking. On cessation of the drug, the tics may fade away if you are lucky, but for some they are permanent.

Tics may be a key symptom of an autoimmune reaction going on inside the brain; a good example being PANS (pediatric acute-onset neuropsychiatric syndrome). These tics are a warning sign and if treated promptly they will fade away in a week or two.

In the case of Monty, aged 19 at the time of writing, we have dealt with rigid behaviors by never letting them become entrenched. We have dealt with stereotypy using NAC every day. Hair twirling is seen as a sign for a haircut, which is a favourite activity for the record. Verbal and motor tics have emerged on a handful of occasions and were promptly treated like a PANS flare up. Scripting, which is when a person with autism repeats some favourite words or phrases, never became a big issue and arises from time to time.

Autism is not static

I recall my doctor mother telling me after I developed the early version of my Polypill therapy, "Okay, now you can stop".

If autism was a static condition that would have been excellent advice. Unfortunately, the condition may evolve and new symptoms appear. In some cases, the new symptoms are much more concerning than the early ones.

There is a phenomenon which I called "double tap autism". This is when a child with early onset autism overcomes many of their initial challenges only to receive a knock-out blow by a later event a few years later. It is a really cruel twist of fate.

For some people this new burden is caused by the triggering of an always present genetic anomaly, like a mutation in a calcium ion channel. For other people it is an autoimmune condition, which really should be treatable. For some people it can be an emotional trauma. Regardless of the cause, a downwards spiral of behaviors then follows.

Very often in severe autism, epilepsy develops during childhood. Quite often the anti-epileptic drugs used actually moderate the child's autism. This is a cloud with a silver lining for some.

The biggest issue for most people is the development of self-injurious behavior (SIB) and aggression towards others. This is unfortunately a learned behavior and once it starts, it will almost inevitably appear again. For many parents the control of SIB becomes their overriding treatment goal.

Tics do appear in some children with autism as they get older. In my blog I did write about what I termed "Tourette's type autism". In this type of autism, where tics were always present, an Italian researcher showed that a significant number of children "recover" with no intervention; the autism just fades away. In some people with autism, they may develop acute onset tics. In my blog I term this as a PANS-like episode, which often responds to a short course of oral steroids. The tics can be either motor tics, like eye blinking, or verbal tics like in Tourette syndrome.

Sound sensitivity and misophonia, which are a common issue in all severities of autism, can get much worse. This is treatable.

Any personalized autism therapy is likely to change over time and may need short-term add on therapies to treat flare-ups.

I refer to my son's baseline therapy as his autism Polypill, but I also developed my Toolkit, to treat the various types of flare-ups that occurred over the years.

Acute onset OCD – PANS and PANDAS

Motor and/or verbal tics are a feature of PANS/PANDAS (Pediatric Acute-onset Neuropsychiatric Syndrome/ Pediatric Autoimmune Neuropsychiatric Disorder Associated with Streptococcal Infections).

In some previously neurotypical people, OCD can develop almost overnight and be accompanied by a loss of cognitive function and also some traits of autism. This condition is known as PANS/PANDAS and is treatable. Best results are found when treatment is not delayed.

People who have already been diagnosed with autism can also suffer acute onset OCD, which may appear as a regression, or autism flare-up. This can be a case of PANS/PANDAS and should be treatable.

Some people diagnosed with autism may rather simply have PANS/PANDAS. People with NMDA receptor encephalitis may end up being misdiagnosed with schizophrenia.

One Christmas after a viral infection, my son, then 12 years old, developed loud verbal tics for the first time in his life. Having already covered the research on PANS and PANDAS in my blog, I opted for a five-day course of prednisone. After a few days, the verbal tics faded away. A few years later a motor tic appeared, it was a kind of eye blinking, it responded to the same therapy and has not re-occurred.

It is definitely a good idea to be aware of the symptoms of PANS. I list the symptoms below from two different sources:

From the International OCD Foundation:
1. Acute sudden onset of OCD
2. Challenges with eating, and at the extreme end, anorexia

3. Sensory issues such as sensitivity to clothes, sound, and light
4. Handwriting noticeably deteriorates
5. Urinary frequency or bedwetting
6. Small motor skills deteriorate – a craft project from yesterday is now impossible to complete
7. Tics
8. Inattentive, distractible, unable to focus and has difficulties with memory
9. Overnight onset of anxiety or panic attacks over things that were no big deal a few days ago, such as thunderstorms or bugs
10. Suddenly unable to separate from their caregiver, or to sleep alone
11. Screaming for hours on end
12. Fear of germs and other more traditional-looking OCD symptoms

From the US National Institute of Mental Health

1. Severe separation anxiety (e.g., child can't leave parent's side or needs to sleep on floor next to parent's bed, etc.)
2. Generalized anxiety, which may progress to episodes of panic and a "terror-stricken look"
3. Motoric hyperactivity, abnormal movements, and a sense of restlessness
4. Sensory abnormalities, including hyper-sensitivity to light or sounds, distortions of visual perceptions, and occasionally, visual or auditory hallucinations
5. Concentration difficulties, and loss of academic abilities, particularly in math and visual-spatial areas
6. Increased urinary frequency and a new onset of bed-wetting
7. Irritability (sometimes with aggression) and emotional liability. Abrupt onset of depression can also occur, with thoughts about suicide.

8. Developmental regression, including temper tantrums, "baby talk" and handwriting deterioration (also related to motor symptoms)

Treatment

Compared to autism, a very refreshing approach is taken to treating PANS, at least in some places. The treatments include: -

Treatment with antibiotics to eradicate the infection, if it is still present.

Immune-based therapies such as

- Plasmapheresis
- Intravenous immunoglobulin (IVIG)
- Corticosteroids, such as prednisone

PANS/PANDAS are only recognized as genuine medical conditions in a minority of countries. There is a diagnostic test called the Cunningham Panel that is available in the US.

Breath holding

Breath holding is a common problem in Rett syndrome, but it also occurs in classic autism. It can be seen as a tic disorder; some might argue it is stereotypy. It is very concerning to parents.

Polydypsia

Polydypsia is compulsive drinking of fluids, usually water. It is a regular problem in severe autism and must be treated because it can become fatal. Drinking vast amounts of water causes low levels of sodium in your blood (hyponatremia) and your heart stops beating.

I wrote an entire blog post about it and how it can be treated. As with anything else in this book, just Google, in this instance "Polydypsia EpiphanyASD" if you want more information and links to the peer-reviewed research.

Epilepsy

Epilepsy is as complex and varied as autism. Usually, it is considered as a comorbidity that particularly can affect those with more severe autism.

I think it might be better considered as a progression of untreated autism in the same way that atopic dermatitis/eczema is the precursor to asthma. Studies have shown that treating people with atopic dermatitis using the mast cell stabilizer Ketotifen lowers the later incidence of asthma in this at-risk group.

In the same way many people with severe autism develop epilepsy around puberty. It would seem entirely plausible that if you modify the neuronal excitatory/inhibitory imbalance as part of autism therapy, you may well lower the incidence of future epilepsy.

Some epilepsy therapies have a secondary effect on moderating autism.

Many of the channelopathies in autism overlap with those known to be present in epilepsy.

Epilepsy deserves a book to itself. A vast amount is known in the research, just like in autism, but much is not translated into therapy. If my son had epilepsy, I would write a book on that subject as well.

Hypokalemic autistic sensory overload

Sensory overload is one well known feature of autism and often blamed for those meltdowns that can happen in public places. Some people blame the noise, some the lighting, but it comes down to not being able to deal with the sensory input. Some older children wear noise cancelling headphones, while others just use their hands to cover their ears.

At the start of my investigation, I looked into whether there are other kinds of sensory overload and indeed there are. I asked the next logical question as to whether these various sensory overloads might be connected.

I conducted a little experiment at home that seemed to confirm that these conditions may relate to the level of the electrolyte potassium and therapeutic improvement comes from producing a sharp increase in it. This suggests some kind of ion channel dysfunction.

The good news is that numerous other parents found the same very simple therapy worked in their child's autism. Troubling sensory issues just faded away. In some people the issues return without the therapy and for others the problem has just gone.

The two related conditions are Hypokalemic Periodic Paralysis (HPP) and Hypokalemic Sensory Overstimulation (HSO). In HPP falling levels of potassium trigger muscle weakness and paralysis; the symptoms disappear after taking an oral potassium supplement.

Hypokalemic sensory overstimulation is characterized by a subjective experience of sensory overload. It responds to oral potassium. It is seen as an ion channel dysfunction that may also occur in some ADHD.

The treatment involves oral potassium of about 250mg. Increasing dietary potassium seems to have no effect – it is the sudden spike in blood potassium levels from a supplement that in needed. When you eat a banana, it does contain about 500mg of potassium, but it is absorbed very slowly into the bloodstream.

I continue to get feedback from my blog that this therapy is effective in others.

This was my test:

1. Find a sound which the person finds disturbing, like a baby crying.
2. Download a recording of this sound.
3. Set up a chair in a fixed location in a room with a powerful sound system
4. Sit the subject in the chair and play the annoying sound at ever greater volume and see at what point the subject reacts strongly (e.g. covers ears, runs away, screams)
5. Repeat the experiment over a few days to establish a steady base-line volume, at which the subject reacts, (for example volume setting 3, when the amplifier to goes 0–10)
6. Give the subject an oral potassium supplement (say 250 mg) and wait 20 minutes

7. Play the annoying sound and measure the volume at which ears are covered.
8. If the volume is markedly higher than the base-line, you established earlier, then you have established Hypokalemic Sensory Overload
9. If the child has a neurotypical sibling, try it on them. They will most likely show no difference with the potassium and do not have Hypokalemic Sensory Overload

I later went on to establish a more potent therapy for sound sensitivity, which is to use Ponstan (mefenamic acid). In our case 250mg once a day is sufficient, in other people the effect lasts for a few hours before fading away. Ponstan affects several different potassium ion channels.

Sensory gating

Sensory gating is an issue in autism, schizophrenia and ADHD. It is the neurological process of filtering out redundant or unnecessary stimuli in the brain; like the child who sits in his classroom and gets bothered by the noise of the clock on the wall and is unable to filter out and ignore this sound. He becomes preoccupied by the sound and cannot concentrate on his work.

This condition is also called misophonia, which is regarded as untreatable.

There are also sometimes advantages to not filtering out environmental stimuli, because you would have more situational awareness and notice things that others ignore. People with autism generally like order, with everything neatly in place. Anything out of its place, be it a dripping tap, an open door, a curtain flapping by an open window needs to be corrected.

There may be times when sensory overload is not a case of too much volume from each of the senses, but rather too many inputs being processed by the brain, instead of some just being ignored. It is more a case of information overload.

Much is known about sensory gating because it has long been known to be a problem in schizophrenia. You can diagnose a sensory gating disorder using an EEG test.

An EEG (Electroencephalography) test measures your brain waves/neural oscillations. In the world of the EEG, the P50 is an event occurring approximately 50 milliseconds after the presentation of an auditory click. The P50 response is used to measure sensory gating, or the reduced neurophysiological response to redundant stimuli.

Abnormal P50 suppression is a biomarker of schizophrenia, but is present in other disorders, including Asperger's, post-traumatic stress disorder (PTSD) and traumatic brain injury (TBI).

Correcting P50 gating

It is known that alpha7 nicotinic acetylcholine receptor (alpha7 nAChR) agonists can correct impaired P50 gating. It is also known that people with schizophrenia have less expression of this receptor in their brains than typical people.

One short term such agonist is the nicotine released from smoking. This likely contributes to why people with schizophrenia can be heavy smokers. The effect is thought to last for about 30 minutes.

Clinical trials using tropisetron, a drug that is an alpha7 nAChR agonist, have shown that it can correct defective P50 gating and improve cognitive function in schizophrenia.

An alternative alpha7 nAChR agonist that is widely available is varenicline, a drug approved to help people stop smoking.

Rather than an agonist that binds to, and then activates the α7 receptor, an alternative strategy is to use a Positive Allosteric Modulator (PAM), which just turns up the volume of the receptors normal response. Galantamine is such a PAM and has shown some promise in reducing deficits in schizophrenia. Galantamine is both a drug and a supplement.

Another therapy in the research shown to improve sensory gating is a low 100mcg dose of roflumilast (Daxas), a PDE4 inhibitor. The same dose has also been patented as a cognitive enhancer. Some people get GI side effects from PDE4 inhibitors.

Food allergy, food intolerance & eosinophilic esophagitis

It is important not to confuse food allergy with food intolerance, both are common in young children. Food allergy prevalence is the greatest during the first years of life where it affects around 8% of infants younger than three years, falling to just 1% of adults.

In this age group, cow's milk allergy is the most common type of food allergy. About 80% of these children develop tolerance by the age of five; however, this group is at risk to develop asthma at a later age. In adults, peanut hypersensitivity is the most common severe food allergy.

The causal role of mast cells in food allergy is indicated by high levels of histamine, TNF alpha, IL-5 and tryptase in blood and stool samples.

This takes us to the concept of the "leaky gut". You have a protective barrier, the intestinal barrier, that is supposed to stop things leaking out of your gut and entering the bloodstream.

Impairment of the intestinal barrier function can be a feature of food allergy and it has been shown that inflammation enhances intestinal mucosal permeability – this leads to "leaky gut". The process is driven by mast cells in the gut. These mast cells are activated by the presence of an allergen, the food you are allergic to. When mast cells encounter the allergen, they release their contents in a process called "degranulation". Mast cell degranulation has been shown to trigger pain and diarrhea. Effective drugs are mast cell stabilizers, like cromolyn sodium.

Food intolerance is a digestive system response, rather than an immune system response. It occurs when something in food irritates your digestive system or when a person is unable to properly digest or break down the food. It is thought that 10% of the population have some food intolerance.

If you are histamine intolerant, you cannot break down the histamine in food. As well as avoiding food that contains histamine, you would have to avoid sodium benzoate and cinnamon which will further aggravate the problem, since they inhibit histamine degradation.

Eosinophilic esophagitis (allergic esophagitis, or just EoE) is usually found in children, but also occurs in adults. The condition is not well understood, but food allergy may play a role. It is an allergic inflammatory condition of the esophagus that involves eosinophils, a type of white blood cell. Symptoms include difficulty swallowing, vomiting, and GERD/reflux/ heartburn.

Treatment consists of removal of known or suspected triggers and medication to suppress the immune response.

It appears that eosinophilic esophagitis is common in autism. According to some medical experts, food allergy and intolerance is no more common in autism than the general population; some parents may disagree.

The diagnosis of EoE is typically made on the combination of symptoms and findings of diagnostic testing.

Prior to the development of the EoE diagnostic panel, EoE could only be diagnosed if gastroesophageal reflux did not respond to a six-week trial of twice-a-day high-dose proton-pump inhibitors (PPIs) or if a negative ambulatory pH study ruled out gastroesophageal reflux disease (GERD).

Treatment strategies include dietary modification to exclude food allergens, medical therapy, and mechanical dilatation of the esophagus.

Eosinophilic esophagitis is a chronic immune system disease. It has been identified only in the past two decades, but is now considered a major cause of digestive system illness. In many cases it likely remains undiagnosed. If it continues, after a few years swallowing becomes difficult, in part because a "ringed esophagus" develops that impedes the passage of food.

There are numerous other GI conditions comorbid with autism, such as colitis, IBD and IBS. In the end I imagine that the molecular basis of some of these diagnoses is actually the same, so you will find the same therapies may be effective.

It looks like that one common factor is the mast cell and, just as in pollen allergy and asthma, stabilizing mast cells yields great benefit. Stabilizing mast cells is complex but involves the flow of calcium ions, Ca^{2+}. By modifying the flow of Ca^{2+} you can prevent mast cells degranulating. This was one of my earlier discoveries, but there is now research showing the L type calcium channels "open" mast cells. Keeping these channels closed is actually quite simple.

It would seem logical that the same approach could be therapeutic to other conditions that are, at least in part, mediated by mast cells.

Eosinophilic esophagitis is called eosinophilic because it is mediated by eosinophils. However it has been established that mast cells also play a role. People with EoE are found to have local mastocytosis and mast cell degranulation in the esophagus.

Food intolerance vs food allergy

Food intolerance, also known as non-IgE mediated food hypersensitivity or non-allergic food hypersensitivity, refers to difficulty in digesting certain foods. It is important to note that food intolerance is different from food allergy.

Food allergies trigger the immune system, while food intolerance does not. Some people suffer digestive problems after eating certain foods, even though their immune system has not reacted – there is no histamine response.

Foods most commonly associated with food intolerance include dairy products, grains that contain gluten, and foods that cause intestinal gas build-up, such as beans and cabbage.

Here are some key points about food intolerance.

Symptoms of food intolerance tend to take longer to appear than symptoms of allergies

The symptoms are varied and can include, migraine, cough, and stomach ache

Some food intolerance is caused by the lack of a particular enzyme.

When it is an allergy, even small amounts result in symptoms, as may be the case with peanuts. Whereas, with food intolerance, tiny amounts will usually have no effect.

Onset typically occurs several hours after ingesting the offending food or compound and may persist for several hours or days. In some cases, symptoms may take 48 hours to arrive.

Some people are intolerant to several groups of foods, making it harder for doctors to determine whether it might be a chronic illness or food intolerance. Identifying which foods are the culprits can take a long time.

Enzyme deficiencies are a common cause of food intolerance.

People who are lactose intolerant do not have enough lactase, an enzyme that breaks down milk sugar (lactose) into smaller molecules that the body can break down further and absorb through the intestine. If lactose remains in the digestive tract, it can cause spasms, stomach ache, bloating, diarrhea, and gas.

People with an allergy to milk protein have similar symptoms to those with lactose intolerance; that is why lactose intolerant individuals are commonly misdiagnosed as allergic.

Histamine intolerance

Many foods and drinks contain histamine.

Usually, the enzyme DAO, and to a lesser extent the enzyme HNMT, break down ingested histamine, preventing it from being absorbed in the gut and entering the bloodstream. Within the brain histamine acts as a neurotransmitter.

Some factors can, however, interfere with how DAO and HMNT work, or how much of these enzymes are present in the gut.

The common food additive sodium benzoate (E211) is a DAO-inhibitor. It is widely used in carbonated drinks, jams, fruit juice, pickles and condiments. Someone who is histamine intolerant will need to learn to avoid such commercially prepared foods.

Other common factors that interfere with DAO and HMNT levels include many prescription drugs, for example:

- airway medications, such as theophylline
- heart medications
- antibiotics
- antidepressants
- antipsychotics
- some diuretics
- muscle relaxants
- pain medications
- gastrointestinal medicines

Pesticides

There is quite a lot written about pesticides like glyphosate and autism. There is even an MIT researcher quoting my blog in her publications. I do not believe she is correct that pesticides are the key driver behind the increased prevalence of autism.

I think it is hardly surprising that pesticides can affect a developing brain, just like the lead that used to be added to petrol/gasoline.

The key time to avoid pesticides and toxic chemicals is during pregnancy and early childhood.

Gluten free?

One long-known feature of autism is the loss of Purkinje cells. These cells are involved in motor skills, and this probably contributes to clumsiness and poor handwriting in many people with autism. For good motor skills you need plenty of Purkinje cells, with plenty of myelin coating their axons.

An extreme cause of Purkinje cell loss in some people is a reaction to gluten, mainly in those with Celiac disease (CD). The process is not fully understood but results in antibodies selectively destroying Purkinje cells and leading to a condition called Cerebellar ataxia.

People sensitive to gluten, but not having Celiac disease, may also experience some ataxia as well as a wide range of autoimmune disorders that can include psychiatric manifestations.

I think some people with autism do have non-celiac gluten sensitivity (NCGS). Those people should feel better on a gluten free diet. A small number of people with severe autism may have undiagnosed Celiac disease.

Gluten related disorders

Gluten-related disorders is the term for the diseases triggered by gluten, including Celiac disease, non-celiac gluten sensitivity (NCGS), gluten ataxia, dermatitis herpetiformis and wheat allergy. The umbrella category has also been referred to as gluten intolerance.

If you have one of the above conditions then avoid gluten.

If you do not have one of the above conditions, you are in the great majority and there is no point spending extra money to avoid gluten.

There is no reliable data, but an estimate is that 10-15% of people have some kind of gluten related disorder.

It is not surprising that a minority of people with autism respond to a gluten free diet, but the majority do not. Your case of autism could fall in either camp.

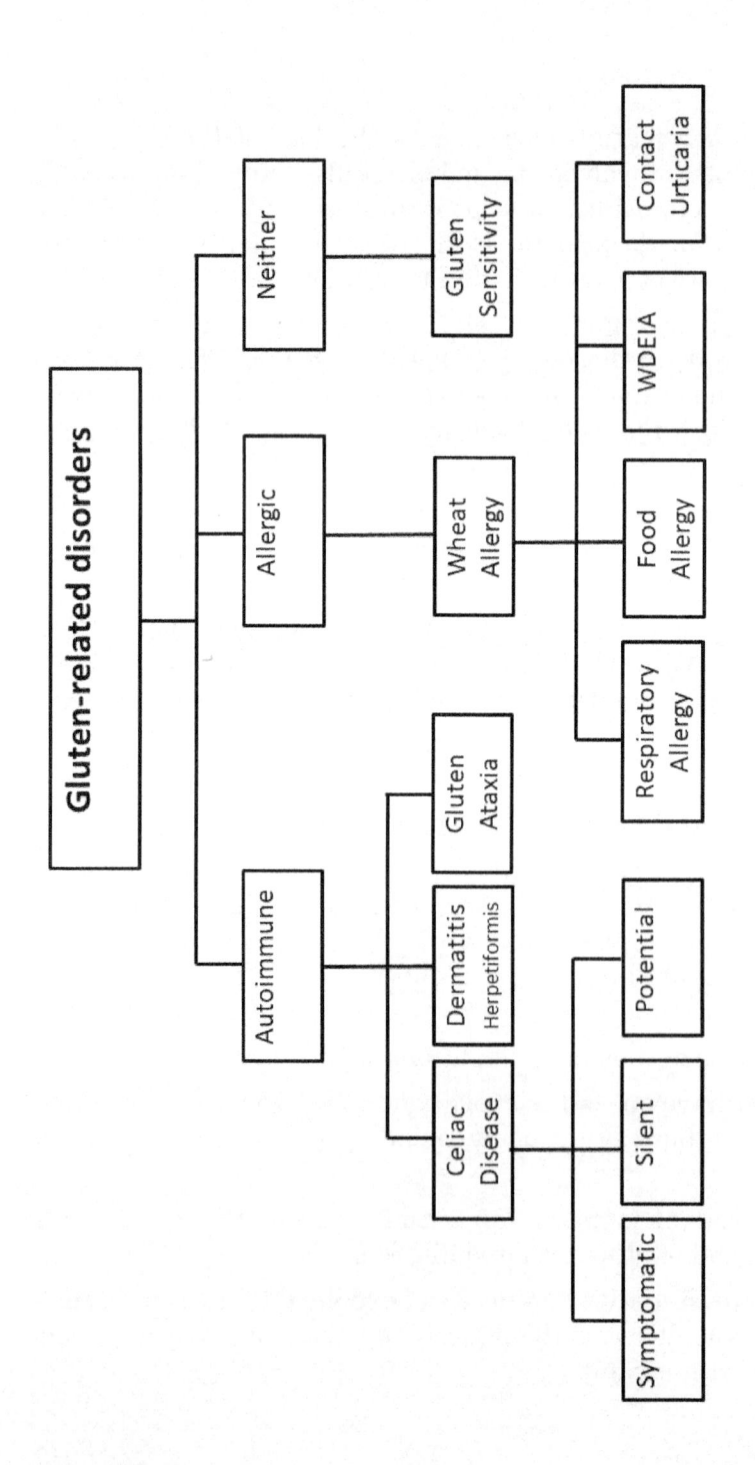

Gluten-related disorders

- **Autoimmune**
  - Celiac Disease
    - Symptomatic
    - Silent
    - Potential
  - Dermatitis Herpetiformis
  - Gluten Ataxia
- **Allergic**
  - Wheat Allergy
    - Respiratory Allergy
    - Food Allergy
    - WDEIA
    - Contact Urticaria
- **Neither**
  - Gluten Sensitivity

WDEIA = Wheat-dependent exercise-induced anaphylaxis

Small intestinal bacterial overgrowth (SIBO) is a serious condition affecting the small intestine. It occurs when bacteria that normally grow in other parts of the gut start growing in the small intestine. That causes pain and diarrhea. It can also lead to malnutrition as the bacteria start to use up the body's nutrients.

If you have severe autism and live in rural China one study suggests you have a 50:50 chance of having SIBO. How common it is in other countries has not been researched.

SIBO is measurable and treatable using mainstream medicine.

Don't treat SIBO if you do not have SIBO.

In the research SIBO was significantly associated with worse symptoms of autism, demonstrating SIBO may significantly worsen the symptoms of already existing autism.

SIBO does not cause autism; but if you have autism SIBO is likely to make the symptoms worse.

SIBO treatment options

For hydrogen-predominant SIBO, the primary treatment is the antibiotic rifaximin.

Methane-predominant SIBO is harder to treat, and it may take longer to respond to treatment. Rifaximin plus neomycin is used for these cases.

If SIBO recurs a nutritionist may advise a FODMAP (low fermentable oligosaccharides, disaccharides, monosaccharides and polyols) diet.

People taking acid reducing drugs for reflux/GERD/GORD might note that PPI-induced dysbiosis is considered a type of SIBO. PPIs are proton pump inhibitors like Nexium that are now more popular than Histamine H2 blockers like Zantac/Ranitidine. So, long term use of drugs to treat reflux may cause SIBO.

Interestingly, apple cider vinegar (ACV) can counter that PPI-induced dysbiosis. Your small intestines need some acid. Your body relies on sodium bicarbonate released by the pancreas to maintain pH levels, but it can only reduce acidity, not increase it. I imagine a swig of anything acidic would likely have a similar effect, although ACV also has non acid-related effects. ACV should be diluted with water and then rinse your mouth with water, otherwise the acid will damage your teeth and your esophagus.

If it is SIBO, get a genuine diagnosis, treat it and avoid it reoccurring.

Rifaximin is yet another drug that is a cheap generic in most of the world, but very expensive in the US.

Rifaximin is also used to treat different types of intestinal dysbiosis caused by proliferation of harmful bacteria. It is quite a hit with some readers of my blog, including those who are doctors treating their own child.

Propionic and butyric acids – SCFAs (short chained fatty acids)

Short Chained fatty Acids (SCFAs) are produced when dietary fiber is fermented in the colon. Acetate, propionate, and butyrate are the three most common SCFAs.

You need fiber and butyrate-producing bacteria for a healthy colon. The fiber and bacteria work together to produce butyric acid. It is called butyric because it smells of butter that has been kept outside the fridge.

Propionic acid is used to cause reversible autism in a mouse model. When propionic acid is infused directly into rodents' brains, it produces reversible behaviors (hyperactivity, dystonia, social impairment, perseveration) and brain changes (innate neuroinflammation, glutathione depletion). In the mouse model, you just feed them some NAC (N-acetyl cysteine) and they switch back to regular happy mice. NAC is an OTC supplement shown effective in autism trials at Stanford University.

Propionic acid leads to PTEN↓ inflammation↑ gliosis↑ mitochondrial dysfunction ↑

We now know the details of what is happening to those mice. To a lesser extent if you produce a lot of propionic acid in your human gut some may well make it to your brain and produce a similar effect.

We know that in autism increasing a protein called PTEN is generally a good thing. Gliosis includes things like activating the brains immune cells (microglia) which we know is bad. Mitochondrial dysfunction reduces the power available to cells in your body and is a feature of many neurological dysfunctions, including some autism.

Modulating the gut microbiome with certain probiotic bacteria and adding fiber like fructo-oligosaccharide (FOS) or inulin does benefit some people. Butyrate is the major fermentation product of inulin, whereas mostly acetate and lactate is produced on FOS.

A popular autism therapy promoted by an American doctor of osteopathy called Nemechek is centered on the use of inulin. He also likes rifaximin. Some people respond well, some badly and some not at all. It will all depend on what is being fermented in the colon and what the underlying cause of autism is in that specific person.

If you lack butyrate, inulin should help you, but you can have too much butyrate.

Eating a balanced diet avoiding junk food looks the best long-term strategy.

Medical food (probiotics) from one end and FMT from the other

There is some very clever research that will hopefully lead to new medical foods, containing specific bacteria, as a means of promoting specific chemical reactions in your gut, which then effect other parts of your body.

One interesting finding discussed in my blog was from UCLA that you could mimic the effect of the ketogenic diet in reducing seizures by using medical food (probiotics) to modify the microbiome. The high fat diet does produce ketones, but it also modifies the microbiome.

At UCLA they showed that people with epilepsy, controlled by the ketogenic diet do not actually need the ketones, they need the altered mix of bacteria in their gut produced by the fatty diet. So, skip the very rigid diet and just eat the bacteria in the form of a medical food.

In my blog we saw how one kind of childhood leukemia can be prevented by taking a particular bacterium in medical food or yoghurt. In effect missing microbes trigger this childhood cancer.

The researcher, Professor Greaves was quoted as saying "The most important implication is that most cases of childhood leukemia are likely to be preventable." His vision is giving children a safe cocktail of bacteria – such as in a yoghurt drink – that will help train their immune system.

Even some expensive drugs have been found to be effective only in the presence of specific gut bacteria. So, alongside the drug give that bacterium?

The microbiota comes from the mother and ideally is augmented by a natural delivery and breastfeeding.

Early use and overuse of antibiotics will disrupt the microbiota.

The body's immune system is calibrated very early in life and if mis-calibrated it will over/under-react for the rest of your life. Early exposure to bacteria is part of the calibration process; this is why having a pet indoors during pregnancy reduces the chance of a child having allergies. Also, good to be exposed to the other animals humans have evolved alongside (domesticated farmyard animals). There is even a product under development to prevent childhood allergies, which is basically barnyard dust and bacteria from untreated milk.

This is a concept called the Hologenone/Holobiont.

It can be summed up as give your body the bugs it evolved to expect, or don't be surprised when things start going wrong and autoimmune diseases develop later in life and autism incidence increases.

FMT/MTT

Another way of colonizing your gut with beneficial bacteria is to repopulate it with someone else's. This is the so-called microbiota transfer therapy (MTT), better known as fecal microbiota therapy (FMT), or more simply a poop transplant (PT, I suppose).

Trials show that taking probiotics orally often has little impact on what is growing in your gut. The effect is often short term and the new bacteria do not colonize their new host.

The idea of taking someone else's feces/poo and inserting into a child with GI problems and autism may not sound very high tech, but in small trials at Arizona State University it has shown to be beneficial and importantly the effect is maintained two years later.

Clearly there is potential to transfer things that might not be beneficial.

In the end I think someone will develop a synthesized lab-made product containing the many billions of "good" bacteria. Ultimately this could be a personalized medical product, tailored to the individual needs of the patient.

Does this only work in people with autism who have GI symptoms? I think it all depends what bacteria you are adding.

Low glycemic diet

Hypoglycemia is low blood sugar that can cause headaches, weakness, and anxiety. Hyperglycemia refers to high levels of sugar, or glucose, in the blood.

Low blood sugar (hypoglycemia) in children may cause uncharacteristic aggression, hyperactivity, the inability to sit still, and the inability to concentrate.

High blood sugar (hyperglycemia) also negatively affects behavior.

Eating foods with a low glycemic index (GI) avoids spikes in blood sugar. This kind of diet is used by people with diabetes, but is actually good for everyone.

A low glycemic index diet reduces symptoms of autism in mice and anecdotal evidence from comments in my blog and elsewhere does give some support for this diet in humans. We also now have some scientific research that also looks inside the brain. The brains of the high-glycemic index diet mice appeared to have greater numbers of activated microglia, those resident immune cells of the brain. Their brains also expressed more genes associated with inflammation, compared to the mice fed the low-glycemic index diet.

The ketogenic diet

I think the ketogenic diet (KD) is the cleverest diet because it will genuinely help different small groups of people, but for entirely different reasons.

We saw that in people with seizures, the beneficial effect does not come from ketones, it comes from the high fat diet changing the microbiome and causing different bacteria to thrive. The researchers at UCLA then showed how this effect finally reaches the brain where it affects GABA and glutamate levels, and so prevents epileptic seizures.

In some people with a problem transporting glucose across the blood brain barrier (as in Alzheimer's) or a problem with converting that glucose into ATP in mitochondria (someone with mitochondrial disease) the ketone BHB becomes an alternative fuel for cells. These people would benefit from the ketones produced naturally in your body, when you follow the high fat ketogenic diet.

In other people the complex and varied anti-inflammatory actions of the ketone BHB are beneficial.

It should be noted that babies fed exclusively on milk are on a simple form of ketogenic diet and so they will be producing BHB. It does not seem to do them any harm.

Chiari 1 "brain hernia"

The Chiari 1 brain hernia occurs when part of the brain is forced downwards into the spinal column. It is supposedly very rare, occurring in only one person per thousand. One study suggests that it is present in 7% of autism cases. It is generally not life-threatening and can be surgically repaired. The symptoms of Chiari 1 do somewhat overlap with those of autism.

You can diagnose Chiari 1 using an MRI scan. Few people with autism ever receive any diagnostic follow up, be it genetic testing, metabolic testing or an MRI scan of their brain. Researchers from the University of Missouri school of medicine published the following paper in 2015.

> ### Chiari malformation I and autism spectrum disorder: an under recognized coexistence
>
> One hundred twenty-five pediatric patients diagnosed with ASD had undergone MRI, and 9 of them had evidence of cerebellar tonsillar herniation. Five patients were symptomatic and underwent suboccipital craniectomy, a C-1 or a C-1 and C-2 laminectomy, and duraplasty with bovine pericardium or Type I collagen allograft. There were no intraoperative complications. All patients showed symptom improvement and/or resolution of presenting

symptoms, which included headache, dysphasia, speech, and irritability.

Many types of autism are associated with accelerated brain growth in early life. If the skull does not grow fast enough, it is logical that part of the brain will be forced downwards into the spinal column.

Dr Manuel Casanova, a neurologist with an excellent autism blog, seems to think that Chiari does not cause autism, but just makes it worse. So, treating it will likely improve behavior and quality of life.

There is a project by the Chiari & Syringomyelia Foundation to analyze the prevalence of Chiari malformation within the ASD population.

Treating self-injury and aggression

When a child is diagnosed very young with autism, the issue that most often concerns parents is the lack of speech. As children grow bigger and stronger the overriding concern often becomes self-injury and aggression.

People with autism of any severity and those of any IQ can engage in self-injurious behavior (SIB). It is very distressing to all concerned and there is no common way of dealing with it. If you intervene to try and stop SIB, you may very well become a victim too.

Our current assistant also has classes at the weekend with severely autistic adults. The policy over there is not to intervene when these adults start hitting their heads with their fists.

In special schools there is always a policy for how to deal with SIB; whatever is done or not done will always upset some parents. Do you use restraint or not? How do you use it, and so on.

People do write to my blog and ask what pill can you take to solve the problem. What I tell them is that if they go to a psychiatrist, they will very likely come home with a prescription for an antipsychotic drug like Abilify or Risperidone. These are approved therapies and may, or may not be effective. They do however have side effects that may not be mentioned; tardive dyskinesia may result in life-long motor tics, obesity may result in type 2 diabetes, elevated prolactin may lead to males growing breasts.

Antipsychotics do not address the underlying cause of SIB, which is usually medical or emotional or some combination. SIB is a learned behavior, which is hard to forget, so it might develop for a medical reason but then just continue.

SIB and worse still aggression towards others will get you excluded from mainstream schools and later in life from group homes. You then may end up with nowhere to live, because in most countries there are very few residential places in psychiatric hospitals that can cater for sometimes violent patients.

I mentioned at the start of this book the advice my doctor mother gave me at the start of our autism adventure: "Make sure he does not get violent when he gets older." It really is good advice, but nobody is going to tell you how to do it!

Over the years I have come across all kinds of solutions that people have found worked in their specific cases. The problem is that none of them are going to work for everyone. Some are quite well documented and some are just mentioned in blogs like mine.

Nicotine patches

A fairly common therapy used by the old DAN! doctors was to use nicotine patches. This is not a crazy idea; it is similar to people with ulcerative colitis smoking or using nicotine patches. The suggested target is the alpha 7 nicotinic acetylcholine receptor (alpha7 nAchR), which is a primary receptor of the cholinergic anti-inflammatory pathway.

Activated alpha7 nAChR exhibits extensive anti-inflammatory and immune modulatory reactions, including lowered pro-inflammatory cytokines and altering differentiation and activation of immune cells, which are important in maintaining immune homeostasis.

L. Reuteri probiotics

In one mouse study L. reuteri probiotics reversed symptoms of autism. It used a model called maternal high fat diet (MHFD). This model mimics the effect of being obese during pregnancy, which causes the pups to be born with autistic behaviors. The pups are born with dysbiosis of the gut microbiota. The researchers looked at what types of bacteria were lacking. Re-introduction of Lactobacillus reuteri bacteria restored social deficits in the pups.

Reuteri is a species of bacteria named after a German called Gerhard Reuter. Lactobacillus means it is a lactic acid bacterium, this is useful to know because it tells you that you can grow it in milk. Within each species there are different strains. Each strain may have unique properties which may allow them to behave like a drug.

L. reuteri DSM 17938 is known to be immunomodulatory. It is sold in a commercial product called Biogaia Gastrus, which also contains L. reuteri ATCC PTA 6475.

L. reuteri ATCC PTA 6475 is also sold by itself as Biogaia Protectis.

One reader of my blog wrote a glowing review of Biogaia Gastrus in the blog and said that other parents in Switzerland had tried it with great success. Following this many parents went out and tried it. One reader in Greece was even given a large amount for free by the local distributor.

The result was that in a small number of people Biogaia Gastrus greatly diminished self-injury (SIB), but in others like my son it triggered immediate self-injury. Fortunately, I did not buy a large supply!

Remarkably, the second bacteria in Gastrus has been shown to stimulate the release of the emotional hormone oxytocin in the brain.

The effect of this bacteria given alone, as Biogaia Protectis, was to make my son go around the playground shaking the hands of the boys and telling them that he liked them and kissing some of the girls.

In the people for whom L. reuteri DSM 17938 was beneficial, a large daily dose was required equal to 5 regular pills. This gets expensive. Fortunately, this bacterium grows in milk, so you can make your own as a yoghurt or kefir. There are videos on YouTube showing how to do this.

BCAAs

Nancy, one of my long-time blog readers, found her game changer therapy in the form of Branch Chained Amino Acids (BCAAs) at the suggestion of another reader Tyler.

> "My son, just turned 26, has had explosive rages with self-injurious behavior for a few years now. Certain things helped in the very short term, then stopped working (Pantogam, vagus nerve stimulation). I started Tyler's recommended regimen of 1 scoop BCAA (XTEND) 2X a day with a morning dose of niagen. The effects were fairly immediate. I took a morning dose of the BCAA myself and found my own mood vastly improved. I continue to take just the morning dose. It has made a world of difference for me. For my son, it has been dramatic. The rages are nearly gone and when they occur, they are over quickly."

Thanks to Tyler, reader Valentina in Uruguay was finally able to solve her son's problem with tardive dyskinesia. This was also achieved using BCAAs, available in all supplement stores.

Tyler's focus had been on targeting kynurenine in the brain to lower self-injury in his son. The research does indeed point to a dysregulation of the kynurenine pathway in people with lifetime aggression and it is known to be dysregulated in autism. The subject is quite complicated and beyond the scope of this book. It is covered in detail in my blog, with graphics and links. Just google "kynurenine pathway epiphanyasd" and it will take you to a post dedicated to this subject.

Tyler later found out that the idea to use BCAAs as a therapy had already been published in the research, not for aggression but as a treatment for tardive dyskinesia, the motor tics eventually brought on by using antipsychotics in a large minority of patients.

Tyler's idea was to use this cheap OTC bodybuilder's supplement to block tryptophan and its metabolite kynurenine entering into the brain, but another effect of the BCAAs is to block tyrosine and phenylalanine. These are both precursors to L-Dopa. Tyrosine is metabolized to L-Dopa and phenylalanine is metabolized to tyrosine. Dopaminergic neurons convert L-DOPA to dopamine, so less L-Dopa means less dopamine. Put simply, in someone with tardive dyskinesia, less dopamine means less tics and eventually no tics. The effect on dopamine is likely what helps people with tardive dyskinesia, which eventually develops in about one in three people taking a second generation antipsychotic drug,

Tyler later stumbled upon the following paper from 2003 that followed his logic.

Efficacy of the Branched-Chain Amino Acids in the Treatment of Tardive Dyskinesia in Men

The branched-chain amino acids share a competitive blood-brain-barrier transport system with the aromatic amino acids. Thus the entry of branched-chain amino acids into the brain is enhanced by increasing their plasma concentration and/or by decreasing their competition for uptake, both of which occur after the ingestion of branched-chain amino acids.

Since the aromatic amino acids are precursors of the amine neurotransmitters, ingestion of branched-chain amino acids can decrease the central synthesis of the neurotransmitters dopamine, noradrenaline, and serotonin. This treatment mechanism has been used successfully in disorders such as hepatic encephalopathy, in which a decrease in the central synthesis of these neurotransmitters is required for a therapeutic effect.

Branched-chain amino acids constitute a novel, safe treatment for tardive dyskinesia, with a strong potential for providing significant improvement in the diseased physiognomy of the afflicted person.

I later wrote in my blog about how the widely available probiotic Lactobacillus Plantarum 299v decreases kynurenine concentration and improves cognitive functions in patients with major depression. I also showed data indicating that there were alterations to the kynurenine pathway in autism. Specifically, increased production of the downstream metabolite, quinolinic acid, which is capable of enhancing glutamatergic neuro-transmission.

We do not know 100% exactly why Nancy's son responded so well to BCAAs, but we do know the beneficial effect has been maintained now for a few years; it remains a game-changer for her son.

The link between MAO-A and aggression

MAOs (Monoamine oxidases) are enzymes that inactivate monoamine neurotransmitters like adrenaline, dopamine, noradrenaline and most importantly serotonin. These neurotransmitters are involved in a number of psychiatric and neurological diseases and some of which can be treated with MAO inhibitors (MAOIs) which block the action of MAOs.

MAO-A is seen in the research as a biomarker for aberrant aggression.

Too much MAO or too little?

Mice unable to produce either MAO-A or MAO-B display features of autism and they have an increased response to stress.

Total congenital deficiency of MAO-A in a human is called Brunner syndrome. It results in antisocial behavior and abnormally high levels of aggression. A low IQ is another key feature of this condition.

Research shows that smoking tobacco heavily depletes MAO-B, mimicking the action of an MAO-B inhibitor. Those who smoke for emotional relief are effectively self-treating with a MAO inhibitor. They could equally well take a MAO-B inhibiting drug.

Pharmacological studies do link MAOs with aggression. MAO inhibitors are widely prescribed for the treatment of a variety of neurocognitive disorders, including depression, and post-traumatic stress disorder. Nonselective MAOIs or selective MAO-B inhibitors have been used to manage suicidal tendencies and impulsive aggressive behavior. MAO-A inhibitors have been used to treat antisocial and borderline personality disorders.

MAO-A deficiency has not only been linked to aggression but also sensory and communication deficits.

Common sense would sum this up as both too much, or too little, MAO has a damaging effect.

MAO-A and the microbiota

In the research it is suggested that there is a role played by the gut-brain axis in the MAO-related modulation of aggression and antisocial behavior. This is an ongoing subject of research.

In the medical world most treatments are for reducing MAO. This is easy to do with existing drugs and they are commonly used as anti-depressants.

In people with too little MAO, they will end up with too much serotonin.

As you can see, in one specific individual it would be very important to use the right type of antidepressant, or the effect will be to make a bad situation even worse.

To figure out with certainty what is going on in a specific person you would need to take a sample of central spinal fluid and consult a clever doctor like Professor Ramaekers.

Approximately 30% of people with autism have high blood serotonin; perhaps a contributing factor is serotonin released by the degranulation of mast cells. It is reported that quite often there is central hypo-function of serotonin in autism, that is low brain serotonin. The endocrine system functions using feedback loops, so high blood serotonin sends a signal to lower serotonin; you could get low brain serotonin but high blood serotonin. Remember that serotonin does not cross the blood brain barrier. The only valid test is central spinal fluid if you want to know what is happening inside the brain.

Palmitoylethanolamide (PEA) and low dose phenytoin

PEA is a supplement widely used in Italy, Spain and the Netherlands to treat neuropathic pain. One of the Dutch neuropathic pain researchers, Jan Hesselink, who writes about PEA also patented the old epilepsy drug Phenytoin to treat neuropathy. Hesselink has also made a case in the literature showing evidence that low dose Phenytoin can also be used to treat aggression. There are published case histories to support the use of PEA to treat aggression.

Both PEA and Phenytoin have multiple and wide-ranging biological effects.

I was contacted by one parent considering using low dose Phenytoin on his adult son with severe autism. This was based on its use in Australia by a psychiatrist called Dr Philip Bird, who published a case history in 2015; he reported on a low dose of Phenytoin to enhance social functioning. He noted a positive effect within 10 minutes of a single sublingual low dose.

PEA is a supplement while Phenytoin is a prescription drug.

Verapamil to treat anxiety and aggression

The use of verapamil to treat anxiety and aggression is primarily documented in my blog. We did try to collect detailed information for one doctor reader of my blog to publish a case series, but she did not get enough parents to participate. In the world of treating autism, people like to remain anonymous and I can understand why.

Verapamil is a calcium channel blocker, widely used to treat high blood pressure. It is usually very well tolerated. Another doctor reader of my blog found that her daughter was a positive responder, but sadly was affected by the rare side effect of gum inflammation.

The effect on anxiety and aggression takes place within about 20 minutes of the first dose and lasts 4–5 hours, so the drug needs to be taken three times a day. Readers of my blog who tried extended-release versions found they were much less effective than the immediate release version.

Verapamil is known as an L-type calcium channel blocker, but it also blocks some potassium channels.

When mast cells degranulate, to release histamine triggered by an allergic reaction, one of the steps requires activation of L-type calcium channels.

In some people, like my son, their aggression is clearly linked to an allergy. Antihistamine drugs are beneficial, but the effect is far less than verapamil.

Some people choose to add other inflammatory drugs to try and completely avoid any aggression. Options include modern antihistamines (Cetirizine, Loratadine etc), mast cell stabilizers (like Cromolyn Sodium, Ketotifen, Rupatadine and Azelastine), Pioglitazone (a drug for type 2 diabetes, trialed in autism), Galavit (an anti-inflammatory drug from Russia) and Hydroxyzine (a first generation antihistamine, also used to treat anxiety).

I later found that there is even a mouse model of self-injurious behaviour. If you activate the L-type calcium channels in mice they will engage in self-injurious behavior.

The L-type calcium channel activator/agonist Bay K 8644 causes the unusual phenomenon of self-injurious biting, particularly when given to young mice. The self-biting provoked by Bay K 8644 can be blocked by pre-treating the mice with dihydropyridine L type calcium channel blockers such as nifedipine, nimodipine, or amlodipine.

However, self-biting in mice is not inhibited by non-dihydropyridine blockers including diltiazem, flunarizine, or verapamil.

If Monty was a mouse, verapamil might not work and I would probably have had to use amlodipine. Interestingly, amlopidine in some human autism seems to raise cognition and improve speech. You can read more on my blog, it is an interesting subject.

N-acetylcysteine (NAC)

I am a big believer in the use of antioxidants to treat autism (and to treat diabetes and other conditions).

For some people with autism the most noticeable effect of NAC is in reducing anxiety and self-injury.

NAC's use to reduce irritability and aggression is documented in the literature. In other people the main benefit is a reduction in stereotypy/stimming.

The effect of NAC lasts about four hours and to give good coverage throughout the day it needs to be given at least three times a day. Extended-release NAC is effective, but the leading producer no longer makes it due to the FDA reclassifying NAC as a drug rather than a supplement.

CBD (Cannabidiol), CBDV (Cannabidivarin) and THC (Tetrahydrocannabinol)

Most people are aware that there is growing interest in the medical use of cannabis. Usually people think mainly of two components: CBD (Cannabidiol), and the mind-altering THC (Tetrahydrocannabinol), but there are hundreds more.

Cannabidivarin (CBDV) is a chemical in the Cannabis sativa plant. It is very similar to CBD. Much of the autism research is focused on CBDV.

For many years there have been anecdotal reports of the benefit of cannabis in autism. Charlotte's Web is one well known product that was initially developed to successfully treat Charlotte Figi, a girl with Dravet syndrome. This syndrome features almost untreatable seizures, speech impairment, intellectual disability, and many symptoms of autism.

From what I am told by my Californian readers, the earlier version of Charlotte's Web, was more beneficial. The later versions had a lower level of THC. Charlotte Figi died in 2020 at the age of 13 from pneumonia, which then caused seizures, respiratory failure, and cardiac arrest.

One of the claimed benefits of cannabis use is reduced self-injury and aggression. There are clinical trials ongoing investigating CBDV and other forms of cannabis. Israel is one major center of this research.

Cluster headaches and other types of severe headache

We all get headaches from time to time, but some people get severe debilitating headaches that may be overwhelming. Some children with severe headaches end up seeing a neurologist. Some people's headaches are linked to an ion channel dysfunction. Mutations have been reported in CACNA1A (calcium channel Cav2.1), ATP1A2 (Na/K-ATPase subunit alpha 2), and SCN1A (sodium channel Nav1.1) genes resulting in the development of hemiplegic migraine.

A minimally verbal person with autism will find it hard to explain a headache to their caregiver.

I remember writing a blog post in 2014 called "Spray fire in my head", that was how my son then described how he was feeling. He wanted to put the fire out inside his head.

If you have pain in your head, it is understandable that you might choose to hit your head.

There are very many different reasons that you might feel intense pain in your head. Some are treated at specialist head ache clinics that your neurologist would be able to advise you about. If you ever had Whole Exome Sequencing check if there are any mutations in ion channels, particularly those widely known to be linked to headaches.

Mast cell degranulation (which happens during an allergy) can trigger migraine pain.

GI discomfort triggering SIB

It is quite common for GI discomfort ranging from reflux to stomach cramps to trigger self-injury. Elsewhere in the book I look at IBS, IBD, EoE, SIBO and other GI problems common in autism.

Tooth-related pain triggering SIB

Not surprisingly some people's aggression is triggered by tooth pain. What surprised me was that the slow process of milk teeth roots dissolving and permanent teeth erupting could also be a trigger.

Inflammatory cytokines like IL-6 are used to signal the roots to dissolve, this is quite a lengthy process. There may be no physical pain caused but the inflammatory cytokine triggers a cascade of changes that worsen behavior, in a similar way to allergy.

This kind of aggressive behavior is likely to respond well to ibuprofen. Once your child has a full set of permanent teeth, you can forget this trigger for SIB.

Electroconvulsive therapy (ECT)

Electroconvulsive therapy (ECT) is used with good results to treat severe self-injury at the Kennedy Krieger Institute in Baltimore. ECT is carried out under general anesthetic, multiple sessions are required and then the child goes home. A few months later the SIB returns and they return to Baltimore for another round of treatment.

Nobody can really know what the mode of action is, but it seems to act like rebooting your old computer to fix a problem. It has been covered in a BBC documentary called *My Child ECT and Me*.

SSRIs like fluoxetine (Prozac)

Many people with autism are taking an SSRI (selective serotonin reuptake inhibitors) like Fluoxetine (Prozac). This might be to treat SIB, anxiety or OCD (obsessive compulsive behavior).

Long term use of an SSRI can be associated with troubling side effects, some of which may become permanent. There is a lot written about these side effects, much by people who are suffering them.

There are many different SSRI drugs and what works well for one person may not work well in the next person.

Sertraline (Zoloft) is another SSRI widely used in autism.

There have been many clinical trials of various SSRI drugs to treat autism, but none of these drugs is yet approved for autism. All use is off-label.

Genetic testing as a tool for personalized medicine

After a few years of writing my blog about autism science, I started to get people sending me their genetic test results. This is usually from Whole Exome Sequencing (WES). What usually happens is that a sample is taken from the child and both parents for analysis at the laboratory. The lab then looks up the list of mutated genes and checks whether any appear on their list of autism genes. If one of more mutated genes are listed as autism genes, you would be informed in a written report.

In most cases you will not be informed about the non-autism genes that have mutations. The reason being that they do not want to raise concerns among their clients/patients.

One problem with this is approach is that each lab has their own list of autism genes and it can be quite a short list. In reality, very many genes will have either a direct or indirect effect on autism. It clearly makes sense to look up all the mutated genes, not just the obvious ones.

Some labs will send you the extended list of all the mutated genes, if asked for it. Other providers will only give you the short report, saying that they have not identified any causal genes that relate to autism.

Single nucleotide polymorphisms or SNPs (pronounced "snips") are like individual spelling mistakes in your DNA. We all have many SNPs and most do us no harm. Most of the SNPs with relatively large effects on common diseases have been identified.

There is a risk of over-analyzing genetic testing results and drawing false conclusions. You might have an SNP in a causal gene, that is actually doing no harm; in which case this gene is not causal in your specific case.

Depending on who you ask, current genetic testing may give you some useful information in autism in 25% to 40% of cases.

Some cases are cut and dry, when there is a specific known mutation in a specific autism gene. You then have a known syndrome that results in autism, among its other symptoms.

One parent sent me their list of mutated genes from WES testing and there were several that could each individually be causal. Which one(s) are relevant in his case?

For most people genetic testing is not going to affect either treatment or the outcome. This is because medicine applied by doctors is decades behind the science and most doctors do not like to engage in experimental medicine.

Genetic testing could be used as a valuable tool in personalized medicine for autism; but it currently is not.

I was asked to speak about the potential use of genetic testing in autism at a conference.

I even contacted someone high up in Google to suggest that a "Gene Screen" application could easily be developed to interpret the results from genetic testing and directly indicate potentially effective therapies.

Personalized Medicine to Treat Neurological Disorders Based on Genetic Testing

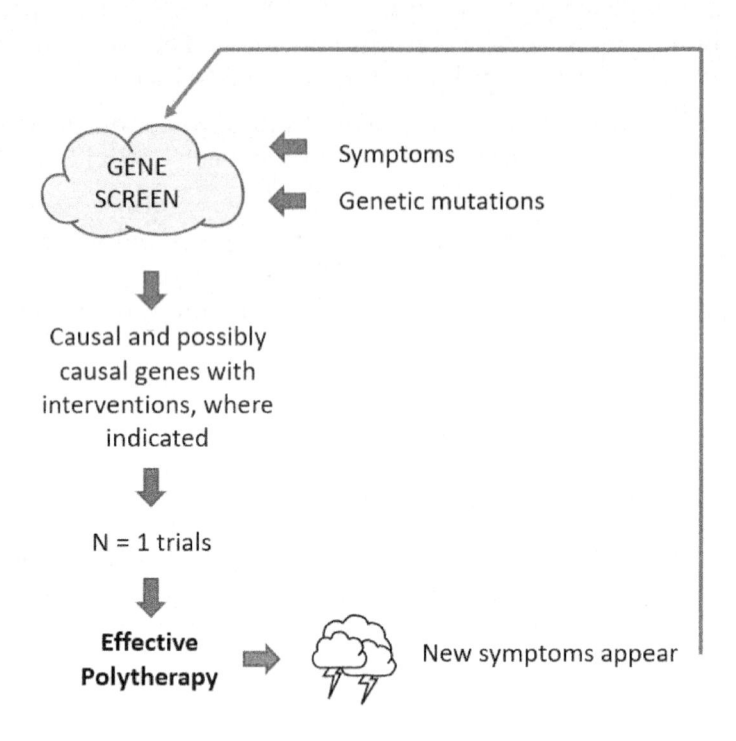

```
         ┌──────────────────────────────────────┐
         ↓                                      │
    ╭─────────╮  ⇐ Symptoms                     │
    │  GENE   │                                 │
    │ SCREEN  │  ⇐ Genetic mutations            │
    ╰─────────╯                                 │
         ↓                                      │
  Causal and possibly                           │
  causal genes with                             │
  interventions, where                          │
  indicated                                     │
         ↓                                      │
    N = 1 trials                                │
         ↓                                      │
   **Effective**    ⇒  ⛈   New symptoms appear ─┘
   **Polytherapy**
```

N is the number of subjects in the trial. In personalized medicine there is only one subject, so it is N = 1.

Because autism is not static, we have to anticipate that new symptoms will appear. When this happens, the process starts again with the new symptom being the target.

The method I used to develop my own personalized autism therapy was more traditional.

Personalized Medicine to Treat Neurological Disorders
Labour-intensive version

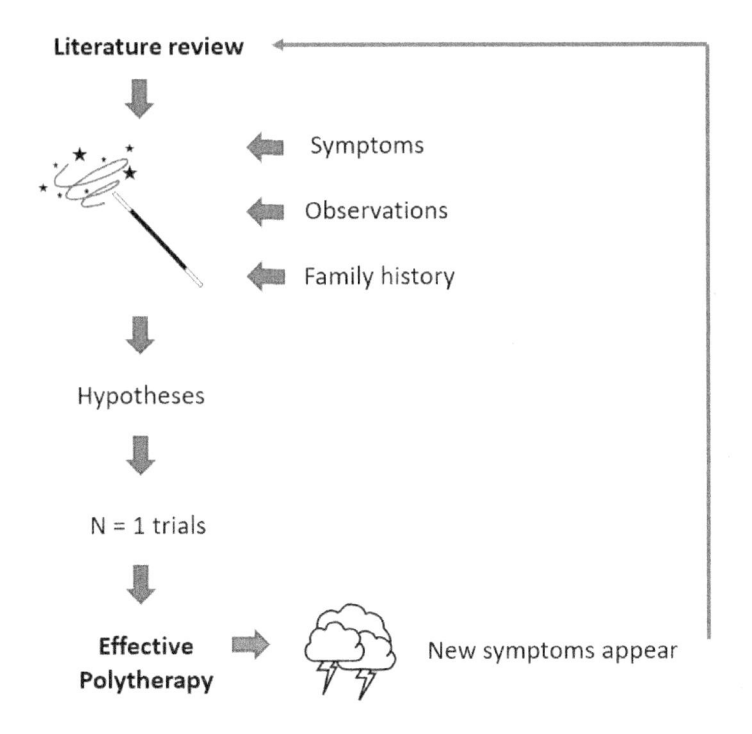

```
Literature review ←─────────────┐
      ↓                          │
   [wand]  ← Symptoms            │
           ← Observations        │
           ← Family history      │
      ↓                          │
  Hypotheses                     │
      ↓                          │
  N = 1 trials                   │
      ↓                          │
  Effective  ⇒ [clouds]  New symptoms appear
  Polytherapy
```

An increasing number of parents of older children are telling me that they only learnt of some key insights into their child's autism when they finally had a lumbar puncture and tested central spinal fluid (CSF). This requires anesthetic and is a rare procedure in children with autism. An MRI is also a comparatively rare procedure that really should be a standard one.

The ultimate hybrid approach would combine all sources of information. It would also screen for all those 116 causes of treatable intellectual disability (116 inborn errors of metabolism).

Personalized Medicine to Treat Neurological Disorders

Hybrid version

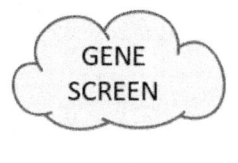

GENE SCREEN

Fast
Definitive for 1 in 4
Partially effective

+

Magnetic resonance imaging (MRI)
Analysis of
Cerebrospinal fluid (CSF)

Needs sedation
Invasive
Possibly informative

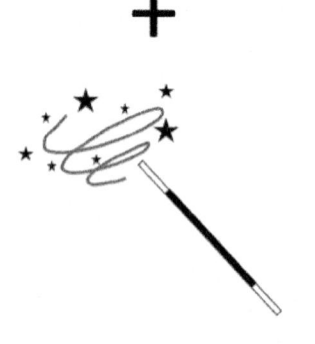

+

"Magic" is very time consuming. Not everyone can do it. Need luck and perseverance.

PETER LLOYD-THOMAS

Part 5

A to Z of Drugs Used in Autism Clinical Trials

The purpose of this section is to show readers that there already exists a large base of information coming from repurposing existing drugs to treat autism.

Many existing drugs have already been tested in at least one randomized double-blind placebo-controlled study in people with autism. Many of these drugs were shown to benefit at least some people with autism. Since there are hundreds of types of autism, even a positive response from a modest subset of those in the trial is actually a big success.

This list does not constitute a recommendation. I have included all the drugs that I found that have been trialed, plus a few more.

I personally would never give my son an antipsychotic drug like Risperidone, even though it has been approved for use in autism by the FDA since 2006. I understand its harmful side effects.

When I developed my son's therapy, I did not limit myself to this A to Z list. I read the underlying research and based on that I decided what I thought might be therapeutic. We live in a very imperfect world and many clever ideas exist in the research but are never followed up.

I do include a "how to use bumetanide guide" written by my friend and collaborator Dr Agnieszka Wroczyńska.

Acamprosate

Acamprosate is a drug to treat alcohol dependence. It blocks NMDA receptors, like mGluR5 (that are upregulated by chronic alcohol consumption) and it also increases the sensitivity of GABA$_A$ receptors (they are down-regulated by chronic alcohol consumption).

A small study in 2010, by the clinician who patented the idea, found some positive effects, with improvements in social relatedness.

A larger follow-on study was planned for 2013, but ten years later had not started.

Amantadine

Amantadine is a drug used to treat Parkinson's disease and other types of dyskinesia. It decreases the effects of glutamate, the excitatory neurotransmitter system which plays an important role in many psychiatric disorders. It does this by blocking NMDA receptors. It increases the level of dopamine in the brain.

It can help control the symptoms of irritability and hyperactivity in autism and also attention deficit hyperactivity disorder (ADHD).

Amantadine is well tolerated in children and adolescents, with an acceptable side effect profile, and is considered safe for long term use.

In a small autism trial in 2001, the clinicians noted an improvement in those taking amantadine, but the parents did not.

In a small retrospective review of the use of amantadine as an add-on therapy to control aggression in autism in 2016, the clinicians concluded that there was a benefit.

Aripiprazole (Abilify)

Aripiprazole is a cheap second-generation antipsychotic drug, developed in Japan.

Aripiprazole is widely prescribed to treat schizophrenia and bipolar disorder. The FDA in the United States has approved aripiprazole to treat irritability in autism.

Aripaprazole works slightly differently to other modern antipsychotic drugs. It targets dopamine receptors and serotonin receptors, but not the same ones and not in exactly the same way.

Like all antipsychotic drugs, it a has a long list of common side effects, the mildest is overeating leading to obesity.

The 2016 Cochrane review of existing clinical trials in autism concluded that aripiprazole can be effective as a short-term medication intervention for some behavioral aspects of ASD in children/adolescents. After a short-term medication intervention with aripiprazole, children/adolescents showed less irritability and hyperactivity and fewer stereotypies (repetitive, purposeless actions). However, notable side effects, such as weight gain, sedation, drooling and tremor, must be considered. One long-term, placebo discontinuation study found that relapse rates did not differ between children/adolescents randomized to continue aripiprazole versus children/adolescents randomized to receive placebo, suggesting that re-evaluation of aripiprazole use after a period of stabilization in irritability symptoms is warranted.

Atomoxetine (Strattera)

Atomoxetine is a drug for attention deficit hyperactivity disorder (ADHD) and bipolar that has been trialed in autism. It increases the levels of the hormones norepinephrine and dopamine in the brain – both of these effects are thought to be beneficial in ADHD.

ADHD is usually treated with stimulants like Ritalin, which work by increasing the level of dopamine in the brain.

In autism trials the conclusion is that atomoxetine can be an add-on therapy and may reduce the severity of autism on the CARS scale by about 4 points, (from 42 to 38 in one study).

Decreased appetite, nausea, and irritability can be the most frequent side effects.

B-12 (methylcobalamin)

Vitamin B-12 is an essential nutrient that plays a key role in critical processes within the body. Your body can store B-12 for years, but severe deficiency can lead to complications like anemia and nerve damage. Mild deficiency is quite common and B-12 levels are routinely tested.

People taking drugs to lower stomach acidity may not be able to absorb B12 and will require a supplement.

B-12 has been shown in trials to improve nerve repair and injections of B-12 in the form of methylcobalamin are a standard treatment in some countries after accidents that result in nerve damage.

For many years alternative doctors have prescribed subcutaneous injections of methylcobalamin to people with autism.

There have been small clinical trials, some at UC Davis. In most people there is either no behavioral improvement, or a modest improvement.

In one study a small sub-group seemed to experience a benefit. That group seems to experience significantly increased plasma concentrations of GSH. That is suggesting that the increase in anti-oxidant capacity provided by B-12 is associated with behavioral improvement.

A subsequent study did not find methylcobalamin affected GSH and the GSH/GSSG ratio.

In 2016 a small trial, funded by Autism Speaks, compared subcutaneous injections of Methyl B12 versus a placebo.

No improvements were noted by the parents using the ABC and SRS rating scales.

The primary outcome measure – the clinician rated CGI-I score – was better in the methyl B12 group than in the placebo group.

The researchers noted that the behavioral improvement in the methyl B12 group was concentrated among 10 out of 17 children whose bloodwork suggested they had a positive biological response. These responders showed increased levels of methionine and other blood chemicals associated with decreased cell and DNA damage.

Hyperactivity and pica, trying to eat non-food items, are common side effects.

Baclofen and arbaclofen/R-baclofen

Baclofen (Lioresal) is a cheap drug to treat spastic movement disorders. It was found, by chance, to improve some people's autism. Baclofen is a mixture of R-baclofen and S-baclofen, both of which activate GABA$_B$ receptors.

Researchers from MIT concluded that the autism benefit comes from R-baclofen and a great deal of money was spent on clinical trials of Arbaclofen/R-baclofen. The drug firm Roche abandoned funding the project due to the trial failing to meet its objectives. Later the Simons Foundation resurrected the project and further trials are now being planned, with different end points. In clinical trials the measure of success is called the end point.

I was contacted by a UK pediatrician years ago who told me that her patients with Asperger's syndrome often respond well to baclofen and that there were no problems with side effects or tolerance. That doctor felt unable to continue with this treatment, since there were no clinical trials or other evidence to support its use. She contacted me for help to justify her continued prescribing. She was not interested to organize a formal clinical trial. Doctors do not like to prescribe off-label.

In 2019, in Iran baclofen was trialed in 64 children aged 3–12 years old, as an adjuvant to risperidone for improvement of hyperactivity symptoms in children with ASD. It was found to be safe and effective.

In Russia, drugs that activate GABA$_B$ receptors are used to treat autism. They have a drug called Pantogam, which is itself a mixture of D-Pantogam and L-Pantogam. L-Pantogam is sold as Pantogam Aktiv. This drug appears not to be suited to long term continuous usage, unlike baclofen.

BH4 (tetrahydrobiopterin)

BH4 is a chemical found in the body that is required for many important chemical reactions. The drug form is used to treat BH4 deficiency usually caused by GTPCH deficiency or PTPS deficiency.

One study showed significant improvements for BH4 relative to placebo with regard to social awareness, autism mannerisms, hyperactivity, and inappropriate speech. Side effects were minimal and similar between both active medication and placebo.

BH4 (Kuvan) is currently extremely expensive.

Bumetanide

Bumetanide is a cheap generic drug used as a diuretic. It has a secondary effect blocking the NKCC2 transporter in the brain and so lowers the level of chloride within brain cells.

Elevated chloride in brain cells causes the key neurotransmitter GABA to work in reverse and cause an excitatory/inhibitory imbalance in the brain. Bumetanide can partially correct this defect.

It is specifically the GABA$_A$ receptor that becomes dysfunctional when chloride levels are too high.

Bumetanide was first investigated in mouse models of autism, before a series of trials began in France. The phase 3 trials took place in multiple centres across Europe and it was predicted to become approved for autism by 2025. Unfortunately, the phase 3 trial failed.

Why did yet another expensive clinical trial for autism fail?

An Italian group that are developing a new version of bumetanide, one that does not cause urination, told me that the problem was that the dose was too low. The trial used a low dose to minimize the urination, but this also inevitably reduces its effect on the brain.

I have been in touch with French bumetanide researchers for a decade and I told them that their trial dose 0.5mg twice a day has no effect on my son. At the age of 9, a dose of 1mg once a day was effective and I later increased it to 2mg once a day. Bumetanide very poorly crosses the blood brain barrier and you need a high level in your blood to get anything significant to enter the brain. The disadvantage is urination, but this is entirely manageable.

Then in 2022 Chinese researchers published a study that showed biological markers that could predict who responds most to bumetanide.

> "three cytokine levels, namely the IFN-γ, MIG and IFN-α2 … These cytokine levels at the baseline could improve the prediction of the bumetanide responders"

The French researchers did not focus their phase 3 trial on severe autism and probably ended up including a large number of people who do not have elevated chloride. Another subgroup had such highly elevated chloride that the trial dosage provided no benefit.

Bumetanide corrects a core defect in autism and, in those who are genuine responders, they experience wide ranging beneficial effects. Those with severe autism are likely to see their measured IQ increase substantially.

Bumetanide is a sulfonamide drug which may trigger an allergic reaction in people who do not tolerate sulfonamide drugs.

A guest post in my blog was dedicated to the safe use of bumetanide in autism.

Since my blog is seen as home to the off-label use of bumetanide, here it is:

The Safe Use of Bumetanide in Children with Autism
Practical Tips for Parents and Professionals

Agnieszka Wroczyńska MD, PhD [1], Peter Lloyd-Thomas Meng, MBA[2]

1 Medical University of Gdańsk, Poland
wroczynska@gumed.edu.pl

2 https://epiphanyasd.com

Updated: 06.06.2019

Bumetanide is a prescription diuretic drug usually used to treat heart diseases or hypertension in adults. It also affects neuronal chloride regulation and was found to improve the quality of life of autistic children targeting core autism symptoms in clinical trials in Europe. Bumetanide has been used off-label in children and adults across the autism spectrum for several years, mostly in France. It is a safe drug with a long history of use in medicine and well-known precautions ensure side effects are avoided.

Details of bumetanide's mechanism of action and its beneficial effects in autism were discussed elsewhere – see the references below. According to the most recent review of bumetanide clinical trials in autism:

> *"Current evidence suggests bumetanide, with close monitoring, may be useful in patients with moderate to severe ASD when traditional behavioral therapies are not*

available or an irritability-modifying pharmacological agent is not required" [James et al. 2019].

Bumetanide treatment should be supervised by a physician. Multinational phase 3 trial of bumetanide for children with autism aged 2–17 years of age started in Europe in 2018. If you live elsewhere and consider bumetanide, this article can be used as a practical companion to ensure safe treatment. It is written for parents and physicians who are not experienced with diuretic use in children or bumetanide itself. While bumetanide's safety precautions can be summarized in short as "drinking more water, eating bananas and if required, use potassium supplementation", this document aims to explain those in detail and provide practical tips for a variety of clinical scenarios.

#1 Myth: Bumetanide is an experimental drug

No. Bumetanide has been used in medicine for years. It's safety profile and recommended precautions are well known and understood. Bumetanide has been studied in both adults and children and found to be well tolerated.

Who can use bumetanide? What should you do before starting bumetanide?

If you are considering using bumetanide, make sure to check with your doctor if there are any contraindications in your child. Bumetanide is a sulfonamide drug. Children with allergy to sulfonamides should not take bumetanide. Another sulfonamide drug commonly used in children is an antibiotic called trimethoprim/ sulfamethoxazole (TMP/SMX), also known as co-trimoxazole. In many European countries co-trimoxazole's brand name is Bactrim. If your child is allergic to co-trimoxazole (Bactrim) or any other sulfonamide drug, then bumetanide should not be used.

It is important to make a distinction between sulfonamide drugs and other sulfur-containing medications and additives, such as sulfates and sulfites, which are chemically unrelated to the sulfonamide group. Allergic reactions associated with sulfonamides are not associated with sulfur, sulfates or sulfites intolerance.

The full list of bumetanide interactions with other drugs is long, but most of the drugs included are not usually used in children.

Children with liver or kidney diseases as well as those with abnormal ECG (electrocardiogram) findings were excluded from the French bumetanide trials. If your child suffers from one of these conditions you need to discuss bumetanide safety with the relevant specialist. Epilepsy does not preclude bumetanide use. In fact, preliminary research showed bumetanide has a positive impact on seizures in temporal lobe epilepsy in adults.

What laboratory tests are needed before and during bumetanide treatment in children?

Bumetanide is a safe drug, provided basic precautions related to its diuretic mechanism of action are taken. One of the most important safety considerations associated with bumetanide use is electrolyte balance. Bumetanide can affect electrolyte blood level and increase potassium loss. Extremely low potassium levels are dangerous, but this is preventable with simple measures in a person using bumetanide.

#2 Myth: Bumetanide use in children with autism is associated with significant risk of dangerous adverse effects.

No. Clinical trials and off-label prescribing experience proved that bumetanide adverse effects can be easily prevented in children. No dangerous symptoms were related to bumetanide in studies on its use in children with autism.

No serious symptoms associated with low potassium levels or electrolyte imbalance were seen in children included into bumetanide trials and case reports so far. However, they might affect a child's well-being and possibly reduce bumetanide's positive behavioral or sensory effect. You may not see the expected results of bumetanide treatment if an adequate potassium level and hydration are not ensured in your child.

That is why it is necessary to test electrolytes levels (potassium, sodium, chloride, magnesium and calcium) before bumetanide introduction and repeat them, especially potassium blood concentration, after the treatment is started.

In the French bumetanide trials several other blood tests were offered to children i.e. g-glutamyltransferase, transaminases, alkaline phosphatases, glucose, uric acid and creatinine. While it is not required to order all of them in a similar way as in the research clinical studies, they are basic and cheap tests, available in most laboratories and it is prudent to check these parameters at least once during early phase of the bumetanide treatment.

In clinical trials children were examined by a physician on a regular basis and had their heart rate, blood pressure and weight checked. Such approach also improves safety of bumetanide use. In turn, all these simple steps increase the chance of experiencing positive effects of bumetanide treatment.

Bumetanide proved to be a safe treatment in the trials. Blood pressure and results of the routine tests did not differ between the bumetanide and placebo groups. Kidney ultrasound did not reveal any abnormalities during treatment. Children in the trials had also ECG (electrocardiogram) done as a precaution. It is prudent to offer a child such test as they are non-invasive and can be done in a stress-free manner.

As bumetanide is a diuretic drug, it is highly recommended to explain its effects prior to treatment and with the use of the communication means used by that child. Social stories, visuals and AAC tools can be helpful for some children. This approach can reduce psychological stress potentially related to the diuretic treatment in children prone to anxiety in new situations.

The diuretic effect of bumetanide is strongest within the first 2 hours of taking the drug. Bumetanide given early in the morning (straight after waking up) lets the child avoid unnecessary toilet visits at school or kindergarten. Giving bumetanide once a day may be much more convenient depending on the person's particular circumstances.

Starting bumetanide – what dose should be used and what to expect?

In the first randomized clinical trial in France the dose of 0.5 mg bumetanide was given twice daily to children 3–11 years old and was found effective in many of them. However, for some people this dose may not be sufficient as actually only about 1% of bumetanide can cross the blood brain barrier and act on neurons. In the 2017 bumetanide study doses up to 2 mg twice daily were trialed. While using higher doses may increase the amount of bumetanide that would reach the brain and so enhance the positive effects of the treatment, it also was found that drug-related adverse event risk is dose dependent and 0.5 mg b.i.d (twice daily) dose was found to be the best tolerated. It is a matter of a careful, individual trial to find an optimal dose for each person.

The benefits of bumetanide treatment can sometimes be seen as early as after 2 weeks, but it is not uncommon to have to wait longer. It is recommended to continue up to 3 months to assess the full impact of bumetanide use. Minor effects may indicate that the child is indeed a bumetanide responder, but the dose needs to be increased.

The beneficial effects seen in a child taking bumetanide are highly variable and individual. In general, this drug targets core autism symptoms and improvements in communication, social skills, including eye contact, speech and sensory issues were reported on bumetanide, as well as stereotyped behaviors decrease, better mood or increased cognition. Many parents can notice more awareness in their children and describe it as if "the fog has lifted". Behavioral improvements were also reported on bumetanide e.g. reduction in aggressive behaviors.

The only known indicator of which people with autism respond to bumetanide, is a previous unexpected negative reaction to Valium (diazepam), or other benzodiazepine drug. These drugs should be calming, but in some people with the GABA neurotransmitter dysfunction targeted by bumetanide, the effect can be agitation and aggression.

How to control hydration in children using bumetanide?

Bumetanide belongs to the "loop diuretics" class of drugs which can lower blood potassium level and increase the body fluid loss. You need to monitor hydration in a child treated with bumetanide. If fluid consumption is increased to compensate for the urination, there will be no significant blood pressure lowering effect from bumetanide, nor will there be dehydration. The daily amount of fluid required varies, but it usually needs to be significantly higher than the volume drank by a child before bumetanide treatment.

Some children drink up to 3 liters (3 US quarts) per day while on bumetanide, others need less. It is safer to err on the side of too much fluid intake rather than too little. Drinking 3 liters of fluids a day in a teenager on bumetanide is not unusual.

In children who still wear diapers/nappies the amount of urination may cause a problem with leakage.

No severe adverse clinical symptoms related to dehydration were found during the bumetanide pediatric trials. However, a child who develops dehydration issues on bumetanide may feel unwell, so it is highly recommended to prevent it.

An easy way to check hydration status in a child is an assessment of mouth mucosa. You can ask your child to present her or his tongue and compare the tongue look with another member of the family. It can be made a good fun for younger children. If the tongue mucosa looks drier in a child on bumetanide, then you need to help the child drink more. Most children automatically drink more fluids, but some refuse to cooperate and drink more. Finding out beverages attractive for your child (e.g. drinking water from a dispenser, juice with ice-cubes etc.) may be useful in such a situation.

Monitoring hydration with weight checks or measuring urine volume, while used in other situations, are impractical in a person on bumetanide.

You can read more on child dehydration symptoms. It is useful to learn about those symptoms as a parent even if you do not plan to use bumetanide.

How to ensure enough potassium intake in a child on bumetanide?

Simple dietary modifications can provide necessary additional potassium and are recommended for every child on bumetanide. Use potassium salt and increase other dietary potassium in your kitchen. Bananas, kiwis, dried fruit, tomatoes are all examples of foods rich in potassium. The daily recommended intake of potassium is 3 to 4 g depending on age. A medium sized banana contains about 0.5g. Most people do not achieve the RDA for potassium but exceed the maximum limit for sodium, which is about 2g.

#3 Myth: Potassium supplements can cause serious heart rhythm issues in children on bumetanide.

No. Recommended potassium daily intake is well above the supplement doses usually used with bumetanide. Provided normal kidney function, there is no significant risk of dietary/oral supplement potassium overdose when typically recommended doses are considered.

Apart from dietary modifications, low dose potassium supplementation can be used in addition to bumetanide from the beginning of the treatment. In the first weeks of bumetanide use it is also necessary to test potassium blood level. In the French trial blood potassium levels were checked before bumetanide introduction and then at 7, 30, 60 and 90 days after the treatment started. You may consider potassium blood level test sooner than after 30 days: it can be scheduled 2–3 weeks after bumetanide introduction to detect low potassium level early. The normal blood level range of potassium is 3,5 – 5,0 mmol/l. In case of abnormally low blood potassium level (which is called "hypokalemia") you need to consult your doctor and add or adjust the dose of potassium supplement for your child. The target is to keep the potassium level well within the normal range. In the first bumetanide randomized clinical trial 22% of children taking bumetanide 0.5 mg b.i.d. (twice daily) experienced benign hypokalemia (low potassium), which was resolved by giving potassium gluconate syrup. In the next French trial the potassium level fell below normal range in 30% of children on that dose, but no serious potassium-related adverse event was seen. A potassium supplement was given to all these children to correct the low blood level.

The potassium dose should be adjusted individually according to blood level and repeat tests may be helpful. As some autistic children seem not to tolerate even minor drops in potassium level, you and your doctor may consider increasing potassium supplementation to keep its level in the upper normal range in those cases.

Side effects of bumetanide and how to manage them:

"Accidents" caused by urination: need to plan ahead. Don't give bumetanide before starting a long car journey or before sleep.

Dehydration has many effects that you may not notice. Make sure your child carries a water bottle and so has easy access to fluids.

Low potassium has many effects and so add potassium to diet as a precaution. Most people are nowhere near the recommended intake of potassium, so add potassium-rich food to diet.

The optimal dose of potassium varies and is highly individual: few children need dietary modifications only, some use as low as 100 mg potassium daily, while some require 500 mg t.i.d. (three times a day) to maintain normal potassium level on bumetanide. Potassium supplements come in different forms e.g. syrup, effervescent tablets, slow-release capsules. Liquid supplements, including effervescent drinks, seem free from the risk of GI distress associated with tablets, which may be especially important in a child who is not able to communicate the pain. It is very hard to do harm by eating too much dietary potassium, because it is absorbed very slowly. Many potassium supplements are absorbed quickly and so giving more than 500mg at once is unwise. Note that in America most potassium supplement tablets do not contain more than 100mg.

It is necessary to actively prevent dehydration and potassium loss while on bumetanide treatment. The good news is that it is easy to achieve with simple steps described above. These precautions become even more important in children who struggle to report thirst and distress due to communication difficulties as well as in situations which make a child prone to dehydration regardless of diuretic use e.g. diarrhea, vomiting, fever or very hot summer temperatures, especially during physical exercise. If such issues occur, you need to be vigilant, consider a doctor's appointment and potassium blood level check with additional supplementation as needed.

In case of persistent low blood potassium concentration it is recommended to check blood levels of magnesium as well. Magnesium deficiency may contribute to hypokalemia (low potassium). If this is the case, supplementing magnesium along with potassium is a solution. Low potassium levels can also be made worse by high sodium levels.

Is long term bumetanide use safe and practical?

Over time, on a proper diet and potassium supplementation, a child treated with bumetanide usually achieves a stable electrolyte balance, so control blood tests are rarely required on long term bumetanide treatment. In fact long term bumetanide use is very practical, and the simple safety precautions required are nothing compared to coping with untreated symptoms common in severe autism e.g. sensory suffering, which may significantly improve on bumetanide.

> **#4 Myth: While on bumetanide every child is required to have often blood draws to check potassium.**
>
> No. Repeated blood draws are required at the beginning of bumetanide treatment to assess individual supplemental potassium needs. Later there is no need to test potassium on regular basis.

If a blood draw is an issue in a child with anxiety or sensory disorders, this is what might help:

- Visuals to reduce anxiety in a child e.g. picture social stories explaining blood draw procedure
- AAC used for communication in a non-verbal or minimally verbal children
- Video modelling or blood draw play at home before the procedure
- Skilled nurse and friendly environment, which can be arranged in advance
- At home blood draw service.

It needs to be stressed that in general, presumed behavioral difficulties should not be a barrier to necessary medical examinations or procedures needed for health in autistic children, as avoiding them can result in increasing the medical risks in a population already prone to co-morbidities and poor health outcomes. It is the responsibility of the health provider and the parent to find the most convenient and effective way to perform the examinations needed. It is not unusual that all medical procedures get easier over the time in a child who uses bumetanide and develops communications skills and improves their cognitive function and awareness.

How to deal with the "bumetanide has stopped working" problem?

After some months or even years some parents may feel that "bumetanide has stopped working". This may well not be their imagination and it can be very disconcerting. A little science is required to explain what may be happening. It appears that bumetanide responders have too many NKCC1 transporters in their neurons and too few KCC2. Only about 1% of bumetanide can cross the blood brain barrier where it blocks the NKCC1 transporter. An inflammatory response elsewhere in the body sends inflammatory signals throughout the body and some reach the brain where this causes an increase in NKCC1 and a reduction in KCC2 expression. This effect can wipe out the beneficial effect of that tiny 1% of bumetanide that is present. You can increase the dose of bumetanide and try and reduce the source of inflammation, which might be as simple as an allergy, or the cause might be harder to identify. There will be many other biological reasons why a shift in NKCC1/KCC2 might occur, so some detective work will be needed. The beneficial effect of bumetanide will then be restored.

Conclusions

Almost all parents whose children were included into the first bumetanide randomized clinical trial in France asked for treatment continuation after the study finished. Safe use of bumetanide for up to 2 years later were reported in this group. According to personal communication, bumetanide has been successfully subsequently used off label for at least 8 years in children and youth with autism, and no long-term issues emerged on long-term treatment. While this treatment does not offer an "autism cure", it could significantly increase the quality of life of autistic persons thanks its potential to bring about improvements in sensory processing and hypersensitivity, cognition and acquiring communication skills (see published studies, linked below, for details on potential positive effects of bumetanide).

If you want to see my science-lite presentation at the Brain Foundation's conference called Synchrony 2020, all about using bumetanide, it is on YouTube.

Just google "Brain Foundation Autism Parent's Perspective: 8 years of Bumetanide Use" or just "Peter Lloyd-Thomas YouTube".

***

Buspirone

Buspirone (Buspar) is a cheap drug used to treat anxiety.

Buspirone is not a benzodiazepine and does not interact with the GABA$_A$ receptor.

Buspirone decreases serotonin levels in specific brain areas while increasing dopamine and norepinephrine levels. It activates a serotonin receptor called 5-HT1A and a secondary effect of that is releasing the emotion hormone oxytocin. Oxytocin is itself a potential autism therapy.

Buspirone is used to treat anxiety in autism. In one trial, and only at the low dose of 2.5 mg, of buspirone there was a meaningful improvement in the ADOS Restricted and Repetitive Behavior score. At a dose of 5mg the effect was lost.

The anxiety dose for buspirone is much higher, 20–60mg, depending on age.

CBD (Cannabidiol) and CBDV (Cannabidivarin)

CBD (Cannabidiol) and CBDV (Cannabidivarin) are both non-psychoactive cannabinoids found in cannabis.

Both CBD and CBDV are being trialed in children with autism. In the case of CBDV the target is to reduce irritability.

To date, the trials that have been complete are small observational studies of CBD that do show a benefit in those that tolerate the therapy. The strongest improvements were reported for seizures, Attention Deficit Hyperactivity Disorder (ADHD), sleep disorders, and communication and social interaction deficits.

Celocoxib

Celocoxib is a cheap anti-inflammatory drug (NSAID - nonsteroidal anti-inflammatory drug) widely used to treat joint pain and arthritis. It is a so-called COX-2 inhibitor.

Celocoxib has been used to treat bipolar, schizophrenia and some types of depression.

Celocoxib is a sulfonamide drug which may trigger an allergic reaction in people who do not tolerate sulfonamide drugs.

There have been many trials of COX-2 inhibitors in neurological disorders. These disorders are associated with unusually elevated inflammatory markers, that can, to some degree, be suppressed using a cheap drug like celocoxib. In effect, it is an immunosuppressing drug.

The problem is that all the NSAIDS drugs also inhibit COX-1 to some degree and this causes their GI (gut) side effects.

Celocoxib is the most selective common NSAID for COX-2 and so should cause the least level of COX-1 side effects. That is why they did not use naproxen or ibuprofen in the clinical trials.

In one autism clinical trial, the combination of risperidone and celocoxib was superior to risperidone alone in treating irritability, social withdrawal, and stereotypy of children with autism.

Clomipramine

Clomipramine is a tricyclic antidepressant. This class of drug is very old and closely related to the first generation of antihistamine drugs, the ones that treat allergy but make you drowsy.

Later versions of antihistamines were modified, so they could not cross the blood brain barrier and so do not send you to sleep.

All this class of drugs have very many secondary different effects and so they are good targets to be repurposed for other uses.

Clomipramine is also used to treat OCD (obsessive–compulsive disorder), and chronic pain. It is a weak serotonin reuptake inhibitor.

In a small study clomipramine produced significant improvement in social relatedness, obsessive compulsive symptoms, and aggressive and impulsive behavior. Others studies were not so positive.

Clonidine

Clonidine is a drug used to treat high blood pressure, but also ADHD (attention deficit hyperactivity disorder). Clonidine binds to alpha-2 adrenergic receptors and so it inhibits the release of the hormone norepinephrine, which is why it is helpful in ADHD.

Clonidine reduces vascular resistance and hence lowers blood pressure.

Clonidine has been prescribed as a sleep aid in children both with and without ADHD.

In an autism clinical trial clonidine was effective in reducing sleep initiation latency and night awakening, and to a lesser degree in improving attention deficits hyperactivity, mood instability and aggressiveness.

CM-AT

A start-up company called Curemark has been developing an autism therapy since 2010, but has never published the results of its clinical trials.

The company proposes that many children with autism exhibit impaired protein digestion, which may or may not manifest from self-restricted diets. The inability to digest protein affects the availability of essential amino acids in the body. CM-AT is designed to enhance protein digestion thereby potentially restoring the pool of essential amino acids. Essential amino acids play a critical role in the expression of several genes important to neurological function and serve as precursors to key neurotransmitters such as serotonin and dopamine.

It appears that CM-AT is a treatment similar to that for Pancreatic Insufficiency. Pancreatic enzyme replacement therapy is used to treat Cystic Fibrosis because the ducts from the pancreas get blocked. A common therapy is Creon, which comes as an enteric coated capsule containing acid-resistant microspheres. This is more effective than sprinkling a powder on food.

There are long-established tests for pancreatic insufficiency.

Testing the level of amino acids in the blood of people with autism has not yielded any consistent meaningful insights.

Secretin is a hormone that regulates the pancreas. In 1998 it was suggested that secretin could be an effective autism therapy, but later it was concluded not to have any benefit. Some alternative doctors do still use it. In one of the patents, assigned to Curemark, the word secretin appears 128 times.

A 2012 Cochrane review concluded:

"There is no evidence that single or multiple dose intravenous secretin is effective and as such currently it should not be recommended or administered as a treatment for ASD. Further experimental assessment of secretin's effectiveness for ASD can only be justified if there is new high-quality and replicated scientific evidence that either finds that secretin has a role in neurotransmission in a way that could benefit all children with ASD or identifies important subgroups of children with ASD who could benefit from secretin because of a proven link between the action of secretin and the known cause of their ASD, or the type of problems they are experiencing."

Many people with autism do supplement with various amino acids and others take digestive enzymes.

Some amino acids can be used as drugs, for example:

- Using the three Branch Chained Amino Acids (BCAAs) to reduce the level of the amino acid phenylanine, which can drive movement disorders/tics
- Threonine is being studied as a possible therapy for Inflammatory Bowel Disease (IBD), because it may increase intestinal mucin synthesis
- Methionine seems to promote speech in regressive autism, but for no known reason

It seems unlikely that there is a one size fits all amino acid therapy, nonetheless it would be great if there was at least one FDA approved therapy.

Cyproheptadine

Cyproheptadine (Periactin) is an old first-generation antihistamine with certain other effects. It is anticholinergic and antiserotonergic, so it blocks the action of the neurotransmitters acetylcholine and serotonin. The anticholinergic effect causes a dry mouth.

It can be used to prevent migraine and to stimulate appetite.

Cyproheptadine is a serotonin 5-HT2A receptor antagonist. Many antipsychotic drugs and indeed psychedelic drugs, like LSD, work by affecting 5-HT2A receptors.

Note that serotonin is the same thing as 5-HT.

Research has shown that 5-HT2A receptor activity is altered in autism and that blocking this receptor (with an antagonist) reduces repetitive behaviors seen in autism.

Many people with Asperger's self-treat by targeting 5-HT2A receptors.

In an autism clinical trial, it was found that the combination of cyproheptadine with a conventional antipsychotic was more beneficial than the conventional antipsychotic alone for children with autistic disorder. The authors stated that "the difference between the two treatments was significant".

D-cycloserine

D-cycloserine (DCS) is an antibiotic used to treat tuberculosis. It is inexpensive in most of the world, but more expensive in the United States.

At low doses, and even intermittent dosing, DCS may have a clever sub-unit specific effect on NMDA receptors that can affect learning, emotions and anxiety.

DCS may improve the negative symptoms of schizophrenia, such as lack of emotional reactions, loss of drive, loss of interest, and loss of fluency of thought.

DCS acts as a dose-dependent agonist or antagonist to the NMDA receptor, and thus its dose needs careful thought. Only low-dose D-cycloserine (50 mg/day) is associated with an improvement in the negative symptoms of people with schizophrenia. Low-dose DCS given once a week improves the extinction of fear in anxiety disorders.

Research suggests that D-cycloserine may be of use in ASD, given the similarity between the negative symptoms of people with schizophrenia and the social impairment of people with ASD, as well as the glutamate dysfunction found in both disorders.

Once a week dosage of DCS persistently improves the negative symptoms of schizophrenia and memory consolidation. This would seem potentially beneficial in some autism, especially those many adults with an autism diagnosis given in childhood who show many symptoms of schizophrenia in adulthood, although they may be oblivious to them.

In one autism study, weekly single doses of 50 mg of DCS significantly increased the sustained benefit from short-term social skills intervention three months after treatment cessation.

Low dose, weekly dosing of DCS should be safe, cheap and simple. It may help in some cases of autism. For schizophrenia it would be an obvious choice to try.

Dextromethorphan

Dextromethorphan is an OTC cough suppressor, but it is a morphine derivative. Dextromethorphan is used in some neuropsychiatric disorders.

Dextromethorphan has very many biological effects; along with its metabolite, dextrorphan, it acts as an NMDA receptor antagonist, making it an attractive candidate for drug abusers.

Dextromethorphan has been researched as a therapy for a vast range of conditions ranging from Parkinson's to stroke, to neuropathic pain and all the way over to epilepsy and autism.

One reason suggested for its effect reducing seizures is through alterations in the subunit composition of $GABA_A$ receptors. If that was true, it would be relevant to autism.

The response in small autism trials has been highly variable, which can be explained by the highly varied (heterogeneous) nature of autism and the numerous modes of action of dextromethorphan. In one small trial the overall result showed no effect, but looking at individuals, there were three responders and one super-responder who showed greater than 50% reduction in the core symptoms measured.

Donepezil

Donepezil is a cheap drug used to treat Alzheimer's, but it is not very effective.

Donepezil increases the level of the neurotransmitter acetylcholine, which is usually thought to be the beneficial mode of action in Alzheimer's - but it is also a so-called sigma-1 agonist.

Donepezil binds and reversibly inactivates the cholinesterases, thus inhibiting hydrolysis of acetylcholine. This increases acetylcholine concentrations at cholinergic synapses.

Another sigma-1 agonist (Anavex) is being developed to treat Rett syndrome and the developer is also proposing it for dementia. Sigma-1 agonists target ER stress and protein misfolding, which play a key role in how brains degenerate in old age. ER stress is a known feature in autism.

In some people with Tourette's syndrome Donepezil reduces their tics. It has been used in ADHD and autism.

The several autism studies to date that evaluated Donepezil gave mixed results. There were people who benefitted, but many did not.

There was an idea to trial Donepezil in Rett syndrome, but there is no record of it being completed.

Fluoxetine

Fluoxetine (Prozac) is a very widely prescribed antidepressant of the selective serotonin reuptake inhibitor (SSRI) class. It has been shown effective to treat OCD (Obsessive–compulsive disorder) and it is widely prescribed in the US to people with autism. Even Temple Grandin says she takes it – just a small dose.

Fluoxetine is FDA approved to treat OCD associated with autism. Fluoxetine can have side-effects, which are dose dependent.

One study in 2019 found fluoxetine no better than a placebo and a Cochrane review in 2013 of nine clinical trials of SSRI drugs (fluoxetine, fluvoxamine, fenfluramine and citalopram) concluded:

> "There is no evidence of effect of SSRIs in children and emerging evidence of harm. There is limited evidence of the effectiveness of SSRIs in adults from small studies in which risk of bias is unclear."

At very low doses, much lower than usually prescribed by a doctor, some SSRI drugs do have a different mode of action that is totally unrelated to serotonin. At low doses (about 1/10th of the normal dose) SSRIs stimulate the production of certain natural steroids in the brain. In particular, allopregnanolone rises and this may change the composition of GABA$_A$ receptors and so modulate neuronal excitability.

If you are interested, search "Low dose SSRIs as Selective Brain Steroidogenic Stimulants (SBSSs)" on my blog.

A trial of the supplement pregnenolone at Stanford University concluded: "Pregnenolone was modestly effective and was overall safe and well tolerated in individuals with ASD". They report that 50% of the trial group were responders. They found that pregnenolone reduced the levels of irritability and associated aggressive behaviors.

Pregnenolone is a precursor to some of the body's own neurosteroids, such as allopregnanolone.

Fluvoxamine

Fluvoxamine (Luvox) is an antidepressant of the selective serotonin reuptake inhibitor (SSRI) class, commonly used to treat OCD (Obsessive–compulsive disorder). It is also a sigma-1 agonist.

In one small autism study half of the patients were categorized as responders. It reduced repetitive thoughts and behavior, maladaptive behavior, and aggression, and it improved some aspects of social relatedness especially language usage. This old study clearly did not impress the Cochrane reviewers, when they assessed its significance in 2013.

Galantamine

Galantamine is a drug used to treat Alzheimer's Disease and vascular dementia. It was developed in Russia, but is now approved in the United States.

Galantamine increases the concentration of the neurotransmitter acetylcholine in certain parts of the brain. This is the same as with donepezil, but the mechanism is very different.

Galantamine is a potent modulator (PAM) of certain nicotinic acetylcholine receptors (nAChRs). This increases the receptors response to acetylcholine. This effect on cholinergic neurons causes an increase in the amount of acetylcholine released. More acetylcholine should boost cognitive function.

In autism, both cholinergic and nicotinic receptors are believed to play a role and some studies have shown that cholinergic and nicotinic treatments have improved attention in autistic children.

It has been hypothesized that galantamine's dual action mechanism might make it a good choice for autism.

It might be expected that galantamine would be more effective in autism than Donepezil. The small studies carried out do indeed bear this out. Galantamine improvements listed included irritability, eye contact, hyperactivity, inappropriate speech and social withdrawal.

Guanfacine

Guanfacine (Tenex) is a drug used to treat both high blood pressure and ADHD.

Guanfacine works by activating alpha 2A adrenoceptors. This lowers blood pressure, but also has a very specific effect in a part of the brain called the prefrontal cortex where it enhances neuronal firing. This second effect is important to people with ADHD.

Sometimes guanfacine is used to treat Tourette's syndrome and sometimes autism.

A study at Emory University showed that extended-release guanfacine appears to be safe and effective for reducing hyperactivity, impulsiveness, and distractibility in children with ASD.

Haloperidol

Haloperidol, is an old typical antipsychotic medication. Haloperidol is used in the treatment of schizophrenia, tics in Tourette syndrome and mania in bipolar disorder

It has well known troubling side effects – some may be irreversible. These tend to be called Extrapyramidal Symptoms (EPS); EPS are bad.

Haloperidol is an antagonist of dopamine D2 receptors at low doses but preferentially an antagonist of serotonin 5-HT2 receptors at high doses.

Antagonism of D2 receptors is more beneficial on the positive symptoms of schizophrenia and antagonism of 5-HT2 receptors is helpful for the negative symptoms.

Haloperidol has sometimes been used in autism to treat severe behavioral problems.

Children with prominent symptoms of irritability, angry and labile affect, and uncooperativeness were the best responders to haloperidol.

Multiple studies found haloperidol improves a variety of behavioral symptoms in young children with autism; but haloperidol treatment frequently leads to acute dystonic reactions, withdrawal dyskinesias, and tardive dyskinesia. The high risk of these side effects has limited the use of haloperidol to patients that do not respond to other treatments.

Second generation antipsychotics like risperidone are favored nowadays.

Insulin-like growth factor 1 (IGF-1) and trofinetide

IGF-1 is a hormone that plays an important role in childhood growth, particularly in the brain. Production of IGF-1 is stimulated by growth hormone (GH). Many growth hormones are disturbed in autism, either elevated or reduced and this varies over time.

In some studies, the level of IGF-1 in spinal fluid were low in autism, but only at an age of five to six years old.

Rapid head growth is a common feature of autism and head circumference is widely measured. Rapid head growth tends to occur between the ages of one and three, which is generally before any autism diagnosis, so we know much less about what is the level of IGF-1 at such a young age.

IGF-1 is seen as a potentially a useful therapy in children with brain disorders, including autism, at a young age when the brain remains highly plastic to encourage self-repair.

Normalizing IGF-1 should reduce neuroinflammation by decreasing secretion of cytokines such as IL-6, alter microglial function and have numerous other effects.

It has been suggested specifically as a therapy for Phelan-McDermid syndrome, where people are missing a functioning copy of the SHANK3 gene. It was also proposed as a therapy for girls with Rett syndrome.

In a small trial in 2014 children with Phelan-McDermid syndrome were treated with IGF-1 and significant improvement was noted in both social impairment and restrictive behaviors. IGF-1 was found to be well tolerated and there were no serious adverse events in any participants. A larger trial is planned.

A trial in 2016 at Harvard comprised girls with Rett syndrome, aged 2 to 10 years old; it concluded that there was worsening of some behaviors, but improvements in social, communication, and symbolic behaviors. There was a reduction in breath hold length. Overall, the trial showed that while IGF-1 was well tolerated, none of the primary outcome measures showed significant improvement.

A small trial is planned using young children with non-syndromic autism.

Trofinetide (NNZ-2566) is a modified version of IGF-1 (called an analog); it can be taken by mouth, whereas IGF-1 has to be injected. Trofinetide has been trialled in Rett syndrome. It is showing some promise. It has been suggested that early treatment is needed. In Fragile X, a trial in people aged 12–45 years old has also showed clinical improvement with trofinetide.

I wrote a lot about growth factors in my blog. An interesting potential treatment for Rett syndrome is actually NGF (Nerve Growth Factor), which is known to be consistently reduced at all ages in this syndrome. I did report about the Nobel Laureate who discovered NGF and later self-treated using home-made NGF eye drops, to maintain her mental function into her very old age. Your eyes are part of the central nervous system (CNS) and so provide an entry point for drugs targeting the brain.

Levels of growth factors in blood do not correlate with those found in spinal fluid; only the levels in spinal fluid are relevant to what is going on in the brain.

Ketamine

Ketamine is a sedative. It blocks certain NMDA receptors and this results in the anesthetic and hallucinogenic effects, but Ketamine has dozens of other effects.

There have been case studies using either oral ketamine or intranasal ketamine to treat people with severe autism. In a 2016 case report from Albert Einstein College, the autistic person received ketamine as a sedative at the dentist. When he woke up, and for the next 36 hours, he was markedly improved and able to speak in full sentences for the first time.

Intranasal ketamine is being trialed in Cincinnati on adults with autism, looking for improvements in social and communication impairment.

Leucovorin

Folic acid is an essential B vitamin required by the body, but to be used by the body it has to metabolized to a usable form THF. Some cancer therapy blocks this process and so causes major side effects. Leucovorin is an analog/equivalent of THF and so it was developed to avoid these side effects of the cancer treatment.

Leucovorin (5-MTHF) is also used in the treatment of cerebral folate deficiency, a syndrome in which the use of folic acid from diet cannot normalize cerebrospinal fluid levels of the biologically active form of folate.

The brain's main folate transporter is called FR alpha (Folate receptor alpha). Folate receptor auto-antibodies (FRAAs) can interfere with the transport of folate and cause cerebral folate deficiency. It has been suggested that there may be a link between dairy milk consumption and FRAAs.

Folate abnormalities in autism can potentially be treated in autism using Leucovorin. It is suggested that children with autism and FR alpha autoantibodies (FRAAs) are the ones who should be treated. Confusingly some people negative to FRAAs also respond. UK researchers suggest that oxidative stress in the brain makes folate unstable, which may cause low levels within the central nervous system.

In 2018 a clinical trial by Dr Frye showed that Leucovorin improves verbal communication in children with autism and language impairment particularly in those participants who were positive for FRAAs.

For participants with biomarkers indicating more normal folate metabolism (i.e., FRAA negative, high glutathione redox ratio) improvement in verbal communication was not significantly different between groups. FRAAs predicted response to folinic acid.

A larger multi-center study by Dr Frye's group is planned to be completed in 2023; it is called Leucovorin for the Treatment of Language Impairment in Children with Autism.

Memantine

Memantine (Namenda) is a drug used to treat Alzheimer's. It blocks NMDA receptors and this is usually seen as its mode of action in Alzheimer's, but this is still debated.

Memantine also blocks certain nicotinic acetylcholine receptors (nAChRs). The Alpha-7 nAChR is implicated in cognition and psychiatric diseases, Memantine blocks this receptor, but in a feedback loop the body reacts by producing many more, producing a net increase. It activates dopamine D2 receptors. It blocks serotonin 5-HT3 receptors. Memantine also targets L-type calcium channels.

Memantine has been very extensively prescribed off-label for autism in the United States.

One parent contacted my blog whose child was treated by a prolific memantine prescriber in Iowa. She said that this doctor claims to have treated 3,000 children with autism and has a 99% success rate. In court papers from 2016, it states he has been prescribing it to children with autism for over 10 years, but 3,000 does look like an exaggeration perhaps.

As a result of all the off-label prescribing, Forest Laboratories planned a very thorough series of phase II clinical trials. The doctor in Iowa was expecting a rounding success and vindication from skeptics; apparently he even thought he would end up a guest on the Oprah show.

The first trial had 906 participants and 765 completed the study. The children who were viewed as responders in the first trial (about 60%) then moved onto the next two trials. These trials are extremely expensive.

The trials were terminated early because the sponsor, Forest Laboratories, determined that memantine had failed to achieve the goals of the trial. The problem was that the responders from the first trial went into the next phase and seemed to do as well with the placebo as with memantine.

What can we conclude? Well, the doctor from Iowa did not make it on to Oprah's show.

A drug firm lost a great deal of money betting on a full-sized autism trial.

Quite possibly memantine does have a benefit in some people's autism, but so does a placebo.

I asked one parent what exactly was the benefit she found in her child. I was really surprised by her answer; she uses it because it is the only therapy that controls her son's GI problems. That was one thing for sure that Forest Laboratories was not measuring in their study. I think the child was benefiting from memantine's little known effect on L-type calcium channels. Rezular (R-verapamil) was once developed to treat irritable bowel syndrome (IBS).

Metformin

Metformin is a cheap old generic drug used to treat type 2 diabetes and also PCOS (Polycystic ovary syndrome) a condition in females caused by too many male hormones. PCOS in the mother has been shown to raise the incidence of autism by a factor of 1.5; this should not come as a surprise.

Metformin has broad effects on the metabolism. It improves insulin sensitivity; it reduces the incidence of certain types of cancer and in children with Fragile X it has been shown at UC Davis to raise IQ by about 10%.

The trials in autism have actually been mainly about using metformin to reduce obesity in people being treated by antipsychotics that the FDA approved for autism. In that role it is effective.

The interesting research has yet to be carried out; which types of autism, other than Fragile X, would benefit from this very safe, cheap drug?

Methylphenidate (Ritalin)

Methylphenidate (Ritalin) is an old stimulant drug used to treat ADHD. It is widely abused by students trying to improve their cognitive performance – even Brian, the dog in *Family Guy*, tried it to inspire his writing.

Methylphenidate is a norepinephrine-dopamine reuptake inhibitor. It therefore increases the effects of norepinephrine and dopamine and so can produce increased alertness, reduce fatigue and improve attention.

Interestingly, research shows that long-term treatment with ADHD stimulants amphetamine and methylphenidate decreases abnormalities in brain structure and function found in subjects with ADHD.

There are many common side effects from weight loss to sleep problems to psychosis.

A 2016 Cochrane review of the use of methylphenidate in autism concluded that it might improve symptoms of hyperactivity and possibly inattention in children with autism who are tolerant of the medication, although the low quality of evidence means that they cannot be certain of the true magnitude of any effect. There was no evidence that methylphenidate has a negative impact on the core symptoms of autism, or that it improves social interaction, stereotypical behaviors, or overall autism.

Minocycline

Minocycline is a tetracycline antibiotic used to treat a number of bacterial infections such as pneumonia.

In common with other classes of antibiotic, tetracyclines exert a variety of biological actions that are independent of their expected anti-microbial activity. They have anti-inflammatory and immunomodulatory effects; they can inhibit the formation of new blood vessels and cancer metastasis.

Minocycline may pacify activated microglia in the brain. Microglia are the brain's immune defense and appear to be permanently activated in autism, which will impede their other functions, such as synaptic pruning.

Minocycline has shown a benefit in small trials in Fragile X.

A very small trial in regressive autism at Johns Hopkins showed no benefit. A larger trial in idiopathic autism is planned in Cincinnati.

Minocycline is the only antibiotic seriously trialed in autism, but because of their immunomodulatory effects, many other antibiotics are interesting for autism.

Macrolide-class antibiotics like azithromycin are particularly interesting. A special version of azithromycin is being developed, without the antibiotic property, as a treatment for Cystic Fibrosis. The anti-inflammatory properties of azithromycin are very effective in some lung diseases.

Beta-lactam antibiotics like penicillin have a very special additional effect, they increase the expression of GLT-1. Glutamate is the major excitatory neurotransmitter in the brain and is inactivated by uptake via GLT-1. So, more GLT-1 means less glutamate and that will be good for some types of autism.

Many people with autism report improvement while on certain antibiotics. They should take note of which type of antibiotic and do some detective work.

NAC (N-acetyl cysteine)

NAC is an antioxidant and it also raises the level of the body's main antioxidant GSH. It is used as a drug to dissolve mucus in children and to treat acetaminophen/paracetamol overdose which would otherwise cause liver failure and death.

Oxidative stress is a known feature of autism. A study by Antonio Hardan in 2012 showed that high doses of NAC produced a behavioral improvement in people with autism.

During the 12-week trial, NAC treatment decreased irritability scores from 13.1 to 7.2 on the Aberrant Behavior Checklist, a widely used clinical scale for assessing irritability. The change is not as large as that seen in children taking antipsychotics, but antipsychotics have side effects whereas NAC generally does not.

There have been subsequent trials and case studies, some have showed a benefit and some have not.

I have been using NAC since 2013 and my son definitely is a responder. In him, the main effect is on reducing stereotypy, OCD and related anxiety.

Naltrexone

Naltrexone is used to treat alcohol and opioid addiction. A typical dose is 50mg once a day in adults.

There are many old case reports of naltrexone being used to treat self-injury in autism; a typical one reports that at dose of 0.75mg/kg per day led to significant improvements, as shown by outcome measurements and "Self-mutilating behaviour disappeared completely".

In autism there were trials in the 1990s using full-dose naltrexone:

> "Eight of 13 subjects improved in two or more settings ... Naltrexone offers promise as an agent for modest improvement of behavior and social communication in young children with autism."

In another study 23 autistic children, aged three to seven years, on average, parents' checklists and playroom data could not differentiate between naltrexone treatment and placebo treatment; however, teachers significantly favored naltrexone treatment. They reported a decrease in hyperactivity and irritability. No effects of naltrexone on social and stereotypic behavior could be demonstrated.

Low-dose naltrexone is widely used off-label to treat a wide range of inflammatory conditions such as Multiple Sclerosis (MS), Crohn's disease and various pain conditions. There is a vast collection of peer-reviewed scientific research on low-dose naltrexone, even though your doctor may think it is a quack therapy.

A trial was registered in Israel to investigate low dose usage in autism, but it never materialized. What a pity.

Olanzapine

Olanzapine (Zyprexa) is another atypical antipsychotic used to treat schizophrenia and bipolar. Olanzapine is used to treat aggression and self-injury in autism.

A study in 2020 compared three atypical antipsychotic drugs and concluded that risperidone, aripiprazole, and olanzapine are effective in treatment of irritability, hyperactivity, social withdrawal, stereotypy, and inappropriate speech in autism. The study noted that side effects are more frequent with olanzapine and this should be considered when choosing an antipsychotic for autism.

Oxytocin

Oxytocin is a human hormone associated with emotions, but it is also a birthing hormone released during natural child birth.

The gene that encodes oxytocin is considered an autism gene. Oxytocin plays a role in the switch that should occur just after birth where neurons switch from immature to mature. In many people with severe autism this switch does not flip and neurons remain with high levels of chloride within them, triggering a life-long excitatory/inhibitory imbalance that reduces cognitive function and likely disturbs ongoing development of the brain.

The autism clinical trials have used a nasal spray to deliver oxytocin to the brain.

Each single dose of oxytocin given intranasally seems to increase activity in the neural circuitry and improve social cognitive abilities in autism.

In trials oxytocin is typically given twice a day and is well tolerated. As a chemical oxytocin has a very short half-life of five minutes, although its effects may linger. A better delivery method might improve its effect.

An entirely different way to deliver oxytocin was discussed in my blog. The L. reuteri DSM 17938 bacteria, used in a baby probiotic, causes a signal to be produced in the gut that causes oxytocin to be released in the brain. This seemed a clever way to give the brain a steady increased supply of Oxytocin. The effect is very noticeable in terms of becoming more emotional, at least in my son, he went round the school yard shaking all his classmates' hands and individually telling them they were his friends. He went up to a little girl he knows and kissed her on the head.

The drug Buspirone, mentioned earlier in this section also claimed to cause oxytocin release.

It appears that oxytocin has both short term emotional effects and some long-term benefits.

PDE4 inhibitors - low dose Rolflumilast/Daxas and Ibulilast/Ketas

Rolflumilast and ibudilast are both drugs developed to treat asthma and related conditions like COPD. Both are anti-inflammatory drugs that inhibit PDE4. Ibudilast has been repurposed to treat both ALS/Motor neuron disease and Multiple Sclerosis.

Maastricht University developed low dose roflumilast for cognitive impairments. They showed that a one fifth dose of roflumilast improved cognition in schizophrenia, Alzheimer's, Parkinson's and other types of cognitive impairment. They also showed that it could correct impaired sensory gating, a common feature in autism. When the affected sense is hearing, the technical diagnosis is misophonia. This is when the sound of someone chewing food, or a noisy clock ticking drives someone crazy.

The problem with PDE4 inhibitors is that they are not very selective. They affect other types of PDE and so may have some unwanted effects. They can cause GI/gut problems, specifically they can make you want to vomit, or put more politely, they are emetic.

People taking roflumilast for COPD report that the nausea/emetic effects do usually fade over time.

Ibudilast/Ketas is a Japanese PDE4 inhibitor safely used in teenagers with asthma, so I really doubt it can be severely emetic, but nausea is a known side effect. I expect the effect varies from person to person, as with many side-effects of drugs.

Ibudilast seems promising in multiple sclerosis (MS) because it is both immunomodulatory, so it stops the myelin layer being attacked, and it encourages remyelination.

A low dose of PDE4 inhibitor looks an interesting choice for autism and some people do indeed use it for autism.

Pentoxifylline

Staying with PDE inhibitors brings us to pentoxifylline, a xanthine derivative used as a drug to treat muscle pain.

Pentoxifylline is a non-specific PDE inhibitors. It inhibits many types of PDE, not just PDE4.

During the 1970s in Japan, pentoxifylline was used to treat autism in a series of published trials, with what appears to have been remarkable success. None of the studies used placebos and a control group, but they all report super-responders, responders and non-responders. Even in the worst case, a third of children were responders.

In 1970s Japan autism meant severe autism.

A double-blind placebo-controlled trial of pentoxifylline added to risperidone in 2010 showed it provided beneficial effects on aberrant behavior in children with autism.

> "The difference between the two protocols was significant as the group that received pentoxifylline had greater reduction in ABC-C subscale scores for Irritability, Lethargy/Social Withdrawal, Stereotypic Behavior, Hyperactivity/Noncompliance and Inappropriate Speech."

One researcher thinks the beneficial effects are due to immunomodulation; this is certainly plausible, but the drug has numerous other totally different effects.

Pentoxifylline is a nonselective phosphodiesterase (PDE) inhibitor which raises intracellular cAMP, activates PKA, inhibits TNF and leukotriene synthesis. It reduces inflammation and innate immunity. In addition, pentoxifylline improves red blood cell deformability and reduces blood viscosity. It decreases blood clot formation.

Pentoxifylline facilitates synthesis and release of serotonin and inhibits its uptake.

PDE (phosphodiesterase) inhibitors are covered extensively in my blog and some are interesting potential autism drugs.

Improving blood flow is often the mechanism of action of cognitive enhancing drugs. Pentoxifylline is going to increase cerebral blood flow.

Some readers of my blog with teenage children find pentoxifylline a beneficial therapy. The studies actually suggest its greatest benefit is in younger children.

I was recently contacted by Dr Robert Charles Powell, a US doctor who has written extensively about the off-label use of pentoxifylline to improve cognition. He had discovered this by chance when he himself had been prescribed the drug for other reasons. He even wrote a book about it, called Pentoxifylline: A Versatile Off-Patent Medication Best Not Overlooked.

Unfortunately, pentoxifylline remains overlooked. Dr Powell is now looking into its potential to treat teenagers with autism. For updates, read my blog.

Some readers of my blog use pentoxifylline for their child with autism; in at least one case the child is now an adult.

Pioglitazone

Pioglitazone is a cheap generic drug widely prescribed to improve insulin sensitivity in type 2 diabetes. It was withdrawn from sale in France and Germany due to concern about bladder cancer, subsequent research disputed this association.

Pioglitazone stimulates PPAR-gamma (peroxisome proliferator-activated receptor gamma) and to a lesser extent PPAR-alpha. This has some profound effects on the metabolism.

In 2007 there was a small study published of children treated with 30 or 60 mg pioglitazone for three to four months. There were no adverse effects noted and behavioral measurements revealed a significant decrease in four out of five subcategories (irritability, lethargy, stereotypy, and hyperactivity). Improved behaviors were inversely correlated with patient age, indicating stronger effects on the younger patients.

A small study in 2018 found a statistically significant improvement was observed in social withdrawal, repetitive behaviors, and externalizing behaviors. Forty-six percent of those enrolled were deemed to be global responders.

To determine safety, three different doses were used 0.25 mg/kg, 0.5 mg/kg, and 0.75 mg/kg once daily. There were no serious adverse events at any dose.

In 2018/9 two papers where published, the first showing pioglitazone treatment corrects social and communication deficits, as well as elevated plasma IL-6 levels and in the second paper pioglitazone was shown to reverse cognitive impairment. In both cases these were in animal models and treatment started soon after birth.

There is a question about upper respiratory tract infections and Pioglitazone, but I found a study treating obese people with asthma, where the placebo was associated with upper respiratory tract infections while Pioglitazone was not. In the same study the placebo caused a loss in weight, but participants were told the trial drug might cause weight gain; they probably all cut back on their calorie intake.

My son takes Pioglitazone as an add-on therapy during spring and summer. This is to tackle what I called "dumber in the summer" in my blog, when cognition, aggression and broader autism get worse, due to allergy.

Pregnenolone

Pregnenolone is a steroid used by the body to make other hormones.

It has many effects directly and via its metabolites. It will reduce the sensitivity of $GABA_A$ receptors and increase the sensitivity of NMDA receptors, so it could affect the excitatory-inhibitory (E/I) balance in the brain.

Some of the effects of taking pregnenolone as a supplement are equivalent to the effect some SSRI antidepressants have at tiny 1/10th doses, where they do not increase serotonin, but rather increase pregnenolone-related steroid hormones in the brain.

Antonio Hardan and colleagues at Stanford applied this neurosteroid approach to try to improve the E/I imbalance common in autism.

In their study pregnenolone was modestly effective and well-tolerated in individuals with autism. It was less effective than an antipsychotic, but we know antipsychotics are not well tolerated.

Propranolol

Propranolol is beta-blocker drug used to lower blood pressure.

In psychiatry, propranolol is used to treat performance anxiety, polydipsia (drinking too much water) and aggressive behavior.

Propranolol inhibits the sympathetic nervous system by blocking the beta receptors on the nerves of the sympathetic system; by blocking the action of these nerves, propranolol reduces the heart rate and is useful in treating abnormally rapid heart rhythms.

Autonomic nervous system (ANS) impairment has been increasingly recognized in autism. Abnormalities in pupillary light reflex, resting heart rate, heart rate response to social cognitive tasks, respiratory rhythm, and skin conductance suggest that autonomic dysfunction is common in autism and may play a role in the social, behavioral, and communication problems.

An imbalance in the sympathetic and the parasympathetic nervous system (dysautonomia) and the resulting autonomic storms is a frequent occurrence in girls with Rett syndrome. Propranolol has been used to manage hyperactivity of the sympathetic nervous system in Rett syndrome.

The first autism trial using propranolol was back in 1987 at the Harvard Medical School. In eight adults with autism the immediate result across all patients was a rapid diminution in aggression. As time on the drug increased, subtler changes in speech and socialization emerged. The researchers speculated that these effects may be the result of a lessening of the autistic individual's state of hyperarousal. As the individual becomes less anxious, defensive and "dearousing" behaviors are relinquished and more social and adaptive behaviors appear. There was also an improvement in language.

After that promising start, not much happened. A story that repeats.

There have been cases studies, mainly in adults with autism.

A small trial in 2019 showed a cognitive benefit in adults with autism and even showed effects visible on an MRI scan. Those researchers plan a larger study, funded by the US DOD, that will include younger people.

At Rutgers, a trial using high dose propranolol to treat severe and chronic challenging behaviors in adolescents and adults with autism spectrum disorders was due in 2021.

As I highlighted in my blog, propranolol has some entirely different effects. It blocks the sodium ion channels Nav1.1, Nav1.2 and Nav1.3; these can all play a role in epilepsy, headaches and indeed autism. The ion channel Nav1.1 is encoded by the gene SCN1A, mutations in which cause Dravet syndrome. Dravet syndrome causes severe, hard to treat epilepsy, intellectual disability and features of autism. Both low dose clonazepam and potassium bromide can be used to treat Dravet syndrome.

Some people report a benefit from very modest doses of propranolol. Some autism studies use high doses of propranolol.

In some countries propranolol is used to calm nerves before driving lessons or a driving test. Monty's big brother got very anxious during his driving lessons and he found a small dose of propranolol very helpful.

Riluzole

Riluzole is a remarkably inexpensive drug to treat ALS/Motor Neuron Disease. As with almost all drugs to treat neurological conditions, it is actually very minimally effective, potentially extending life in ALS by just a few months.

Riluzole stimulates glutamate reuptake by increasing activity of the glutamate transporter GLT-1. If you have too much glutamate, as in ALS, riluzole may help.

In reality this is a very crude intervention, because the problem is usually specific to a particular glutamate receptor. Riluzole will affect them all.

Penicillin antibiotics also increase the expression of GLT-1 and so in people whose autism moderates while taking Penicillin or other beta-lactam antibiotics, riluzole might be interesting.

There have been several trials of riluzole in autism. Some are imaging studies looking at the excitatory-inhibitory (E/I) imbalance and some are trials measuring behavioral effects.

In an imaging study comparing adults with autism to typical adults, riluzole increased the prefrontal cortex inhibitory index in autism but decreased it in controls. There was also a significant group difference in prefrontal functional connectivity at baseline, which was abolished by riluzole within the autism group. The researchers claimed that the results show that E/I flux can be 'shifted' by a drug and that abnormalities in functional connectivity can be 'normalised' by targeting E/I, even in adults.

A trial of riluzole in 2013, as an add-on to the antipsychotic risperidone, showed improved irritability, in children with autism. However, it significantly increased appetite and weight gain.

In 2018 a trial investigating irritability in autism found five weeks of riluzole was well tolerated, but had no significant effect on the target symptoms.

Riluzole has effects other than reducing glutamate. It affects $GABA_A$ receptors, NMDA receptors and some sodium ion channels.

I did not find riluzole helpful, but then my son has never experienced an autism benefit when taking penicillin/beta-lactam antibiotics. It produced lethargy, which is exactly what you would expect if you damp down excitation in the brain. Many anesthetics work the other way on the E/I balance; that is they increase the inhibition side (amplify the effect of GABA), to the point you fall asleep.

Risperidone

Risperidone (Risperdal) is an atypical antipsychotic. It is used to treat schizophrenia, bipolar disorder, and irritability associated with autism. It is actually an FDA approved therapy for autism.

Atypical antipsychotics are second generation drugs which have less troubling side effects than haloperidol. Nonetheless, these second-generation drugs can still have severe side effects like tardive dyskinesia and they can trigger severe weight gain.

Risperidone works by blocking dopamine and serotonin receptors in the brain.

A review of seven clinical trials in autism found that risperidone is effective in the treatment of symptoms of ASD and that one in every three ASD children and adolescents has benefits from treatment with risperidone. However, treatment with risperidone increased the incidence of adverse events, particularly in weight gain.

Sertraline

Sertraline (Zoloft) is a cheap antidepressant drug of the selective serotonin reuptake inhibitor (SSRI) class. It is also prescribed to treat social anxiety and OCD (obsessive compulsive disorder).

Sertraline is FDA approved to treat OCD associated with autism.

For many years, sertraline at regular doses has been used to treat people with mild autism/Asperger's. Anecdotally, some people seem to benefit profoundly, but it is a small minority.

At low doses, about a one tenth of the standard dose, sertraline ceases to have an effect on serotonin but has a secondary effect increasing the level of the steroid hormone allopregnanolone in the brain. This neurosteroid modifies the effect of the $GABA_A$ receptor, implicated in autism. This same receptor plays a role in anxiety and depression. An expensive new therapy uses synthetic allopregnanolone to treat women with post-natal depression.

Search "Low dose SSRIs as Selective Brain Steroidogenic Stimulants (SBSSs)" on my blog.

In 2016 a small trial was carried out in young children with Fragile X. This randomized controlled trial of six months of sertraline treatment showed no primary benefit with respect to early expressive language development and global clinical improvement. However, in secondary, exploratory analyses there were significant improvements seen on motor and visual perceptual subtests, the Cognitive T score sum on the MSEL, and on one measure of Social Participation on the Sensory Processing Measure–Preschool. Further, post hoc analysis found significant improvement in early expressive language development as measured by the MSEL among children with ASD on sertraline.

A clinical trial in 2019 at UC Davis concluded that in idiopathic autism, there was no benefit from taking low dose Sertraline over the placebo.

A trial at Stanford was carried out using oral pregnenolone, which should have a similar effect to low dose sertraline in modifying the level of neurosteroids. The trial was in adults with autism and it reported a modest benefit.

Simvastatin (plus atorvastatin and lovastatin)

Simvastatin (Zocor) is a cheap generic drug to lower cholesterol, but it has other remarkable effects. In people with Multiple Sclerosis (a disease featuring by a loss of myelin), simvastatin reduces brain shrinkage by 40% when taken long term. This is a drug that people would think might make MS worse, because myelin is made from cholesterol.

Also of interest, Smith Lemli Opitz syndrome (SLOS) is a single gene autism, caused by a defect in the DHCR7 gene. This gene encodes an enzyme your body needs to synthesize cholesterol. Simvastatin somewhat surprisingly upregulates expression of DHCR7 and so can be a helpful therapy in children with SLOS.

The three common statins that are fat soluble and so can enter the brain are simvastatin, atorvastatin and lovastatin. They all have slightly different "bonus" effects.

If you have Fragile X the research shows you may benefit from lovastatin, but you may need to start at an early age to benefit.

In Neurofibromatosis type 1 a study showed 25% responded to simvastatin.

An autism clinical trial of simvastatin, as an add-on therapy to the antipsychotic risperidone, found improvements in hyperactivity and noncompliance.

I chose to use atorvastatin. It has numerous potential benefits including on the expression of autism genes like PTEN and BCL-2; as well, it has been shown in numerous studies to be anti-inflammatory and neuroprotective. It improves recovery chances from traumatic brain injury (TBI) and can suppress a cytokine storm. Most importantly, it works. It is very well tolerated. It seems to affect very specific aspects of cognition and behavior. It seems to remove an inhibition to do things for yourself, as if before the person simply got "stuck". They know perfectly well how to complete a process, but without prompting they will not do it. Atorvastatin removes this inhibition after one dose and on cessation the inhibition returns. I call it cognitive inhibition and, if untreated, it would be a major impediment to learning anything at school and in applying daily living skills.

Sulforaphane (plus Indole-3-carbinol, I3C)

Sulforaphane is a chemical produced when you eat broccoli in the presence of an enzyme called myrosinase, which is present in broccoli before you cook it. Sulforaphane is not stable at room temperature, so no supplement actually contains sulforaphane, it hopefully contains what you need to make it in your body (glucoraphanin and myrosinase).

Sulforaphane activates the switch Nrf-2 that turns on your anti-oxidant genes, this in turn increases the amount of serotonin in the brain. This is why broccoli supplements improve mood and even create short term euphoria is some people (in my son, but not in me).

Sulforaphane is also an HDAC inhibitor, so it may affect the expression of certain important genes. This is why in studies sulforaphane has been shown to be chemoprotective. A modified version, which is stable at room temperature, is being developed to treat prostate cancer and will also be trialed in autism.

A widely reported study in 2014 showed that sulforaphane, derived from broccoli sprouts, substantially (and reversibly) improved behavior in young men with autism.

Since broccoli products are supplements rather than drugs, you cannot know whether they contain the myrosinase needed to actually make sulforaphane.

Broccoli is also a rich source of Indole-3-carbinol (I3C), which itself appears to be chemoprotective. I3C affects the estrogen metabolism and it may benefit women with lupus, an auto immune disease associated with estrogen.

I3C increases expression of the cancer and autism gene PTEN. PTEN is a tumor suppressor and in some cancers, like that of the prostate, it gets turned off, allowing the cancer to grow.

There clearly is a lot packed into broccoli.

Of note is that in people who have cancer you do not want to reduce oxidative stress, for example by activating Nrf-2 with healthy food. Cancer cells are fast growing which makes them vulnerable to oxidative stress. You need healthy eating to avoid getting cancer in the first place.

Some people with autism lack PTEN and in some people they produce a mutated version. You would only want more of the "clean" PTEN protein.

Some people with autism respond well to broccoli supplements, although some report the effect fades over the years unless you increase the dosage. For others the same supplements do absolutely nothing.

Suramin

Suramin is an old anti-parasite drug used to treat African sleeping sickness and river blindness. It is taken intravenously and does have some side effects.

Suramin has been proposed as a unifying autism therapy, based on studies in both mouse models and humans. A larger trial is planned.

Two companies are developing Suramin products as potential autism therapies and an interesting intranasal version is in the pipeline.

The research is driven by Dr Naviaux at UC San Diego, who proposes his cell danger response as a common mechanism in autism and other diseases like CFS/ME (Chronic Fatigue Syndrome / Myalgic Encephalomyelitis).

Naviaux is one of the cleverest researchers looking at autism and his research papers are unusual in that they show knowledge/insights from far outside his narrow research interest. Hopefully his theory proves correct.

Topiramate

Topiramate is an epilepsy drug, also used to prevent migraine.

It affects very many different targets, from sodium ion channels, to calcium channels, to $GABA_A$ receptors. It has an effect on carbonic anhydrase enzymes that may lead to kidney stones. It has the side effect of reducing appetite.

Topiramate was trialed in autism as a way of reducing the obesity caused by antipsychotic drugs. In a small trial of 10 children variable degrees of weight reduction were observed in four patients, two subjects showed weight increase. Behavioral adverse effects were observed in three patients causing rapid withdrawal of the medication. The authors recommended topiramate be used with caution in autism because this population has a high risk of behavioral disruption.

When trialed as an add-on therapy with risperidone in 2010 there was an improvement found in scores for irritability, stereotypic behavior and hyperactivity/noncompliance.

In 2015 there was a small case series with two adult females with autism, who were obese due to being treated by antipsychotic drugs. In those two cases topiramate was found to be safe and effective with minimal cognitive and noncognitive side effects.

You do wonder why they don't just stop giving antipsychotic drugs. They are generally not needed.

Valproate

Sodium valproate (Depakote) is used to treat epilepsy, bipolar and prevent headaches. It has a long list of possible side effects.

Nobody knows for sure how valproate reduces seizures. It is considered to "increase GABA". It affects sodium channels, often implicated in seizures and also the potassium channel Kv7.2 which regulates neuronal excitability. Seizures are just neuronal hyperexcitability. Valproate is also an HDAC inhibitor, meaning it can change which genes are turned on or off, via a process called epigenetics.

It is known that valproate taken during pregnancy can lead to the child developing autism; furthermore, 10% of children will have physical birth defects and 40% will have development/learning problems.

One of the most used animal models of autism is produced by injecting valproate into the pregnant mother to produce a pup with features of autism.

In a small autism clinical trial in 2001, 10 of 14 participants were rated as having responded well to the treatment and it was generally well tolerated. Improvement was noted in core symptoms of autism and associated features of affective instability, impulsivity, and aggression. All patients with an abnormal EEG and/or seizure history were rated as responders.

In 2018 a larger trial of sodium valproate treatment, compared to placebo, resulted in significantly greater improvement with valproate versus the placebo. Valproate appeared to be well tolerated. There were significantly more responders at week 12 in the valproate sodium group than in the placebo group. It is important to note that the effect of valproate increased over time.

Valproate can activate genes that are regulated by DNA methylation. Valproate might have long-term effects on gene expression, which might be similar to the consequences of genetic alterations.

Low dose valproate and also low dose phenytoin, another anti-epileptic drug (AED) have been used as autism therapies.

Many people with severe autism go on to develop epilepsy, I remember being warned about this when my son was diagnosed with autism. Some parents do report that when their child starts taking their anti-epileptic drugs (AEDs), their autism moderates.

Vasopressin

Vasopressin is a hormone with three totally different effects, influencing social behavior, blood pressure and urination.

In autism studies one idea has been to use intranasal vasopressin. At Stanford they found that this improved social skills in young children compared to a placebo.

Meanwhile, the Swiss drug producer Roche created a new drug (Balovaptan) that blocks Vasopressin Receptor 1A in the brain, which they believe will improve social behavior in autism.

The Stanford nasal spray will activate the very receptors that Roche are trying to block.

Balovaptan failed in its clinical trial and was abandoned.

An analogue of vasopressin already exists as a nasal spray in your pharmacy, desmopressin, which is given at night to prevent bed-wetting.

I was contacted by a parent of a little girl with autism who was prescribed desmopressin by the neurologist and it produced significant gains.

I am not sure why Stanford uses a compounded version, rather than try the off the shelf product.

Care would have to be taken if you took bumetanide together with vasopressin/desmopressin because of the risk of low sodium. This should be an entirely manageable risk.

VSL#3 and Vivomixx

VSL#3 and Viviomixx are expensive combinations of probiotic bacteria that are widely used to treated conditions like inflammatory bowel disease but also other autoimmune conditions. They have been used in numerous clinical trials.

A trial in autism is planned using Viviomixx at University College London in people with autism and co-morbid gastrointestinal symptoms.

There are case reports showing a benefit in autistic patients treated with VSL3#3/Vivomixx for their chronic GI problems.

There have been no trials in people with autism and regular GI function.

Part 6

Preventing Autism
What to Do About the Autism Tsunami

Many people are familiar with the commonly used term, the autism epidemic, and the profound increase in the rate of autism diagnosis in recent years.

In my blog I went into some detail looking into this subject. By far the most knowledgeable researcher is a French psychiatrist and epidemiologist called Éric Fombonne, long based in North America. He writes very well.

There are several factors at work.

In the United States and much of the world, the diagnosis of autism is based on a reference book called the Diagnostic and Statistical Manual of Mental Disorders – DSM for short.

Over the years DSM has evolved. Only in 1973 was homosexuality removed as a mental diagnosis.

When it comes to autism, over the years, milder and milder types have been included in DSM. It became less socially acceptable to diagnose people with intellectual disability (ID), so some people were diagnosed with autism instead. Classic autism is severe autism with comorbid ID.

As schools got better at handling pupils with special needs and were able to get extra funding based on a diagnosis of those needs, both the schools and the parents wanted more people to be diagnosed.

Éric Fombonne has written that when his group have retested children with an autism diagnosis, they found many who do not warrant the diagnosis.

In the United States, the CDC's figures even include children with school-diagnosed autism; no medical assessment ever being made.

Even by compensating for all the above factors, the informed opinion is that there still has been a genuine increase in autism, rather like there has also been an increase in all autoimmune disease. Something really is going on, but what?

In my blog I looked at all the factors. Vaccines are such a net benefit to society and have saved millions of lives, you have to tread carefully.

I rather liked the statement made by a Chinese researcher about their Covid-19 vaccines, "No vaccine is 100% effective and no vaccine is 100% safe". Some collateral damage is inevitable, you just need to be sure it is very small, compared to the benefit of the vaccine.

We know that mitochondrial disease can be triggered in predisposed very young children by some kind of viral stress. From the team at Johns Hopkins, now widely cited, we know that mitochondrial disease can lead to an autism diagnosis. Dr Jon Poling and his friends from Johns Hopkins won a vaccine case that claimed his daughter's severe autism was caused by her vaccinations triggering mitochondrial disease. This is all a matter of record. The logical question is how many other people are similarly affected. This is a question that may never be thoroughly answered to everyone's satisfaction.

Parents want to blame something for what happened to their child, which is very understandable.

Public health does not want anything to undermine faith in early childhood vaccines, which have saved many millions of lives around the world.

Personally, I would like the truth, which is likely that a small percentage of children are predisposed to a risk from early childhood vaccination. As the Chinese researcher candidly told us "No vaccine is 100% effective and no vaccine is 100% safe".

If you rule out vaccines as the primary cause, you do not have to look far to find rational explanations for the increase in autism prevalence.

When you understand what is driving the increase, you can start doing something to mitigate it.

Why prevent/minimize future autism?

If you are the Oscar-winning actor Sir Anthony Hopkins or the billionaire Elon Musk, you are very likely quite content to carry the diagnosis of Asperger's syndrome, which nowadays has been subsumed into the autism spectrum.

When I started my blog about treating severe autism, I was surprised how many people contacted me who were parents of someone with an Asperger's diagnosis, or someone with an Asperger's diagnosis themselves. Some Aspies really are not happy with their autism and some struggle. Many Aspies are self-treating their autism and many hang out on Reddit forums, where they exchange tips.

Talk to anyone who teaches at a special school for severe autism and they will tell you about the parents, and how many have mild, or not so mild, Asperger's-like symptoms. Since autism is polygenic, it would be strange if this were not the case.

I am always amused when mildly autistic, but obsessed, self-advocates get into arguments with parents advocating for their children with severe autism. The self-advocates dispute that the so-called neurotypical parents have a right to talk about autism. Little do they know that many of those parents would have little difficulty getting an autism diagnosis themselves. They have the Hopkins/Musk type of autism, that they do not let define them. They actually do have a life, in spite of their Asperger's-like symptoms.

A little bit of autism, giving you attention to detail and the drive to complete tasks, looks like a good thing – far from a disability. It helped Sir Anthony Hopkins memorize his movie scripts. However, too much of a good thing produces a severely disabled individual.

Autism is not just polygenic but also multifactorial, as a result there are many external influences that can increase how autistic someone is.

I think it is common sense to say that preventing a problem from developing is much wiser than trying to solve it later on. This is a recurring issue in both life and medicine.

Robert Naviaux, at the University of California San Diego, has suggested 50% of autism might be prevented by identifying babies born with what he sees as a defective Cell Danger Response (CDR) and then correcting that response. He views most chronic illness as being caused by the CDR blocking the body's own healing mechanisms from working effectively. I hope he eventually proves his theory and commercializes his anti-purinergic therapy. If he is right, it would trigger a medical revolution. Naviaux is an expert in mitochondrial medicine, metabolomics and genetics. If you read his papers, you will see that he is one of the very few researchers with a broad in-depth knowledge of the entirety of autism, rather than just one tiny area.

In my blog I reviewed the ideas of Knut Wittkowski, a biostatistician looking at the scientific data to find critical overlapping points where an effective therapy might be possible. Knut looked at the progression of autism in very young children. He identified certain potassium ion channels as likely to be key in determining the severity of autism that will result in adulthood. He looked for an existing drug that affects these ion channels that could be repurposed. He is developing a modified version of Ponstan (mefenamic acid), a pain relief drug, to permanently shift the developmental trajectory of those diagnosed very young with autism. In many countries mefenamic acid is a cheap pediatric drug used to treat pain and lower temperature. Knut is developing the therapy using a modified version of Ponstan, so that it is patentable. His idea is to switch non-verbal autism towards much milder autism, by using his therapy until critical phases in brain development have been completed.

Even if both Naviaux and Wittkowski are proven wrong, there are many other ways to reduce the incidence/severity of autism in those yet to be born.

In the research we now see that preventative measures reduce the risk of cancer, dementia, heart disease and many other conditions. We also see how some interventions are only effective when started very early.

In the case of autism we have seen that it is often influenced by a myriad of factors that on their own might have been harmless, but when taken together they produce multiple hits that cause the brain to develop differently.

Much research looks at these individual factors that increase the risk of autism. The lay public often do not understand when they see a headline on their smart phone and they miss the point completely. For example, the research does link being born via a cesarean to an elevated chance of developing autism. You then see a comment like, "My four kids were all born via cesarean delivery and none have autism – so the research is wrong," or "My child has autism and was delivered naturally." Perhaps a cesarean raises the chance by just 10%, so you still have a 98% chance of having a child without autism, unless you have other existing risk factors.

There is no single cause of autism, but understanding the many factors that contribute to autism allows you to think about reducing its incidence.

You can also look how researchers make their animal models of autism, whatever they are doing in their labs, mothers might want to avoid doing during pregnancy.

A very common model of autism is called MIA (maternal immune activation). This is to mimic a mother who gets sick during her pregnancy.

If you are interested in browsing through the numerous models of autism and see how many are reversible, use Google to look them up.

https://gene.sfari.org/database/animal-models/genetic-animal-models/

Among the hundreds of models, here are some I found interesting:

- Maternal stress
- Maternal obesity
- Diesel particles
- A germ-free environment
- Use of the common anti-epilepsy drug valproic acid

Many mothers do not like the fact that nearly all the autism models are based on females. Paternal stress does not have a mouse model in the SFARI database, but the research has shown than epigenetic markers from paternal stress are passed to their offspring. Paternal age is just as important as maternal age as a risk factor.

The germ-free environment is interesting, because it supports the hygiene hypothesis. This suggests that in our modern ultra-clean lives we lack of exposure to the bacteria humans have evolved to expect. This then results in a dysfunctional immune system and contributes to the huge rise in all autoimmune diseases, including autism.

It has been shown that keeping a pet dog indoors during pregnancy reduces the incidence of asthma in the child. Not surprisingly, nobody has studied this in autism.

Consider the effects of owning a dog prior to starting a family. It reduces your level of stress and it makes you exercise, so improving your health and reducing the likelihood of obesity. Most importantly it ensures a future mother and her future baby are exposed to the bacteria from domesticated animals that our bodies have evolved over thousands of years to expect. This exposure to bacteria conditions and calibrates the baby's immune system, which can only be done very early in life.

Don't go for long walks beside busy roads; breathing in diesel particles is one cause of autism and has its own mouse model.

If you are a female with epilepsy, don't take the drug valproic acid if you might get pregnant. One of the classic models of autism is where a pregnant mouse is injected with this common anti-epilepsy drug to produce a pup with autism.

There are hundreds of other mouse models of autism.

We can return to my simplified model of autism and instead of looking how to treat it, we can look at how to prevent it.

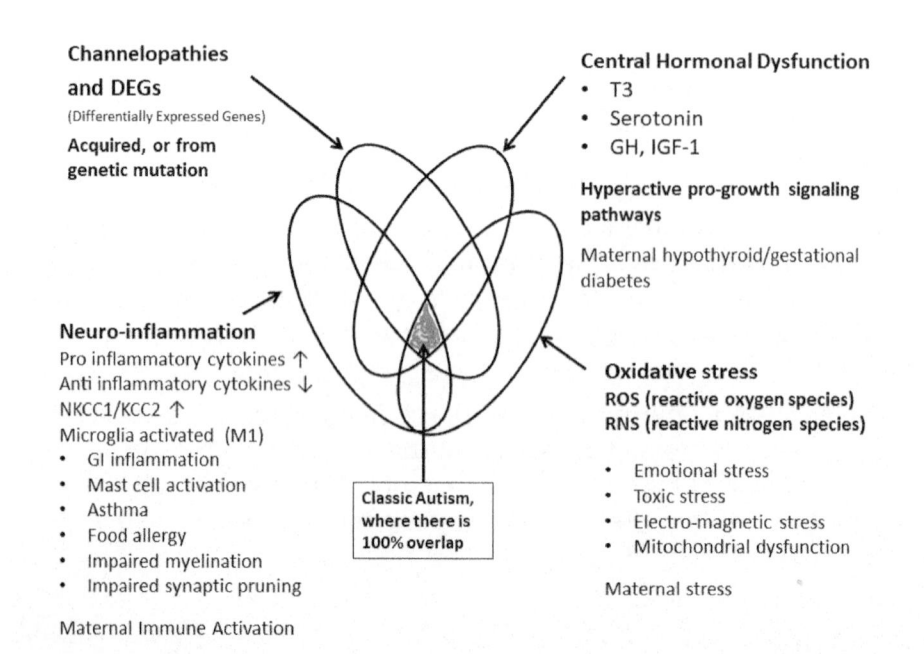

Channelopathies and DEGs
(Differentially Expressed Genes)
Acquired, or from genetic mutation

Central Hormonal Dysfunction
- T3
- Serotonin
- GH, IGF-1

Hyperactive pro-growth signaling pathways

Maternal hypothyroid/gestational diabetes

Neuro-inflammation
Pro inflammatory cytokines ↑
Anti inflammatory cytokines ↓
NKCC1/KCC2 ↑
Microglia activated (M1)
- GI inflammation
- Mast cell activation
- Asthma
- Food allergy
- Impaired myelination
- Impaired synaptic pruning

Maternal Immune Activation

Classic Autism, where there is 100% overlap

Oxidative stress
ROS (reactive oxygen species)
RNS (reactive nitrogen species)

- Emotional stress
- Toxic stress
- Electro-magnetic stress
- Mitochondrial dysfunction

Maternal stress

Channelopathies and differentially expressed genes

Many parents carry mutations in autism genes that are passed on to their children. The parent is unaffected, one child is unaffected and yet the other child is affected and develops autism.

Genetic defects are often more about probabilities rather than certainties.

Some types of autism are caused by a critical single gene that is mutated.

Most autism is polygenic and multifactorial. Some of these factors you can influence and some you cannot.

If you abuse drugs, alcohol and even cigarettes, this affects not only how your genes are expressed, but also those of your heirs. If a male uses cannabis he epigenetically "tags" the autism gene DLGAP2 in his DNA. He then passes on sperm with epigenetic tags on the DLGAP2 gene, which then appears as tags in the DNA of his offspring.

If your grandparents were heavy smokers, they have passed on epigenetic tags from their DNA, that reduce your capacity to deal with oxidative stress.

We all have inherited baggage in our DNA, which we then may go on to combine with someone else's inherited baggage in their DNA.

In some parts of the world siblings with disabilities get hidden away at home specifically not to impede the marriage prospects of the siblings. This may be cruel, but so is natural selection.

Some disabilities are inherited and some are not. Cerebral palsy is almost never caused by inherited genetic dysfunctions. Idiopathic autism is caused by a cocktail of inherited genetic/epigenetic defects, random new genetic errors and a myriad of environmental influences.

A sibling of someone with severe autism, who desperately hopes to have unaffected children, should definitely think hard about who he/she chooses to combine DNA with. A good choice would be someone with no psychiatric disorders in their family, and no other major risk factors.

The fact that Asperger's and bipolar disorder have not disappeared over the centuries is because some features are attractive to mates. Genuine Aspies are highly intelligent and bipolar is associated with creativity and so both groups have traits that could lead them to be successful and hence attractive to potential mates.

It is entirely predictable that people with Asperger's, schizophrenia or bipolar have a higher risk of producing children with severe autism. Combining two people with these diagnoses at least doubles the risk.

While he was still a teenager, my neurotypical elder son did ask me how to avoid autism in his children. I suggested developing a taste for calm beta females who like animals.

I do get occasional questions about reducing the risk of autism. It has become a research topic and some doctors are already implementing their pet ideas.

In practical terms, you cannot change your genes or those inherited epigenetic markers. Maybe this will change in future. But there are things you can do.

Antioxidants before/during pregnancy? For the mother or the father?

We know that oxidative stress is a driver of much disease, including autism. This can be minimized by lifestyle changes and indeed with a little pharmacological help.

It is suggested that reducing oxidative stress prior to conception and during pregnancy may offer protection against autism and other conditions.

I was interested to see a study that used the over the counter (OTC) supplement NAC to treat mothers who suffer unexplained pregnancy loss. The antioxidant showed a significant increase in the "take-home baby rate". I was really just looking for safety information to see if NAC was considered safe to be given during pregnancy. NAC had only positive effects

N-acetyl cysteine for treatment of recurrent unexplained pregnancy loss

Pregnancy could be associated with a state of oxidative stress that could initiate and propagate a cascade of changes that may lead to pregnancy wastage. This process of oxidative stress may be suppressed by the antioxidant effect of N-acetyl cysteine (NAC). The current study aimed to evaluate the effect of NAC therapy in patients diagnosed with unexplained recurrent pregnancy loss (RPL). The study was a prospective controlled study performed in the Women's Health Centre, Assiut University, Egypt. A group of 80 patients with history of recurrent unexplained pregnancy loss were treated with NAC 0.6 g + folic acid 500 microg/day and compared with an aged-matched group of 86 patients treated with folic acid 500 microg/day alone. NAC + folic acid compared with folic acid alone caused a significantly increased rate of continuation of a living pregnancy up to and beyond 20 weeks. **NAC + folic acid was associated with a significant increase in the take-home baby rate as compared with folic acid alone.** In conclusion, NAC is a well-tolerated drug that could be a potentially effective treatment in patients with unexplained RPL.

"Take-home baby rate" sounds like a "Peter-ism" that I would use, but that is how the researcher described it in his published abstract.

There was indeed a paper published that suggested that the prospective father might want to take antioxidants to lower the risk of autism.

Male preconception antioxidant supplementation may lower autism risk: a call for studies

The idea is to reduce *de novo* mutations (DNMs) occurring within the paternal germline that are linked to autism.

This then takes us to a US fertility clinic, where they noticed a connection between parents with reproductive difficulties and families with autism. They had two websites:

http://www.preventmiscarriage.com/

http://www.preventautism.com/ no longer functioning

"At Braverman Reproductive Immunology, we believe Autism Spectrum Disorder (ASD) and various pregnancy and infertility complications (listed below) appear to have the same cause. In fact, we have found that a large number of patients who present to our center with the below complications already have a child with ASD.

This discovery started us on the journey to see if ASD itself could be prevented while treating other associated conditions. We believe treatment for these common issues will not only prevent the pregnancy complications listed below, but may also prevent ASD in the group of patients that have already had a child with ASD."

After a few years, when it went out of fashion to talk about treating, curing or preventing autism, the autism site was discarded. A pity, but not unexpected.

In the US, Talk About Curing Autism (TACA) rebranded as The Autism Community in Action. The Defeat Autism Now! (DAN) movement was shut down, by the Autism Research Institute. Cure Autism Now merged into Autism Speaks to paint the world blue.

In the UK the Treating Autism charity rebranded as Thinking Autism.

Behind the scenes there has been pressure. Severe autism is rather suffering from cancel culture, where liberal media and tiny activist groups are pushing an agenda where disability is cool and just another identity, like being gay or not sure what gender you are. Treating autism has become a threatening concept to these groups. Fortunately it did not hinder me.

Dr Braverman did not mention oxidative stress, but perhaps he should have.

We know that maternal inflammation is one of the easiest ways to cause autism in mouse models (that MIA model – Maternal Immune Activation).

We have some research to show that the risk of autoimmune disease can indeed be reduced and indeed that the risk of progression from minor to more major autoimmune disease can also be minimized.

We even have a tiny study showing that immuno-modulatory therapy using a probiotic during pregnancy can reduce incidence of ADHD and autism. For me ADHD is just a case of autism-lite.

A possible link between early probiotic intervention and the risk of neuropsychiatric disorders later in childhood: a randomized trial

Background:
Recent experimental evidence suggests that gut microbiota may alter function within the nervous system providing new insight on the mechanism of neuropsychiatric disorders.

Methods:
Seventy-five infants who were randomized to receive Lactobacillus rhamnosus GG or placebo during the first 6 months of life were followed-up for 13 years. Gut microbiota was assessed at the age of 3 wk, 3, 6, 12, 18, 24 months, and 13 years. The diagnoses of attention deficit hyperactivity disorder (ADHD) and Asperger syndrome (AS) by a child neurologist or psychiatrist were based on ICD-10 diagnostic criteria.

Results:
At the age of 13 years, ADHD or AS was diagnosed in 6/35 (17.1%) children in the placebo and none in the probiotic group. **The mean numbers of Bifidobacterium species bacteria in feces during the first 6 months of life was lower in affected children than in healthy children.**

Conclusion:
Probiotic supplementation early in life may reduce the risk of neuropsychiatric disorder development later in childhood possible by mechanisms not limited to gut microbiota composition.

The idea of using a probiotic bacterium to reduce the incidence of autism fits well with the hygiene hypothesis that blames our overly clean homes and lifestyles for the rise of autoimmune diseases. A probiotic is just putting back a bacterium to replace those we all used to have.

At the University of Colorado researchers used a known stress-protective microbe called Mycobacterium vaccae to see if they could prevent autism in an animal model. They found that it prevented the expression of ASD-like behavior in the model. This was summed up as "Exposure to 'good bacteria' during pregnancy buffers risk of autism-like syndrome."

We also have the studied effect of having a pet dog at home. Humans have been living alongside dogs and farm animals for thousands of years and have become accustomed to their bacteria. The researchers found that early life exposure to "doggy dust" protects against allergic disease

House dust exposure mediates gut microbiome Lactobacillus enrichment and airway immune defense against allergens and virus infection

Early-life exposure to dogs is protective against allergic disease development, and dog ownership is associated with a distinct milieu of house dust microbial exposures. Here, we show that mice exposed to dog-associated house dust are protected against airway allergen challenge. These animals exhibit reduced Th2 cytokine production, fewer activated T cells, and a distinct gut microbiome composition, highly enriched for Lactobacillus johnsonii, which itself can confer airway protection when orally supplemented as a single species. This study supports the possibility that host–environment interactions that govern allergic or infectious airway disease may be mediated, at least in part, by the impact of environmental exposures on the gastrointestinal microbiome composition and, by extension, its impact on the host immune response.

I recall another study that looked at treating people with eczema to see if you could reduce the chance of progression to asthma. Using ketotifen the trial showed that it was indeed possible.

Prevention of asthma by ketotifen in infants with atopic dermatitis.

To evaluate the prophylactic effect of ketotifen against the onset of asthma we selected 121 infants with atopic dermatitis, without any history suggestive of asthma (cough and/or wheezing). Sixty-one children received ketotifen twice daily. Those who weighed less than 14 kg received 0.8 mg; 14 kg or more, 1.2 mg. Sixty children, a placebo syrup indistinguishable from the active syrup. Both groups were followed for 1 year, with bimonthly evaluations. The criteria for onset of asthma were two different episodes of wheezing treated with bronchodilator drugs. Both groups were comparable regarding age, sex, weight, onset, and duration of atopic dermatitis and age at the onset of asthma. During the 1-year study, asthma was observed in eight children of the ketotifen group (13.1%) and in 25 children of the placebo group (41.6%). **Side effects were negligible** and routine laboratory tests disclosed no significant alterations. **Ketotifen is a very useful drug for prevention of asthma in children with atopic dermatitis**.

What is the conclusion?

It looks clear that you can take simple steps to minimize future autoimmune disease and indeed neurological conditions including autism. Have a pet at home, ideally a dog, because they are messier than cats. Go for nature walks and get some exposure to a wide range of animals, just like your grandparents or great grandparents did. Horses, cows, sheep, goats and chickens have been contributing their bacteria to humans for thousands of years, because we all used to live in contact with them.

The critical time to do this is before pregnancy, during pregnancy and in the first few years of the child's life.

The microbiome comes from the mother

I attended a presentation by an Italian gastroenterologist, with a career-long interest in autism. What remains in my mind from his talk is his phrase "The microbiome comes from the mother."

The microbiome is the name given to all the bacteria living inside your gut.

The fetus is exposed to the mother's bacteria because she is its home for nine months and then during a natural delivery the baby gets a liberal dose of bacteria during the birth process. The mother is another rich source of good bacteria.

If the baby is born via a cesarian section and fed on formula milk, she fails to inherit important parts of her mother's microbiome.

Somali autism clusters

This then takes me back to an issue I looked at long ago in my blog, which was the reason for the Somali immigrants to Sweden and the US (Minnesota and San Diego) having so many children with autism. This even got termed the Swedish Disease by the migrants, who claimed to have never seen autism back home in Somalia.

The exposure to bacteria in Somalia is completely different to living in Stockholm or Minnesota. The female born in Somalia develops an immune system calibrated by the typical exposure in a poorer African country. She then moves to super clean and tidy Scandinavia, where she is no longer exposed to the same bacteria. Her fetus is expecting bacteria typical in type and magnitude to that found in East Africa, not a social housing complex in Sweden, so a maladapted immune system is produced. An immune system that cannot differentiate between tiny threats and serious threats, will significantly increase the risk of autism, as well as all other autoimmune diseases.

Some researchers thought that the reason for the Somali autism hot spots was a lack of vitamin D from sunshine. That might potentially apply to Sweden and Minnesota, but hardly San Diego.

A Norwegian study in 2022 found that recent immigrants from poor countries has a seven fold increase in the likelihood of their children being diagnosed with autism and significantly, the autism had a much higher score on the ADOS scale of severity, compared to the ethnic Norwegian babies.

When I last wrote about this subject in my blog, I received a flood of comments from people who had migrated to North America or the United Kingdom and then had a child with severe autism. They commented that others they know who had migrated had also produced children with autism. I guess I touched a raw nerve. They are anecdotes that would seem to support the Norwegian study.

One interesting point that arose was that some people's autism symptoms improved when they went back to their original country. India was a case in point and one reader moved back permanently.

Hormonal dysfunction

We know that gestational diabetes increases the risk of autism and we also know that the mother being hypothyroid increases the risk. In some cases, the hormone dysfunction is a consequence of an autoimmune dysfunction.

We also know the female hormones estrogen and progesterone are extremely neuro-protective.

I am intrigued by experimental therapies to improve the outcome in traumatic brain injury (TBI), like in a car crash or a skiing accident. What tends to happen immediately after the accident is that the body mounts a massive over reaction, a cytokine storm, that ends up doing irreversible damage.

In models both progesterone and estradiol have been shown to improve outcomes in TBI.

The level of these hormones is supposed to increase substantially during pregnancy.

In past times hormones were given to some pregnant mothers, but this went out of fashion. Perhaps this should be revisited?

We have the surge of the hormone oxytocin that the baby is supposed to receive at birth. This surge is relevant to the GABA switch when shortly after birth this neurotransmitter is supposed to switch from excitatory to inhibitory and the neurons mature. If the baby is born by cesarian, there will be no oxytocin surge for the baby. Maybe some women during natural childbirth fail to release sufficient oxytocin? Perhaps all new-borns should receive a dose of oxytocin?

Low folate in pregnancy

The US Center for Disease Control (CDC) tells the public why folic acid is important before and during pregnancy.

> "When the baby is developing early during pregnancy, folic acid helps form the neural tube. Folic acid is very important because it can help prevent some major birth defects of the baby's brain (anencephaly) and spine (spina bifida)."

Research by Professor Ramaekers and his associates in the US has focused on low levels of folate in the brains of people with autism. This resulted in the finding that 75% of people with autism appear to have antibodies to the Folate Receptor A (FRA). FRA is responsible for the transport of folate into the brain. The antibody test is a way to identify central folate deficiency, which will cause a range of metabolic failures inside the brain. In many people these negative effects are at least partially reversible by very high doses of calcium folinate (Leucovorin).

Ramaekers found that often one, or indeed both parents of children with autism have antibodies to the Folate Receptor A. He proposed that treating future parents who have these antibodies by boosting their levels of folate might prevent future autism. Both parents can be treated prior to a planned pregnancy and the mother during pregnancy. I was rather surprised to hear that he actually started doing this.

Are such large doses of calcium folinate safe during/before pregnancy?

Thanks to Google we can see that in 1992 a study found quite a high dose was totally safe.

Calcium folate in pregnancy. Therapeutic efficacy

An open, randomised multicentre study was carried out to compare pregnant women, treated with calcium folinate 15 mg/day starting from the 12th or 20th week of gestation, with an untreated group. The results obtained confirm the efficacy of calcium folinate treatment on the trends of parameters analysed (serum and endoerythrocytic folatemia, hemoglobin and sideremia) which remained within the normal range. **Moreover, no adverse effects of any type were reported during the study.**

Good luck to Professor Ramaekers! We did correspond in the past; he liked my presentation on eight years of bumetanide use in autism at a conference.

Preventing regressive autism secondary to mitochondrial disease (AMD)

It is on open secret that doctors at Johns Hopkins have identified a variant of regressive autism called Autism secondary to Mitochondrial Disease (AMD).

It remains unclear how rare this is and absolutely nobody serious is going to research it, if they ever want to receive a research grant in the future.

In people with a genetic predisposition to mitochondrial dysfunction, an immune over-reaction to an insult like a viral infection can trigger mitochondrial disease. This will present itself as autism and quite possibly severe autism, in a previously unaffected child.

Those doctors treating AMD use mild immuno-suppressing drugs before any future vaccinations.

How do you minimize the chance of AMD? Any activation of the immune system can potentially overload the mitochondria in the brain, but this can only really happen while the brain is the power-hungry organ it is during the first three or four years of life.

Researchers at Northwestern University wrote how "at its peak in childhood, the brain burns through two-thirds of the calories the entire body uses at rest."

A five-year old's brain uses twice as much glucose as that of a full-grown adult. After the age of five, the brain gradually reduces its energy requirement. Up to that age, the brain is vulnerable to any power outage, it does not have any spare capacity.

The researchers suggest that humans evolved to grow slowly during early childhood to free up fuel for energy-guzzling childhood brains.

In a person with already impaired mitochondrial function, they are like an old house where the fuses keeping blowing if you turn on all the appliances at the same time. In the human brain there are no fuses, so it does not switch off but rather incurs damage in terms of neuronal death and loss of myelin.

Once you reach the age of six it is almost unheard of to develop regressive autism. There is a good reason for this, you have already safely past the critical period for the onset of AMD. If your fuses did not blow by the age of six, you are out of risk.

307

To help avoid AMD, never use paracetamol/acetaminophen in a baby, child or a pregnant woman. This drug will reduce a fever but it also depletes GSH the body's main antioxidant, just when it needs it most. Use something like ibuprofen.

Studies, including one funded by the US National Institute of Health suggests acetaminophen/paracetamol exposure in pregnancy is linked to a higher risk of autism and ADHD. In my blog I refer to ADHD as autism-lite.

Vaccines are given in multiples, so as to save time and money and to improve their take up. You might expect giving them one-by-one would actually make them more effective, as well minimizing any collateral damage. In Japan they stopped using the MMR vaccine in 1993, but now they suffer outbreaks of these diseases, because not enough people received all their individual vaccines.

Diagnosing who has a predisposition to AMD is not so easy at this time, but you would imagine that younger siblings of a child with AMD might be at elevated risk. The DNA for your mitochondria comes exclusively from the mother.

The expert on AMD is Dr Richard Kelley, formerly Head of Department at Johns Hopkins, but now retired.

His advice on treating AMD can be found online by entering into Google:

> "Evaluation and Treatment of Patients with Autism and Mitochondrial Disease"

You do have to wonder why his paper was never published in a medical journal. I can think of no rational explanations, that are not conspiracy theories.

Take Home Message

In this book you have read about many existing drugs that can be repurposed to benefit people diagnosed with autism. Much of this is well documented and you can verify it for yourself.

Within my blog I discuss even more potentially useful therapies, from published scientific research.

I encourage you to seek out the treatments that might work in your specific case. The reward of doing this is that you may significantly improve your child's life prospects and your own future. Others have done this successfully and I hope that many more will follow them.

There is no one autism, hundreds of factors can lead to such a diagnosis. This makes autism very difficult to treat, because what works wonders for one child may be completely ineffective in another. Just because something is difficult does not mean you should not attempt it.

Where nothing is ventured, nothing is gained.

epiphanyasd.com

There is a vast amount more information in my blog, with direct links to all the research papers. Many issues were not covered in this book. The epiphanyasd blog contains more than 600 posts and 17,000 comments. This book has 96,000 words, the blog has a few million. The blog is indexed and it is searchable, so you do not need to read it all!

Good luck!

PETER LLOYD-THOMAS

Index

ABA, 3, 8, 9, 11, 12, 13, 15, 16, 17, 18, 19, 20, 21, 26, 49, 61, 62, 63, 66, 92, 94, 103, 108, 109
ABBLS, 15
Abilify, 204, 225, 244
Acamprosate, 244
Acetaminophen, 87, 274, 308
ADHD, 24, 41, 110, 112, 113, 114, 184, 187, 189, 212, 213, 244, 245, 259, 260, 261, 265, 267, 272, 273, 301, 308
ADNP, 170
AEDs, 103, 288
Afghanistan, 152
Aggression, 50, 72, 205, 207, 223, 225, 226, 228, 230, 231, 232, 233, 234, 235, 244, 253, 266, 275, 280, 281, 288
Agmatine, 23, 55, 73, 177
ALA, 137, 152, 160, 200
Allergy, 50, 117, 134, 208, 209, 210, 214, 215, 217, 232, 235, 250, 258, 260, 280
ALS, 110, 111, 277, 282
Alzheimer's, 74, 99, 110, 111, 120, 139, 153, 168, 169, 170, 171, 172, 173, 176, 177, 199, 224, 264, 266, 271, 277

Amantadine, 105, 244
AMD, 127, 128, 152, 171, 172, 307, 308
Antibiotics, 106, 208, 216, 222, 273, 274, 282
Antihistamine, 119, 232, 260
Antipsychotic, 50, 79, 103, 204, 216, 225, 228-9, 244, 245, 262, 263, 267-8, 274-5, 280, 282, 283, 285, 287
Apple cider vinegar, 219
Aripiprazole, 244
Army, 74
Asperger, 11, 41, 49, 53, 58, 59, 77, 78, 79, 83, 84, 90, 93, 96, 97, 108, 111, 113, 114, 161, 164, 165, 173, 188, 189, 190, 191, 201, 202, 214, 247, 263, 283, 293, 298, 301
Asthma, 32, 107, 133, 139, 147, 187, 191, 208, 210, 211, 276, 277, 279, 296, 303
ATEC, 98
Atomoxetine, 105, 245
Atorvastatin, 55, 72, 284, 285
ATP, 74, 138, 148, 151, 153, 224
Autism Research Institute, 57, 84, 98, 200, 300

311

Autism Society of America, 57, 84
Autonomic nervous system, 280
Autophagy, 110, 168, 170, 171
Azithromycin, 106, 273
B-12, 245, 246
Baclofen, 246, 247
Baron, 79
Basmisanil, 167
Bay K 8644, 233
BCAAs, 228, 229, 262
BDNF, 142
BEIP, 85, 184
Belchertown, 81, 82
Beta lactam, 106
BH4, 105, 247
BHB, 74, 153, 154, 224
Biogaia, 227
Biomarker, 101, 102, 214, 230
Biotin, 69, 70, 174, 175
Biotinidase, 70, 175
Bipolar, 59, 66, 79, 109, 110, 111, 112, 113, 122, 135, 144, 161, 163, 168, 185, 187, 189, 244, 245, 267, 275, 283, 287
Boat, 36
Brain bank, 120
Breath holding, 208
Broccoli, 286
Brunner syndrome, 230
Bumetanide, 3, 5, 1, 13, 20, 45, 46, 49, 55, 71, 72, 105, 145, 153, 168, 195, 197, 248, 249, 250, 251, 252, 253, 258, 259, 289, 307
Buspar, 259
Buspirone, 105, 259, 276

Butyrate, 167, 220, 221
CAM, 104
Cancer, 146, 286
Cannabidiol, 233, 234, 259
Cannabidivarin, 233, 234, 259
Carnitine, 152, 155
CARS, 98, 245
Casanova, Manuel, 87, 225
Catterall, William, 73
CBD, 233, 234, 259
CBDV, 233, 234, 259
Celiac, 136, 217
Cell Danger Response, 294
Celocoxib, 259, 260
Cerebral folate deficiency, 70, 108, 174, 270
Cerebral palsy, 56, 298
Cesarean, 295
Channelopathy, 124, 143, 181, 185, 297
Charlotte Figi, 234
Charlotte's Web, 234
Chez, Michael, 201
Chiari, 121, 224, 225
Childhood Autism Rating Scale, 98
Childhood Disintegrative Disorder, 178
Childhood schizophrenia, 79, 112
Cinema, 27
Ciprofloxacin, 106
Clemastine, 157, 159
Clinical trial, 3, 63, 98, 99, 100, 104, 125, 126, 137, 173, 234, 236, 245, 246, 247, 249, 252, 260, 261, 265, 271, 276, 283, 289
Clomipramine, 105, 260
Clonazepam, 73, 80

Clonidine, 105, 260, 261
CM-AT, 102, 261
CNN, 128
Complex 1, 148, 151, 153
Compulsions, 114, 115
Copaxone, 160
COPD, 107, 139, 147, 276, 277
Coplan, James, 90, 91, 92, 94, 95
Corpus callosum, 22, 57, 68, 120, 145, 181
Cost, 60
Covid, 25, 33, 34, 129, 292
Crete, 175
Crohn's, 118, 275
CRP, 101
Cyproheptadine, 105, 262
Cytokine storm, 285, 305
DAN, 33, 47, 49, 84, 98, 200, 201, 226, 300
Dancing, 21
DAO, 215, 216
D-cycloserine, 105, 263
DEGs, 143, 146, 147, 156
Dementia, 168
Dentist, 28
Depression, 74, 96, 157, 159, 166, 207, 229, 230, 259, 283
Dermatitis, 211, 217, 303
Desmopressin, 289
Dextromethorphan, 105, 264
DHCR7, 180, 284
Diamox, 152, 153
Diary, 14, 50
Dickinson, 80
DJ-1, 139
DLGAP2, 297
DMF, 158, 159

Doctor, 32, 47, 54, 200, 201, 202, 221
Donepezil, 105, 119, 264, 265, 266, 267
Down syndrome, 41, 78, 167, 179
Dravet syndrome, 76, 80, 179, 180
Drowning, 27, 37, 64, 120
Dyslexia, 24, 41, 161
Dysmaturational, 108, 115
E/I, 67, 73, 280, 282, 283
ECT, 235
EEG, 213, 288
Electroconvulsive therapy, 235
elF4E, 170
Endoscopy, 106, 118
Eosinophilic esophagitis, 208, 209, 210
Epigenetic, 69
Epilepsy, 72-4, 78, 80, 83, 95, 103, 107, 119, 143, 144, 153, 160, 181-2, 186, 198, 205, 210-1, 221, 231, 251, 264, 281, 287, 288, 295
EpiTED, 88
European Medicines Agency, 39, 45
Fallon, Joan, 101-2
Fein, Deborah, 92, 93, 109
FG syndrome, 57
Fluvoxamine, 105, 266
Flying, 35, 36
FMT, 221, 222
Folinic acid, 270
Fombonne, Eric, 190, 291, 292
Food allergy, 214
Food intolerance, 208, 209, 214

FOS, 221
FRAA, 270
Fragile X, 48, 67, 101, 121, 166, 168, 169, 179, 269, 272, 273, 284
Frye, Richard, 152, 270
GABA, 5, 145, 167, 224, 248, 253, 283, 287, 305
Galantamine, 105, 119, 214, 266, 267
GAPS, 199
GERD, 118, 119, 209, 210, 216, 219
GI, 33, 50, 80, 85, 134, 210, 214, 222, 223, 235, 256, 260, 272, 277, 289
Giurgea, Corneliu, 107
Glutathione (GSH), 87, 129, 136-7, 139, 246, 274, 308
Gluten, 199, 215, 217
GPx, 136
Grades, 4, 20, 44
Great Ormond Street, 80
Guanfacine, 105, 267
H. pylori, 106
Haircuts, 28
Haloperidol, 105, 267, 268, 283
Harvard, 55, 85, 101, 176, 184, 269, 281
HDAC, 147, 167, 285, 287
Headache, 223, 234, 235, 281, 287
Headsprout, 14, 52
Heller's syndrome, 178
High school, 4, 12, 20, 22, 24, 25, 44, 56
Histamine, 119, 167, 209, 215, 216, 219, 232, 260
HNMT, 215

Holiday, 3, 32, 34, 46, 75, 203
Hologenome, 191
Home schooling, 42, 43, 44
Homocysteine, 168, 173
Humira, 96, 118, 135
Huntington's, 110, 170-1
Hypokalemic periodic paralysis, 124, 153
Hypokalemic sensory overload, 124
I3C, 285, 286
IBD, 117, 118, 119, 210, 235, 262
IBS, 117, 119, 133, 134, 210, 235, 272
Ibudilast, 159, 276, 277
Ibuprofen, 73, 87, 129, 135, 235, 260, 308
IED, 114
IGF-1, 142, 268, 269
IL-10, 134
IL-6, 134, 135, 235, 279
Indole-3-carbinol, 285, 286
Inflammation, 1, 101, 106, 117, 119, 122, 129, 133, 135, 158, 209, 223, 232, 258, 278, 301
Institutionalization, 94
Intellectual disability, 24, 41, 68, 83, 92, 97, 98, 145, 162, 163, 170, 174, 175, 182, 189, 202, 234, 239, 281, 291
Inulin, 221
IP3, 171
iPad, 21, 38, 44, 50, 143
IQ, 49, 54, 55, 67, 88, 89, 90, 91, 92, 97, 103, 109, 115, 161, 162, 163, 164, 167,

185, 188, 190, 225, 230, 249, 272
Irena, 3, 17, 18
Irritable Bowel syndrome, 117
Ivermectin, 106, 200
IVIG, 61, 96, 208
Johns Hopkins, 70, 77, 80, 86, 87, 94, 127, 128, 152, 155, 171, 178, 182, 273, 292, 307, 308
Kanner, Leo, 57, 77, 78, 84, 178
Karolinska Institute, 76
KCC2, 145, 258
Kelley, Richard, 94, 95, 127, 128, 152, 154, 155, 171, 308
Kennedy Krieger, 235
Ketamine, 269
Ketogenic diet, 74, 153, 154, 160, 199, 221, 224
Ketotifen, 119, 211, 233, 303
Krigsman, Arthur, 118
Kynurenine, 228, 229
L. Reuteri, 226
Lactobacillus Plantarum 299v, 229
Learning Disability, 161
Leucovorin, 55, 105, 138, 270, 306
Levi-Montalcini, Rita, 172
LGBT, 58, 59
Life expectancy, 57, 75, 80
Lilian, 3, 15, 16, 21
Lioresal, 246
Lord, 87, 88, 89, 95
Lovastatin, 284
Low Glycemic Diet, 223
Lunch, 13
Macrocephaly, 57, 100, 121

MAO-A, 230, 231
MAPS, 33, 85, 86, 200
Matryoshka, 54, 55
MCI, 168
Mebendazole, 160, 200
MECP2, 48, 67
Mefenamic Acid, 74, 213
Meldonium, 152, 153
Memantine, 100, 105, 110, 201, 271, 272
Metformin, 105, 272
Methylcobalamin, 245, 246
MIA, 122, 134, 295, 301
Microbiome, 69, 160, 191, 221, 223, 302, 304
Microcephaly, 100, 121
Microglia, 133, 156, 159, 196, 221, 223, 273
Mini-brains, 123
Minocycline, 105, 273
Misophonia, 205, 213, 277
Mitochondrial disease, 70, 127, 148, 171
MMR, 85, 308
Mouse model, 80, 120-2, 157, 160, 186, 220, 233, 295
Movie, 28, 52, 54, 293
MRI, 120, 121, 156, 177, 181, 184, 197, 224, 239, 281
mTOR, 170, 171, 182
Myelination, 155
NAC, 55, 67, 72, 115, 117, 122, 137, 160, 173, 174, 204, 220, 233, 274, 299
NAG, 160
Naltrexone, 105, 274, 275
Namenda, 100, 110, 201, 271
National Autistic Society, 79
Naviaux, Robert, 106, 286, 287, 294
Nazi, 78, 79, 80

Nelson, 85, 184
Nemechek, Patrick, 49, 201, 221
Neurodiversity, 58, 59
Neurofibromatosis, 284
Neuron, 110, 144, 156, 277
Nexium, 219
NGF, 142, 168, 172, 173, 269
Nicotine, 119, 167, 214, 226
Nimodipine, 233
Nitric oxide, 73, 176, 177
Nitrosative stress, 137-9, 174
NKCC1, 144, 145, 258
NKCC2, 248
NMDA, 69, 167, 244, 263, 264, 269, 271, 280, 282
Nrf-2, 139, 285, 286
Obsessive Compulsive Disorder (OCD), 114-6, 206-7, 236, 260, 265-6, 274, 283
Olanzapine, 105, 275
Oligodendrocyte, 156, 157, 158, 159, 160
OPC, 159
Oxidative stress, 69, 129, 135, 137, 138, 139, 147, 148, 149, 159, 171, 173, 176, 200, 270, 286, 298, 299, 301
OXPHOS, 148, 149, 150
Oxytocin, 105, 191, 227, 259, 276, 305, 306
P50 gating, 214
Palmitoylethanolamide, 231
PANDAS, 69, 73, 206, 208
PANS, 69, 73, 204, 205, 206, 207, 208
Paracetamol, 87, 129, 274, 308

PARK7, 139
Parkinson's, 110, 139, 159, 169, 185, 244, 264, 277
PCOS, 133, 142, 272
P-Cresol, 69
PDA, 114
PDD-NOS, 97, 114, 188, 189, 190
PDE4, 159, 214, 276, 277
PEA, 231, 232
PECS, 8, 9, 42, 54
Pediatrician, 8, 45, 90
Penicillin, 106, 282
Pentoxifylline, 105, 159, 277, 278, 279
Periactin, 262
Peroxynitrite, 138
Pesticides, 216
Phenytoin, 231, 232, 288
Piano, 22, 23, 27, 44, 46
Pioglitazone, 105, 233, 279, 280
Piracetam, 107
Pitt Hopkins, 146, 147, 179
PMD, 149, 150, 151
Poling
  Hannah Poling, 86, 128
  Jon Poling, 86, 107, 128, 129, 292
Pollen, 134, 210
Polydypsia, 208
Ponstan, 74, 75, 213
Potassium bromide, 80, 198, 281
Potassium, 72, 74, 80, 124, 125, 143, 144-5, 198, 211, 212-3, 232, 250-7, 281, 287, 294
Powell, 278
PPI, 219
Prednisone, 73, 206

Pregnenolone, 266, 280
Prevotella Histicola, 160
Probiotic, 118, 221-2, 226
Prognosis, 87, 90-4, 181
Propionic acid, 69, 122, 220
Propranolol, 105, 280, 281
Prozac, 103, 236, 265
PTEN, 146, 220, 285, 286
Purkinje, 217
Rain man, 57, 68, 85
Ramaekers, Vincent, 231, 306, 307
Ranitidine, 219
RAS, 110, 182
Reflux, 33, 118, 134, 209, 210, 216, 219, 235
Regression, 3, 10, 18, 38, 87, 95, 128, 154, 178, 206, 207
Regressive, 155, 178, 307
Rett, 5, 48, 67, 95, 96, 101, 172, 173, 179, 208, 265, 268, 269, 281
Reye's syndrome, 87
Rifaximin, 219, 220, 221
Riluzole, 105, 282
Rimland, 57, 84, 85, 98
Risperidone, 103, 204, 225, 268, 283, 285
Ritalin, 103, 245, 272
Roflumilast, 159, 214, 277
Roger, 108, 174
Rolflumilast, 276
ROR alpha, 68
SCFAs, 122, 220
Schizophrenia, 53, 59, 77, 79, 97, 106, 110-3, 122, 135, 144-6, 155, 161-8, 182-9, 213-4, 244, 259, 263-4, 275-7, 283
School, 1, 3, 4, 9-28, 38-9, 41-6, 51, 52, 56, 58-60, 65, 70-

3, 81, 83, 97, 113, 126, 143, 166, 175, 189, 190, 196, 201, 204, 252, 276, 285, 292, 293
Schwann, 158
Schweckendiek, 158
Scripting, 116, 204
Selenium, 136, 137
Self-injury, 50, 72, 205, 225, 228, 233
Sensory, 123, 206, 207, 211, 212, 213, 284
Sensory overload, 124, 125, 211, 212, 213
Shank3, 180
Sharapova, Maria,152
SIB, 50, 114, 205, 225, 226, 227, 235, 236
Siblings, 28, 50, 55-8, 82, 119, 154, 298, 308
SIBO, 134, 219, 220, 235
Siegel, 42
Sies, Helmut, 138, 139
Simvastatin, 105, 180, 284, 285
Skiing, 24, 26, 33, 305
SLOS, 180, 284
SMD, 149, 150
Smoking, 107, 118, 119, 146, 187, 214, 226, 230
Sodium benzoate, 216
Somali, 304
Son Rise, 49
SpectrumNeeds, 150
Spermidine, 171
SSRI, 236, 265, 266, 280, 283
Stem Cells, 123
Stereotypy, 55, 67, 72, 114-7, 166, 203-4, 208, 233, 260, 274-5, 279
Stimming, 116, 203, 233

Stockholm, 75, 304
Strattera, 245
Strictly Defined Autism, 188, 191, 192
Sukharev, Grunya, 77
Sulforaphane, 137, 198, 285-6
Suramin, 71, 106, 200, 286
SWAN, 49
Swedish Disease, 304
Swimming, 27
Tardive Dyskinesia, 228, 229, 268
Tauopathy, 169, 170
TBI, 214, 285, 305
TCF4, 146, 147
Tetrahydrobiopterin, 247
Tetrahydrocannabinol, 233, 234
THC, 233, 234
Theatre, 27
Thioredoxin, 139
Tics, 4, 69, 73, 103, 109, 114-6, 204-6, 225, 228-9, 262, 265, 267
Timothy Syndrome, 181, 182
TNF, 96, 118, 134, 135, 278
Topiramate, 105, 287
Tourette's, 93, 108-9, 115, 116, 205, 265, 267
Tracking Devices, 64
Treatable ID, 174
Trichotillomania, 114, 203, 204
Trofinetide, 268, 269
Tropisetron, 214
TSC, 139, 169, 170, 180
Turner syndrome, 68, 143
Ulcerative colitis, 1, 118-9, , 226
Vaccines, 76, 84, 86, 87, 128, 292, 293, 308
Vagus, 119, 133, 228
Valproate, 104, 105, 287, 288
Varenicline, 214
Vascular, 175, 176, 177, 261, 266
Vasopressin,
VEGF, 142
Verapamil, 55, 62, 72, 171, 198, 232-3, 272
Viviomixx, 160, 289
VSL#3, 160, 289
Wakefield, Andrew, 85-6, 118
Wandering, 37, 63, 63
Whole Exome Sequencing, 48, 61, 197, 235, 236
Wittkowski, Knut, 294
Wnt, 160
Wroczyńska, Agnieszka, 249
Yu, 200
Zantac, 219
Zappella, Michele, 108, 115
Zoloft, 103, 236, 283
α7nAChR, 226

Printed in Great Britain
by Amazon